TOM WRIGHT was taken to his first game aged nine, a friendly against Leicester City at Easter Road in February 1957. Little did he realise that football, and Hibs in particular, would become such a major influence in his life from that day on. Wright has now been a Hibs supporter for over 50 years, and has the scars to prove it. Previously the Secretary of the Hibs Former Players' Association, Wright is now the official club historian and curator of the Hibernian Historical Trust. He is the author of *Hibernian: From Joe Baker to Turnbull's Tornadoes*, *The Golden Years: Hibernian in the Days of the Famous Five* and *Leith: Glimpses of Times Past* and he is co-author of *Crops: The Alex Cropley Story*.

ERIC STEVENSON comes from a staunch Hibs background – his uncle was a founder member of the Bonnyrigg Hibs Supporters Club. As a schoolboy in 1960 he signed briefly for Hearts, then fulfilled his dream of becoming a Hibs player. Between 1960 and 1971, he made 257 appearances and scored 53 goals. Eric's intricate close ball control allowed him to regularly outwit the opposition and win a number of penalties. After an eventful career in football, culminating with a spell at Ayr United United 1971–73, his wife Agnes ran a successful business in Bonnyrigg for many this day he is a fanatical Hibs supporter.

Hibs Through and Through

The Eric Stevenson Story

ERIC STEVENSON

with

TOM WRIGHT

Luath Press Limited

EDINBURGH

www.luath.co.uk

First published 2016

ISBN: 978-1-910745-67-0

The paper used in this book is recyclable. It is made from low-chlorine pulps produced in a low-energy, low-emissions manner from renewable forests.

Printed by Bell & Bain Ltd., Glasgow

Typeset in 10.5 point Sabon by Main Point Books, Edinburgh

Contents

To my wife Agnes, daughters Sonya and Nadia,
and grandchildren Owen, Aidan, Connor, Lucy and Logan.

Acknowledgements

MY THANKS TO Gavin at Luath Press for suggesting a name for the book which in the circumstances was so very appropriate. Most of the photographs in the book are from my own personal collection. The Summer Cup final image is courtesy of the family of the late Peter Caruthers. My thanks also to Tom Purdie for the use of the two photographs on page 73 (Eric playing in the Scottish Juvenile side against at Muirton Park and in his early days at Easter Road). Every effort has been made to locate image copyright holders and to trace sources of media quotes.

Introduction

FOR OVER TEN years Eric Stevenson was probably the best uncapped player in the entire country.

Born at Eastfield near Harthill, Eric comes from a Hibs background, his uncle a founding member of the Bonnyrigg Hibs Supporters Club. Stevenson had been signed by Hearts as a schoolboy, but a contract irregularity later saw the Tynecastle club fined £150 and manager Tommy Walker £75. Hibs, who had been keeping a close watch on the situation, soon stepped in to contract the player to Easter Road. It was a deal that was to pay long term dividends for both parties, Stevenson a lifelong Hibs supporter, realising his life's ambition to play for the club, Hibs reaping the reward of over ten years' sterling service from one of the best players ever to wear the famous green and white jersey. Making an almost immediate breakthrough into the first team, barring injuries he would be an almost automatic first choice over the next decade.

During his time at Easter Road Eric would play, with and against, some of the biggest names in the game, taking part in many memorable matches that are still spoken about today, including games against Napoli, Liverpool and Leeds in European competition and many other unforgettable domestic fixtures and a League Cup final.

Equally capable on either wing, he was usually to be found wearing the number 11 jersey, his mesmerising close ball control consistently bemusing the opposing defenders. An intelligent player with a great football brain, he knew the game and his deceiving, but deadly bursts of pace down either wing would help set up many goals for the likes of Joe Baker, Neil Martin, Jim Scott, Colin Stein and later Joe McBride. He also had an eye for goal himself, as he showed when scoring two of Hibs goals in a 4-0 defeat of Hearts at Tynecastle in 1965, when all four were scored in the opening ten minutes of the game.

Slightly built, his intricate close ball control would also help him win a number of penalties for his side. Eric insists that he never dived, although he did not try too hard to stay on his feet.

During his time at Easter Road he would play under a succession of managers from Hugh Shaw to the irrepressible Eddie Turnbull. Much admired by the latter who had earlier tried to sign the player for Aberdeen. Unfortunately personal difficulties meant a move to Ayr United shortly after Turnbull's return to Easter Road as manager in 1971.

Although retiring prematurely at the age of almost 31 to concentrate on his business interests, a time when he should have been approaching his best, Eric is still fondly remembered by those who saw him play and remains a great favourite of all the Hibs fans who were fortunate enough to have witnessed him at his very best. He left the game with only a single appearance for the Scottish Inter-League side, scant reward for his undisputed talents.

He remains to this day a fanatical Hibs supporter. This was never better demonstrated than when he was fined two weeks' wages by the then Ayr United manager, Ally MacLeod, for missing a game one Saturday. Where was Eric that day? At Hampden, watching Hibs beat Celtic in the League Cup Final. That, says Eric, was money well spent.

A member of the Hibernian Former Players Association, in 2012 the popular Eric Stevenson was inducted into the Hibernian Hall of Fame and still attends games at Easter Road today.

Tom Wright

CHAPTER ONE

Early Days

I WAS BORN on Christmas Day 1942 in the small coal mining village of Eastfield, near Harthill in North Lanarkshire. At that time the Second World War had well over two years to run, but with the industrial towns and cities like Glasgow and Clydebank not all that far away, a sleepy village like Eastfield didn't seem to be of much interest to Adolf Hitler and his German bombers. Eastfield was just one of the numerous small towns and villages in the area that depended almost entirely on the pits for its very existence, an industry that for centuries had proved so vital to the country's economy. Coal had been mined in Scotland for hundreds of years, but it was the coming of steam in the late 18th century that created an almost insatiable demand for the fuel. More and more mines started to spring up, employing, particularly in the mid-1800s, men, women and even children as young as five, many of them Irish immigrants who had fled to Scotland to escape the great potato famines that were ravaging Ireland. It was dirty and dangerous work with many serious accidents, often with fatal consequences. Scotland's worst ever mining disaster occurred at nearby Blantyre in 1877 when 209 men and boys lost their lives. By the beginning of the 19th century, in Lanarkshire alone there were 200 pits, the industry reaching its zenith just prior to the Great War. By 1947 and nationalisation, there were just 190 mines of varying sizes in the whole of Scotland. By the 1980s only five remained, the closing of the pits forcing a great number of decent hard working miners to look elsewhere for employment.

My mother Christina, or Teen as the family knew her, came from mining stock, her father spending his entire working life at the pit. At the beginning of the war Teen had become engaged to a lad called Alistair, who also lived in the village and worked at the mine. Alistair would eventually be called up for military service and posted overseas. These were difficult times, the population uncertain of just what the future had in store, and unfortunately Teen found herself in the family way, as it was quaintly described at that time, me being the result.

There was obviously no way that Teen's condition could be kept a secret for long in a small village like Eastfield, but to be fair to Alistair who was always very good to me when I was growing up, on his return from the forces he agreed to stand by my mother. Perhaps understandably though he struggled to come to terms with another man's child and I was sent to live with my gran and grandad Cove, who also lived in the village.

I have very few memories of Eastfield in the early days, although I can still vividly remember coming home from school one day to be told that my gran had died. I was still very young and obviously there was no way that my grandad could manage to look after a young child on his own so once again I was on the move, this time to live with my mother's sister Nan and her husband Tam Clark, who for some unknown reason was called Elk by his friends. Like countless other, Tam had spent his entire working life at the pit, but with several of the mines now on the verge of closure he and many of the other men from the surrounding areas were forced to look elsewhere for work.

It must have been around 1948 or 1949 that uncle Tam and several other men from the village went looking for fresh employment, either at the then modernised Lady Victoria pit at Newtongrange or at Bilston Glen. In our case it meant moving into a corporation house in Bonnyrigg which was only a few miles from Edinburgh. Nan and Tam already had a family of their own in Henry who was four years older than me, but I quickly settled in to my new surroundings and to be fair to them I was treated no differently to Henry whom I had taken a liking to immediately. Some time later two half-sisters Christine and Mary would arrive on the scene.

I remember that Tam was always full of encouragement for us youngsters. Once during the local Poltonhall Gala I was leading in a race when I was pushed from behind by another boy, causing me to stumble, so could only manage to finish in second place. The other boy was declared the winner, but my uncle wasn't having any of that. He stormed over to the judges' table claiming that clearly I had been pushed and that the decision should be reversed and he got his way. That was the kind of guy Tam was, always full of support.

We lived in a four-in-a-block upstairs-downstairs house in Pryde Avenue which I imagine would have been a far cry from a miner's house in Eastfield. This house actually had its own bath, a world away from the customary large tin tub in front of the fire that the miners had been accustomed to.

I managed to settle into my new surroundings immediately, attending the local primary school, and have nothing but happy memories from early childhood. For a youngster, life in my new environment was idyllic, our out of school hours usually spent playing football either in the local park or in the street with my pal Daniel Hughes. In those relatively care free days it was normally the latter, and only rarely would our games be disturbed by a passing vehicle of any sort, usually only the coal lorry or the very occasional visitor to the area who actually owned a car.

I was aware from the very beginning that Tam and Nan were not my real parents, something that didn't bother me in the slightest, but there could be the occasional confusion over my surname. One day at school the teacher asked an Eric Clark to stand up, and it was only when I was nudged by a classmate that I realised, much to my embarrassment, that the teacher was actually addressing me. Other than that I really enjoyed my time at school. One of my last acts at the primary school was to play the part of a page boy complete with wig, tights, the whole caboodle, in the Coronation celebrations in 1953. God knows what my pals must have thought of me. Although I was no scholar I couldn't have been all that thick, as the pupils involved in the pageant were usually selected on their academic ability.

Another vivid memory I have from school is watching, either in the cinema or on a neighbour's television, as we didn't own one ourselves till much later, Hungary defeating England 6–3 at Wembley, particularly the famous Puskás goal when he drew the ball back with sole of his boot to leave full-back Alf Ramsey floundering on the ground, before firing a fierce shot past goalkeeper Gil Merrick into the top corner of the net. That evening all us boys were out in the street trying to emulate the move.

It was around then that I was considered old enough to visit my mother on my own, although at that time I still didn't know that she was my mother. I was only about nine or ten when I was first put on the bus to St Andrew's Square in Edinburgh. There I would catch the bus to Harthill where I would be met by my grandad, later making the reverse journey home. It sounds a terrible thing now to let a lad that young travel such a distance by himself, but these were more innocent times and nobody ever thought much about it.

At that time Hibs were by far the best team in the country, and one day Big Tam and a few of his pals, who all drank at the Anvil pub in Bonnyrigg High Street, decided to form a local branch of the Hibs Supporters Club. During the immediate post-war years, Hibs were a huge draw and were well capable of attracting crowds of 30 or 40,000, often more, and soon the supporters club was thriving. The bus would leave from the High Street in Bonnyrigg for both the home and away games and would invariably be packed, stopping at nearby Dalkeith to pick up more fans. I don't know in the early days if the club would have been officially affiliated to the Hibernian Supporters Association that had been formed in 1946, but by 1952 with Tam as chairman and Alex McQuaid as secretary, they had been accepted as full members, one of almost 40 supporters clubs throughout the Lothians and Fife. From what I can remember, monthly meetings were held in the church hall at Poltonhall, the occasional Sunday excursions always eagerly anticipated by the children.

Came the magical day when along with Big Tam, Auntie Nan, Henry and my pal Robert Healy, who has now sadly passed away, I was taken to my first game. I could only have been seven or eight and unfortunately I have no memory of who Hibs were playing that day, or even the score, all I know is that the entire proceedings made a great impression on me, and started a passion for the game that remains as strong today. A passion for Hibs in particular, but also for all things football. In the '50s the Scottish game was experiencing arguably the greatest period in its history and there was no bigger draw than the Hibs. During the war thousands of young men serving abroad had been deprived of their traditional Saturday afternoon pastime of watching their favourite sides in action, and the game in the immediate post-war years attracted supporters in unprecedented numbers. Nearly everyone worked on a Saturday morning, and with few of the leisure pursuits that are available or acceptable nowadays, like betting shops, TV, or even going shopping with the wife, it was common practice for the men to have a few pints after work in the local pub, then it was off to watch their heroes in action.

After that first game my appetite had been whetted. I wanted more, and soon I was attending games both home and away, with the possible exceptions of Parkhead, Ibrox or Tynecastle (places that my uncle Tam considered to be unsuitable for youngsters of my tender age). My main problem was that I would burst out crying on the rare occasions that Hibs lost. Apparently I was well known for it. The men on the bus would try to cheer me up, but uncle Tam would always insist jokingly that he was not bringing me back. I particularly remember one away trip to Methil to see Hibs play East Fife who were then one of the top teams in the country. On the way Tam bought me a ticket for the customary sweep that was always held on the bus. I remember drawing a player called Eddie Turnbull who fortunately scored the first goal that afternoon to make me a winner. Little did I know then that not only was I to become great friends with Eddie in later years, but would actually line up alongside him in practice matches at Easter Road.

For home games the bus would park in one of the many side streets near the ground and in those more innocent days we would be given the admission money and complete with our autograph books would be allowed to run ahead, hoping to get a lift over the turnstiles from a passing adult which would allow us to keep the money. Once inside the ground we would make our way to the top left-hand corner of the 'Dunbar End' where we knew we would find our grownups. It was the perfect spot to watch the Hibs international left winger and future Scotland manager Willie Ormond making his mazy runs up the left wing, little realising that within a few years I would be pounding that same furrow myself.

Willie was a talented outside-left whose direct style of play was perhaps in direct contrast to the exquisite ball skills of Gordon Smith on the other wing, but he was no less effective. Capped half a dozen times for the full Scotland side and nine times for the Scottish League, he helped Hibs win three championships between 1948 and 1952. At that particular time the Famous Five was in full flow, each one a Scottish International in his own right and it was something to see them at their very best as they swept through the opponents defence with consummate ease.

Inside-left Eddie Turnbull, who as I have already mentioned would later become a great friend, was considered to be the workhorse of the side, but he was far more than that. A rugged, but determined competitor with a great engine and thunderous shot, his never-say-die attitude inspired the side on the rare occasions when things were going against them, and it was only later when I played alongside him in training at Easter Road that I realised just how good a player he really was.

The other inside position was filled by the diminutive Bobby Johnstone who was considered by many to be the brains behind the legendary forward line. Johnstone, who hailed from Selkirk in the Borders, made one of his first appearances for the side in a league game against Queen of the South at Easter Road in 1949, in what was the first ever outing in a competitive match by a forward line that would shortly become known universally as 'The Famous Five'. A two-footed player, 'Nicker' was blessed with exquisite ball skills and a great football brain, it was often said that he could open the proverbial can of beans with his educated feet. Capped 13 times for Scotland at full level, Bobby joined Manchester City in 1955 leaving Hibs and the Scottish game much the poorer. At Main Road he would become the first ever player to score in consecutive FA Cup finals in 1955 and 1956. Later in his career he would return to Easter Road, helping the then England International Joe Baker to a record haul of 42 goals in a single season, before leaving to join Oldham after a disagreement with the Hibs chairman Harry Swan. Much to my great disappointment I would miss playing alongside this mercurial talent by only a few weeks.

The legendary Gordon Smith is perhaps rightly acclaimed as Hibs greatest ever player. An integral member of what is still considered by many to be Scotland's greatest ever forward line, Smith played well over 700 games for the club, scoring 364 goals in all matches while helping his side to three league titles between 1948 and 1952. Later in his career the Scottish International would create his own piece of football history by becoming the first player to win league championship medals with three different clubs, none of them the two big Glasgow sides, before retiring from the game aged almost 40. There is no doubt that Smith, with his film star looks and bewitching ball control was the darling of the Hibs fans, but I only had eyes for one, someone who would also become a great friend in later years, centre-forward Lawrie Reilly. Perhaps he lacked the delicate ball skills of some of the others, but Lawrie would end his career at the almost obscenely young age of only 29 due to injury, as Hibs' top goal scorer of all time in official games. Nicknamed last-minute-Reilly because of his penchant for scoring late goals, often for Scotland, I can still remember him standing, legs splayed with the ball at his feet, almost inviting the defender to come and try to take it from him.

In our street games or down the local park I was always Lawrie Reilly, and would spend hours on end, often on my own, kicking a small rubber ball against a wall pretending that I was playing for Hibs against Hearts. At the time I had no idea that I had anything special to offer as a football player, although looking back my brother Henry and his friends who were all a good few years older than us, would let both myself and Bobby Nesbit join in their often 12 or 13-a-side games in the local park. I don't think that would have happened if we'd not been any good. Indeed, although I was still only very small I would regularly take them on and beat them and I'm sure that helped me gain their respect.

Henry was a very good player. He played for the Edina Hearts under-21 side, and would later sign for Hearts. Although he would fail to make the grade at Tynecastle he did manage to play several games for Dunfermline before moving to Berwick Rangers. Later he would become a police officer in Grimsby of all places.

It was only in the final year that the primary school had a football team. We weren't a bad side reaching a cup final only to lose, but it was after I had moved on to Lasswade High that I really started to take the game seriously. Nearly all of the school side were later selected for trials for the County. About the only two players who were not picked was a lad named George Peden, who would later sign for Hearts, and myself. Ironically, as far as I am aware, we were the only two who went on to play professionally.

Near the end of my schooldays I managed a few games for a local amateur team, but was soon invited to join the Edina Hearts under-17 juvenile side, probably at the recommendation of my brother Henry who at that time was still playing for the under-21s. Edina Hearts were run by a lad called Davy Johnstone who had been on Hearts books at one time and still had connections at Tynecastle and also a guy named Johnny Smart who would later train the Hibs youngsters at Easter Road in the evenings. Unfortunately, at that time I still had the physique of a fag paper seen sideways, and I didn't get many games. It was only later when I was farmed out to the local Easthouses Boys' Club and playing against lads of my own age and stature that I really started to come into my own. By then I knew I was good, and playing in my favourite position of inside-left it didn't take me long to become the best player in the team. I was recalled to Edina Hearts after a player called Fred Jardine left to join Dundee. Jardine would later go on to have quite a good career in the game. Although he would make only a few appearances at Dens Park, Fred would spend almost a decade with Luton Town before ending his career at Torquay United.

I really enjoyed my time with Edina, although I'm not sure if the secretary didn't rate me or was merely trying to encourage me psychologically, but all he seemed to do was criticise. I was getting better and better however, and before long I was one of the main men in the side. I still lacked a physical presence, but had learned to rely on speed of thought and action to avoid most of the hard tackles that came my way. We had a very good side, winning the league and also the Lord Weir cup in my first season, and from a squad of around 14 or 15 players I think that only two or three did not go on to sign for Hearts. I had not been at Edina long when, probably due to the influence of Davy Johnstone, I was invited along to Tynecastle to train with the youngsters a couple of evenings a week. At this time because I was playing so often I rarely managed down to Easter Road to see the Hibs. Although I do remember after one of our games being extremely upset to discover that they had lost to Clyde in the 1958 Scottish Cup Final. However, for me it was no real problem to be training with the Easter Road side's greatest rivals or in wearing the maroon and white jersey.

One evening after training I was taken by Davy Johnstone to see the Hearts manager, Tommy Walker, in his office at Tynecastle. I was still only

16, but can vaguely remember signing the piece of paper that was put in front of me without really looking at it or realising just what I was signing. I was far more interested in being informed that I would now be paid £3 per week, money luckily that my uncle Tam insisted that I put directly into the bank.

It was while I was at Edina Hearts that I was capped for the Scottish Juvenile side to play Ireland at Muirton Park in Perth. To say I was surprised to be selected would be an understatement. I believe that someone had called off at the very last minute and that I had been hurriedly called into the team, but I was in extremely good company. Several of the side that evening would later go on to play professionally, including Willie Henderson who would later star for Rangers and Scotland, Alex Ferguson – I wonder whatever happened to him! – and Andy King, who would later join Kilmarnock. I remember being met at the door of the team's hotel before the game by Ferguson who welcomed me into the set-up and even then he seemed to be the main man. I have very little memory of the game itself, but I still have the framed jersey hanging on the wall at home as a permanent reminder of a very special day in my life.

By now it was time to leave school and no deep consideration was required as far as work was concerned. It was merely accepted that I would follow the family tradition and go down the pit. After passing the basic exam, I started work at the Lady Victoria pit in Newtongrange. At that time, far too young to work on the coal face itself, all the recent school leavers would spend the first few weeks separating coal from the conveyor belt at the surface as part of our training. We did get taken down to see the working conditions at the face where some of the digging still took place by hand, but were never allowed to stray far from the bottom of the shaft, where our job would soon be to couple and uncouple both the empty and full wagons. We were also expected to attend college one day each week, but that didn't last long as I was thrown out for fighting – only from the college, I have to say, and not the pit. I am not normally aggressive by nature, but for some reason this guy in the class had been niggling me for ages. Finally I snapped and belted him. Funnily enough, as so often happens, we later became great friends.

I was still only 16 and training two nights a week at Tynecastle with the part timers. The legendary former Scotland player Jimmy Wardhaugh who worked for a newspaper during the day, would normally train alongside us in the evenings, as did another first team regular, Billy Higgins. Being young and somewhat impetuous, one night I shimmied Higgins, putting the ball through his legs as he tried to tackle me. The big mistake I made was in going back to try to do it again. This, perhaps understandably, was too much for the experienced Higgins, who clattered into me, only for Andy Kelly, a young player who could look after himself, to step in, remonstrating that I was far too small for that kind of treatment. Jimmy Wardhaugh however was something else. Then approaching the veteran stage of his career, his still mesmerising ball control made him great to watch, and brought back memories of standing on the Easter Road terracing watching him display his magical ball control in games against the Hibs, as incidentally did Willie Fernie of Celtic who was yet another player that I admired greatly.

When I was on the back shift at the pit and couldn't make the evening training sessions at Tynecastle I would usually join the full timers at Saughton Enclosure on Tuesday and Thursday mornings. One morning there was a full-scale practice match with the first team taking on the reserves. Much to my surprise I was selected to play for the reserve side and found myself lining up at outside-left in direct opposition to right-back Bobby Kirk in a forward line that consisted of the great Gordon Smith, manager Tommy Walker – (who although he was getting on a bit, you could still see that he had been some player) – Willie Bauld and Jimmy Wardhaugh. For a 16-year-old to be playing alongside these legendary figures in the Scottish game was like going to heaven.

At that time Hearts were by far the best side in the country. At the end of the season they would win the league cup and also the league championship for the second time inside three years. After his controversial free transfer from the Easter Road side during the summer, Gordon Smith would not only collect his first ever cup winner's medal in senior football after Hearts victory over Partick Thistle in the League Cup final at Hampden, but would also win another league championship medal to go alongside the three he had already won at Hibs. Centre-forward Willie Bauld was something special. Although he could often appear lethargic on the field, he had a great football brain and the uncanny ability to place headers with great accuracy. I thought my future team mate at Hibs, Neil Martin, was exceptional in the air, but I have to admit that Bauld was the best that I have ever seen. I have already mentioned 'twinkle-toes' Jimmy Wardhaugh who was almost impossible to dispossess on the run with the ball at his feet, a superb master of the dribble. The side was packed with so many exceptional players, including Alex Young who would go on to achieve legendary status on Merseyside with Everton, the fans favourite Johnny Hamilton, goalkeeper Gordon Marshall who would soon join Newcastle and the ever reliable John Cumming to name, but a few.

I thoroughly enjoyed my time at Tynecastle. It was a great experience for one so young and I always received great encouragement from everyone at the club. One morning I was standing outside the ground waiting for the bus to take us to training at Saughton Enclosure. It was an extremely cold day and I was wearing only the thin training gear that had been supplied by Edina when I was surprised to be approached by Willie Bauld who asked if I didn't have anything heavier to wear. When I replied no, he told me to wait there and in no time at all he came back out with his own tracksuit top. Before I could thank him, my pal Archie Kelly nipped in to say impishly: 'What a cheek Willie, he's a Hibs supporter and his hero is Lawrie Reilly. You ought to hear him tearing you to ribbons.' I could only stand there embarrassed, but Willie just laughed and walked away. He was one of the nicest guys you could ever wish to meet, and what a player.

At Hearts I took part in just the one reserve game, against Hibs of all teams. That evening at Tynecastle I faced several of my future Easter Road colleagues, Desmond Fox who scored a hat trick, Pat Hughes, John Fraser, Duncan Falconer and most notably Jim Scott who would soon become one of my best pals. I was at outside-left in a Hearts side that contained several players with first team experience including goalkeeper Wilson Brown, Danny Ferguson, Billy Higgins, Jimmy Murray and Ian Crawford, but that didn't stop us from going down to a heavy 6-2 defeat.

The teams that evening were:

HEARTS: BROWN, FERGUSON AND LOUGH, FRASER, OLIPHANT AND HIGGINS, LIVINGSTONE, MURRAY, BLUE, CRAWFORD AND STEVENSON (LISTED AS A TRIALIST).

HIBS: MUIRHEAD, FALCONER AND MACKAY, NICOL, HUGHES AND DAVIN, FRASER, FRYE, BUCHANAN, FOX AND SCOTT.

It was around this time that a scout from Wolves started to turn up at the house. The English side had just won consecutive First Division championships and with players of the calibre of the England captain Billy Wright, Ron Flowers and goalkeeper Malcolm Finlayson and were a team to be reckoned with. I wasn't really interested in a move to England, but the scout kept insisting that at least I should come down and look the place over. I still wasn't interested and it was only when I was told that I could take a pal down with me that I agreed and the next thing I knew both Peter Nesbit and myself were both on the train bound for Wolverhampton. At Molineux we were met by a couple of lads we knew from the Bonnyrigg area who were already on the ground staff who made us welcome. The following day I took part in a wee bounce game that lasted no more than half-an-hour playing alongside Norman Deeley who was then a first team regular. While getting changed back at the ground I was notified that manager Stan Cullis wanted to see me in his office. Cullis, a former rugged England centre-half, explained that although I had been asked down only to look the place over, he had been given a good report by Deeley and he wanted to sign me there and then. Incredibly, I was offered the same basic wage as the first team squad including the current England captain, Wright. I was not sure and asked for time to think it over. As we were leaving the ground my pal Peter asked if I had received any money. We were absolutely skint so I went back and asked Cullis if I would be getting any expenses for my trouble, at which he pulled out a £20 note from a huge wad in his pocket. Although we had barely turned 17, working down the pit we had already been well grounded in the drinking culture that was prevalent among miners and we both immediately headed for the nearest pub and a couple of pints of lager.

Back in Scotland, Edina Hearts were having a good season. We were still involved in several cups and were due to play on the following Wednesday. I was well up for the game, but had been puzzled to receive a letter from the SFA a couple of days before notifying me that as I had signed a contract with Hearts I was now a professional footballer. That evening when I turned up with my boots I showed Davy Johnstone the letter to be told that as I was now a professional I could no longer play for Edina. This was news to me. As far as I was aware the only thing I had signed was a form saying I was to be paid £3 per week. It later turned out that although I was not old enough to do so, the form I had signed earlier had been a full professional form which had been kept in a drawer until I had turned of age, something that was totally against the rules at that time. Although Hearts insisted that they had done nothing wrong they were eventually fined £75 and manager Tommy Walker £150.

My uncle Tam had not been all that keen on me working down the pit and a few months earlier he had contacted Tommy Walker to see if the club could find me a job, a move that may well have meant me remaining at Hearts. Although he had been told by Walker to leave the matter with him, no more was heard about it and I never went back to Tynecastle again as a Hearts player.

The whole sorry saga stretched out over several months during which time I was not allowed to play for anyone. For weeks the event filled many column inches in the back pages of the newspapers, one well known sports reporter, Bob Scott of the *Daily Express* even started labelling me 'The Rebel', a nickname that would stay with me for several years.

It later turned out that Eddie Turnbull who was then the trainer at

Easter Road had been well aware of the situation at Tynecastle for some time, and out of the blue one day I was contacted by the Easter Road scout George Smith who told me that he knew I was a Hibs fanatic and asked that if he could get things sorted out would I be interested in signing for the club? I explained about the Hearts contract wrangle, but was told not to worry. The other problem was that I had been receiving £3 each week and would have to pay the money back. Once again I was told not to worry as I would be reimbursed by Hibs.

During the long months of inactivity I had also been contacted by Jimmy Murphy who was then assistant manager to Matt Busby at Manchester United. At that time United were still recovering from the disaster at Munich that had occurred only a couple of years before, but they still had some great players on their books including Noel Cantwell, Johnny Giles and Bobby Charlton. Murphy tried his hardest to persuade me to sign for the Old Trafford side, telling me that perhaps I didn't realise just how big a club United were. They had obviously had me watched several times, but I was already in enough trouble over the contract situation, and besides didn't really want to leave home. Murphy tried everything to convince me that I would be making the right move in joining United, but it was only after he finally realised that my mind was made up about signing for Hibs, that he eventually gave up and wished me well in the future. The Aberdeen manager Tommy Pearson also turned up at my doorstep in person one evening, as did the legendary George Young who was then the manager of Third Lanark, but they both received the same answer as Murphy. My mind was made up: I wanted to sign for the Hibs.

It was only much later that I learned I could have taken my pick from almost anybody as there had been a long list of top clubs all keen for my signature. I could well have joined Rangers. Apparently their scout had turned up to watch me one day and later told Davy Johnstone that they would have signed me in a minute, but after seeing the name Edward McConville Stevenson on the team lines he had wrongly assumed that I was a Catholic and left. That didn't bother me in the slightest. It had taken some time, but at last it looked as if I had achieved my boyhood dream of wearing the famous green and white of Hibs.

I believe that the contract fiasco at Hearts eventually went some way in addressing an anomaly regarding the signing of young players in Scotland. The earlier introduction in England of an apprentice professional scheme had meant that clubs down south could sign schoolboys at 15, while in this country the rules that existed at that time prevented our clubs from signing a boy on a full professional contract until he was 17. This obviously gave an unfair advantage to the English clubs. Possibly because of the Hearts situation, the rules would eventually be changed to bring the Scottish clubs more into line with their English counterparts.

CHAPTER TWO

Signing for Hibs
and Disappointment in Rome
1960–61

THE CONTRACT SITUATION with Hearts dragged on all through the summer
months and well into the following season while I sat twiddling my thumbs,
unable even to turn out for Edina. I just wanted to play football. Hearts
themselves had made no contact at all during this time. In their eyes they
had done nothing wrong and still considered me to be their player. The
Scottish League agreed, but the SFA saw things differently and although
I didn't know it the time I was now a free agent. I don't know the exact
circumstances regarding the contract situation, but the next thing I knew I
was being invited down to Easter Road for signing talks.

Extremely nervous, but also very excited, I remember climbing the
stairs at Easter Road accompanied by my uncle Tam to meet manager
Hugh Shaw and chairman Harry Swan. Unfortunately, it would not be
the last time I would be invited up to the boardroom to meet Harry Swan!
Hugh Shaw, who had played for the celebrated Hibs side of the mid-
1920s that had reached successive Scottish Cup finals before leaving to
join Rangers, had been manager at Easter Road since the sudden death
of his predecessor Willie McCartney in 1948. During his tenure he had
overseen the halcyon post-war days at Easter Road when, fronted by
the legendary Famous Five forward line, the club had won three League
Championships and had also been Britain's first ever representatives in the
inaugural European Cup in 1955.

Shaw, who was rarely seen without his collar and tie, was a true
gentleman in every sense of the word. Perhaps a throwback to a different
generation, he rarely took much to do with the day-to-day training itself,
leaving that side of things to Eddie Turnbull who had retired from playing
to take over as trainer in 1959. Apart from the very occasional visit to the
dressing room before training to have a quick word, we would rarely see
the manager except on match days.

Chairman Harry Swan, on the other hand, was the main man – Mr Hibs. Along with the secretary, Wilma, he ran the day-to-day operations at the club. Like Shaw, Harry Swan was rarely seen in the dressing room, and if truth be told although he was a small man in stature, he had such a presence that I was probably more frightened of him than respectful. It didn't take me long to accept the contract put in front of me, full time football and far more money than I had been earning at the pit, but in fact there was never any doubt in my mind that I was going to sign, and I was now a Hibs player.

The first thing I did was to hand in my notice at the Lady Victoria. I was absolutely delighted to be exchanging my pit boots for football boots and almost the next thing I knew I was boarding the early morning bus from Bonnyrigg, bound for Easter Road. By that time the golden years of the late 1940s and early '50s, when Hibs had generally been recognised as the best side in the country, were well in the past. The club was now in what was, for the want of a better phrase, generally described as in a state of transition. There were still some very good players at a club that had lost only narrowly to Clyde in the Scottish Cup final a couple of seasons before and there was no air of despondency around the place and certainly no lack of ambition.

I was still very shy, but was welcomed by all the senior players who soon made me feel at home, particularly John Grant and Tommy Preston who immediately took me under their wing. Perhaps being that bit older they had recognised immediately that I would be a good addition to their regular drinking school. Grant, who had been capped twice for Scotland only a couple of years before was a particular help to me in the early days. Both he and his defensive partner, Joe McClelland, had been the full-back pairing at the club for a couple of years. John was very strong, could tackle, was good in the air and had a fair bit of pace although his distribution could sometimes let him down. When fit he was probably the best defensive full-back I ever played with.

McClelland was more a rugged type of defender prevalent in the game at that time, although I think that Joe himself often had delusions that he was Maradona. His dad would turn up to watch him every Saturday, and even if Joe hit a bad pass into the crowd, something he did with regularity, he was always ready with an excuse. Nicknamed 'Walkie-Talkie' by the rest of the players because he rarely stopped talking, possibly his best ever excuse came after Hibs had been beaten 6-1 by Rangers in a League Cup game at Easter Road. While the rest of the players were down in the dumps after the heavy defeat, Joe was quite happy that the player he had been marking had not managed to get on the score sheet, totally oblivious to the fact that outside-right Willie Henderson had made most of the goals. He was another great lad though, just one of many at Easter Road at the time.

Then approaching the veteran stage of his career, Tommy Preston was still some player. Although a bit on the slow side, he was blessed with a brilliant football brain and had scored many important goals for the club. Another great guy, after he moved back to left-half behind me on the wing, he would just give me the ball and would often say that I kept him in the game for an extra couple of years.

Finally, what is there to say about Joe Baker? Nicknamed Roy-of-the-Rovers by the other players, he had the looks of a film star and was always surrounded by the girls wherever he went. He had a bit of a ruthless streak on the field and didn't suffer fools gladly, but was a genuinely nice guy who treated everyone the same, whether it was the kit man, Tommy Scotland, or the Lord Provost of Edinburgh. Although I was just a young boy he didn't differentiate, and treated me no differently from all the other lads. Joe was a one-off. He had it all. Strong, good in the air, fast with the ball at his feet, he could shoot with both feet and could tackle. Although not quite as aggressive as Lawrie Reilly, to my mind he was probably the better of the two and without doubt he was the glamour player at Easter Road.

I arrived at the ground early that first morning full of a mixture of excitement and trepidation and was probably the first in the place. There was no one around to meet me and being extremely shy I just sat in the corner of the dressing room. Probably understanding just how nervous I was feeling, I appreciated the gesture when Jimmy McDonald, an outside-right who had signed from Wishaw Juniors the previous season, came over and introduced himself. Jimmy was great pals with Joe Baker and the pair travelled through from the west each morning. We became good friends, but sadly, although he was a fairly prolific goal scorer for the reserves, Jimmy would fail to make the breakthrough into the first team and would be released at the end of the following season.

As I've already mentioned, while working at the pit I had grown accustomed to the drinking culture that was prevalent amongst miners, and even at the age of 15 I would often pop into the local Jug Bar for a couple of pints with my pals. At Easter Road I soon became great friends with Jim Scott, and both Scottie and I would be welcomed with open arms into the post-match drinking school of Tommy Preston, John Grant, Joe McClelland and Ronnie Simpson.

Not long after signing for the club, a couple of mates and myself attended a Sunday night dance at the Bilston Glen Miners' Club. Obviously someone must have contacted chairman Harry Swan because immediately on arriving at Easter Road the following morning I was informed that I was 'wanted' upstairs. I arrived in the boardroom to be confronted by a far from happy Swan who asked as to my whereabouts the previous evening. He obviously knew the answer so I told no lies. Asked if I had been drinking, I replied that I had a few. At that he almost erupted. 'I'm warning you now,' he ranted, 'for years I've had nothing but trouble from one player, and I don't want another.' A reference, I later found, to the former Famous Five forward Bobby Johnstone, who had left the club in mysterious circumstances just a few weeks before I arrived. I don't know if Harry thought that Selkirk where Bobby lived and Bonnyrigg were close to each other, but I had never been in Johnstone's company, although I had heard that he could drink for Scotland. It was his second spell at the club and some of the older players would tell me that Bobby would sometimes be out on the town on a Thursday and Friday evening before a game. Come the Saturday he would often play for just 15 or 20 minutes, but what a 20 minutes, managing to lay on many of Joe Baker's club record 42 league goals in a single season. However, back to Harry Swan. Suffice to say, being young, the chairman's advice regarding the perils of drink went in one ear and out the other.

My first ever appearance in a Hibs jersey was in a reserve Penman Cup tie against Cowdenbeath at Easter Road on Wednesday 5 October 1960. I can't remember much about the game itself except that we drew 2-2, the Hibs goals scored by John Fraser and Johnny McLeod. But if I remember rightly the press were fairly kind to me the following morning suggesting that I had showed promise and could earn a quick promotion to the first team. The Hibs side that evening featured several players who already had, or soon would, feature in the first team, namely:

WILSON, FALCONER AND MCCLELLAND, DAVIN, EASTON AND YOUNG, MCLEOD, FRASER, BUCHANAN, STEVENSON AND ORMOND.

I already knew goalkeeper Willie Wilson from playing against him for Lasswade against Musselburgh High School, and later for Edina Hearts against Musselburgh Windsor, and had always been impressed. Willie was some keeper, and who knows just how good he would have been, but for a serious back injury that ultimately affected him throughout his career. He had made his debut at the start of the 1959–60 season at Dens Park just days after signing, when he replaced the off-form Jackie Wren who had just conceded six in a comprehensive home league cup defeat by Rangers. During only his second first team appearance a few days later he had the misfortune to be in goal when Motherwell's Ian St John managed to score a hat trick in just two-and-a-half minutes at Easter Road. Nevertheless, Willie had performed well and kept his place in the side. There is absolutely no doubt in my mind that he would have got better and better, but for the back injury received in a game against Dundee a few months later, when according to some he had been rushed back playing before he was ready. In later years he would often make a great save, but struggle to get back for the follow-up. Despite that he went on to give the club more than ten years' service before leaving to join Berwick Rangers in 1969.

I found John Fraser to be a gem, a great guy who is still a good friend. Although, as his nickname would suggest, 'Bacardi' liked a drink, he was not one of the hardened 'clique'. He had joined the club several years before as yet another potential replacement for the great Gordon Smith before moving back into defence. A very good full-back, he was also more than passable on either wing, and when moved into the centre he could certainly score goals. John served the club well for over 12 years as a player before returning later as trainer to the great Turnbull's Tornado's side of the early 1970s.

Willie Ormond was another player that I always had a lot of time for. Although he was well aware that potentially I could eventually take his place, he was always a great help to me in passing on advice and we became great friends, remaining so until his premature death in 1984 aged only 57. Willie liked a laugh and was always joking. He treated the younger players more like a father and one of my favourite memories of him was after the game in Barcelona when he decided to take both Jim Scott and me out on the town. I don't know if Willie thought that he was looking after a couple of inexperienced youngsters, but at the end of the night the roles were reversed and it was us who escorted him back to the hotel a tad under the weather.

To my mind many people don't fully realise just how big a club Hibs are. We would often be taken away during the season for a few days training at Gullane, including gruelling sessions up and down the infamous sand dunes, a location the club had been using since the 1920s and long before it was famously 'discovered' by Jock Wallace and Rangers in the 1970s. In the evenings we would be let off the hook and a few of us, including Willie and Sammy Baird, would go for a few drinks at a local hostelry. One night Willie asked me what I wanted to drink. Unsure, I replied that I would just have what he was drinking. One gin-and-tonic turned into quite a few and I don't know yet how we managed to get back to the hotel. I can vaguely remember walking across some fields, it could well have been the golf course for all I knew, before entering the hotel by the back door. Although nothing was said to me personally, in the morning Eddie Turnbull gave both Ormond and Baird a right rollicking. In their playing days Turnbull and Ormond, who both hailed from the Falkirk area, had been great buddies, but I remember Willie telling me later that, 'The bastard's changed since he became the trainer.'

It would be easy to give the impression that it was nothing but fun, but all the players took the playing side extremely seriously. After spending time down the pit, for me every day was like a holiday. The only down side as far as I was concerned was the training. I hated training, always had, and always would until the day I retired from the game. Under the eagle-eye of Eddie Turnbull, we would spend hours either running up and down the huge main terracing at Easter Road or sprinting endlessly around the pitch. That may well have been okay for the bigger and stronger boys, but I was still just a slip of a lad and often found it hard going. Eddie however, seemed to have taken a liking to me from the beginning, and sensing that I was struggling, he would sometimes say, 'Okay Eric, that's enough for you.' This would immediately bring the lighthearted comment from Tommy Preston that I was 'the 'f***ing teacher's pet'.

The newspaper article had been right regarding the quick promotion. Just days after my debut for the reserves I was surprised to be taken aside by Eddie Turnbull who informed me that I would be playing for the first team against St Johnstone at Muirton on the Saturday. The club had been struggling since the beginning of the season failing to win any of the previous six games, and had not won since a 6-1 defeat of Airdrie in mid-August. In an attempt to change things, in midweek goalkeeper Ronnie Simpson had been signed from Newcastle United and Sammy Baird from Rangers. Simpson, who had been the youngest ever player to feature in a competitive Scottish game when he lined up for Queens Park against Hibs in 1945, aged only 15, was now reckoned to be at the veteran stage of his career, but he was still some goalkeeper. Although he was not the tallest, he was great in the air and could punch the ball further than most people could kick it. He was also great in one-to-one's with the opposing forwards, saving the ball with every part of his body including his feet. Like most goalkeepers, Ronnie loved to play outfield during training and was brilliant on the left wing. He also had something of a reputation at penalty kicks, saving six out of six in his first season at Easter Road. Ronnie's trick at penalty kicks was to stand slightly nearer one post than the other, seemingly by accident, almost inviting the taker to aim for the larger area, which of course Ronnie had already anticipated.

The former Scottish international Sammy Baird on the other hand had a reputation as something of a hard man, not only on the pitch, and could sometimes be a bit of a bully. He would often try to boss the older players around, and I think that some were physically scared of him. One day when we were golfing at Longniddry, Sammy found himself in a bunker. Thinking no one was looking the next thing I remember was the ball being thrown out of the sand pit. When he realised I had seen what had happened he threatened me in all seriousness, that if I ever told anybody he would batter me. I told my pal Scottie, and he just laughed. Baird later became a bit of a pal although he didn't mix much with us younger lads. He used to travel through from Glasgow with Scottie, whose brother Alex had been a team mate of Baird's at Ibrox, before his move to Everton, and I think he liked me. By the way, apart from Scottie, I didn't tell a living soul about the golf incident. I was no fool!

Before the game against St Johnstone I met up with the rest of the lads at the Scotia Hotel in Great King Street that had been the regular meeting place for as long as anyone could remember. After the traditional pre-match lunch of steak and toast, we all made the journey by bus to Perth, a journey that was anything but enjoyable for me as I was literally a bag of nerves during the entire trip. In the dressing room before the game there were no pre-match tactics or words of advice from the manager and we were just allowed to get on with it. I lined up at inside-left, my customary position at Edina Hearts, between centre-forward Joe Baker and Willie Ormond on the left wing. Again I can't remember too much about the game itself, a 2-0 defeat, except that nerves and a lack of confidence had probably prevented me from performing to the best of my ability, although the newspapers later that evening suggested that I had done ok. I think even Turnbull was fairly pleased. Tommy Preston tried to cheer me up later by saying that I had done alright, but I knew deep down that although their centre-half McKinven was a big strong player I hadn't imposed myself enough on him, although I suppose that that could possibly be put down to inexperience, nerves and a temporary lack of confidence. I also found the pace of the game to be far faster than I had been used to and was knackered at the final whistle. According to the *Pink News* that evening:

> Both Baird and the young Stevenson had done enough to suggest that they can improve matters. After he had settled, Stevenson had some delightful runs, but had played himself out long before the end.

I kept my place in the side for the friendly against Swansea on the Monday evening in a game to inaugurate the Vetch Field floodlights, a ground sadly that is no more. Everything flashed by so quickly that I have little memory of the game except that I managed to score one of the goals in a 4-4 draw, my very first for the club. I was still extremely shy and will always be grateful to Johnny McLeod, who perhaps sensing my unease, asked me to accompany him on a relaxing walk around the town in the afternoon before the game.

Although I had played in the previous couple of games, I was still a bit surprised to be selected to play against Celtic at Easter Road a few days after the Swansea match, and what a shock to the system that would turn out to be. After the pre-match meal at the Scotia, I walked the mile and a half to the ground, a ritual that would continue almost until the day I left the club more than ten years later. Most players are superstitious and I remember in the dressing room before the game hiding in the toilet when the referee came in to check the studs. I usually wore rubber studs so there was never going to be a problem, it was just a strange superstition that I had at the time.

Walking out in front of what was then by far the biggest crowd that I had played before was an exciting, but nerve wracking experience, but unfortunately from then on it was all downhill. The vastly experienced Tommy Preston, John Grant and Ronnie Simpson were all out injured, but even that could be no excuse for the heavy 6-0 defeat. We were absolutely dreadful, and to say that I never got a kick of the ball would be a major understatement. I spent the entire game a virtual spectator as players like Bertie Peacock and Willie Fernie, both of whom I had often admired from the terracing as a boy, appeared to have the ball tied to their feet as they made regular mesmerising runs through our defence, tearing us apart in front of almost 30,000 spectators.

Billy McNeil was just beginning to really establish himself in the Celtic side around that time, but the star of the show was undoubtedly the future Manchester United player Pat Crerand. Everything came through Crerand that afternoon as he ran the game from midfield. I was much too naive to close him down and it was probably Crerand's easiest game ever. About the only memory I have of the game from a Hibs perspective apart from Willie Muirhead picking the ball out of the net six times, was Joe Baker taking the centre seven times, refusing on every occasion to pass the ball to me. Once again the press was fairly kind in suggesting that 'although Stevenson's inexperience was clearly shown at times, his ability to survive hard tackling and charging suggested that he has the spirit and stamina to make the grade.'

At our usual post-match watering hole, the Royal British Hotel on Princes Street, it was a very subdued Tommy Preston, Ronnie Simpson,

John Grant, Jim Scott, Joe McClelland and myself who sat down to drown our sorrows, particularly both of the latter who had actually played in what had been a hugely embarrassing defeat.

I managed to score my second goal in Hibs colours in a 4-2 defeat by Middlesbrough in a friendly at Easter Road the following Wednesday, a certain Brian Clough scoring for the visitors, but it was then back to the reserves for me. I only found out much later that Sammy Baird had taken manager Hugh Shaw aside earlier in the week with the advice to 'take the laddie out or you will waste him'. The experienced Baird could see that although I had been a stand out as a juvenile, continuing to play me at that stage of my development could well have destroyed my confidence and perhaps ruined my career almost before it had started.

Relegation to the second team didn't bother me too much as I still had enough confidence in my own ability to know that I would soon be back. It was during this spell in the second team that I came face to face with my brother Henry on the football field for the first and only time in a competitive game. At that time Henry was playing for a Dunfermline reserve side that murdered us 6-1 at East End Park, a score-line that flattered Dunfermline somewhat according to the papers later that evening. We had been much the better team for 70 minutes before the home side scored four goals inside a fantastic ten minute spell. Watched by my uncle Tam and Nan I managed to score Hibs' solitary counter, described in the following week's match programme as the best move of the game. Receiving the ball near the half-way line, I set off down the left wing, dribbling past three men before crashing an unstoppable shot past the goalkeeper from just outside the penalty area.

It was also around then that I really got to know perhaps the best player that I ever played alongside – Davie Gibson. Davie, who supported Hearts as a boy, joined Hibs from Livingston United in 1956 and had already played several games for the first team and also for the Scottish League against the full Scotland side at Ibrox. He had not yet managed to hold down a regular first team place at Easter Road quite probably due to the fact that he was then doing his National Service with the King's Own Scottish Borderers who were stationed in Berlin. Recently posted to Redford Barracks in Edinburgh to see out the remainder of his time, he would now be more available for selection. It was obvious to me from the start however, that Eddie Turnbull had something against Davie as he didn't seem all that keen to play him. Although he was full of natural talent, one of Davie's problems was possibly that he could be a bit loud and had a tendency not to listen to advice. He was a very confident individual, and although he was still young he could be quite opinionated and would always be the first to question things, a habit that appeared to upset Turnbull. I always enjoyed playing alongside Davie, however. He was an extremely brainy player with a great double shuffle, a great reader of the game, and I felt that we combined well whenever we played together in the reserves.

Hibs had been drawn against Lausanne in the opening round of that season's Fairs Cup, but had been awarded a walkover when the Swiss side were unable to fulfil the fixture. The draw for the second round however, provided mid-table Hibs with a cracker – a game against the Spanish champions Barcelona. Barcelona were then the reigning Fairs Cup holders after defeating Birmingham City in the previous year's final, and were considered by many to be possibly the best club side in the world. At that time teams were allowed to enter both the European and Fairs Cup competitions, and the Catalan's had just become the first side to defeat Real Madrid over two legs to end Real's five year dominance of the European Cup. The draw had obviously created enormous interest, not only in Edinburgh where the Hibs supporters would now have the opportunity of seeing players in the flesh that they had previously only read about, but throughout the country, the whole of Scotland eagerly looking forward to the fixture. Although we knew that facing the Spanish giants would be a daunting prospect, everyone at Easter Road was really looking forward to the match.

The first game was to have been played in Edinburgh, but was cancelled almost at the last minute on account of the heavy blanket of fog that had lingered over the city all day. It had been agreed that it would now go ahead the following evening if conditions had improved, only for Barcelona to announce that they would now be leaving immediately. The game would now take place in Spain a few days after Christmas. With only 13 places up for grabs there was great excitement over who would be making the trip. Although I didn't dare tell anyone, I already knew that I would be going, as part of the deal my Uncle Tam had agreed with Harry Swan when I signed for the club was that I would be taken abroad at the very first opportunity.

Thirteen players, including just one goalkeeper, something that would be considered laughable nowadays, made their way from what was then Turnhouse Airport to Spain. We arrived in Barcelona to find that our pre-arranged light training session at the ground had been cancelled, apparently because the keys to the stadium couldn't be found. Whether this was a typical ploy to upset us I don't know, but it was well known that the habit of attempting to unsettle the away teams was prevalent on the continent at that time. Although I was not expecting to play I trained with the team. It was my first time abroad and a fantastic experience for a young lad from Bonnyrigg who had not yet turned 18.

Both Willie Ormond and myself watched from the stand as the teams took the field in front of well over 50,000 volatile Spanish fans at the Gran Estadio, a ground that had replaced the much smaller all-seated stadium situated nearby. Opened only a couple of years before it was yet to be renamed the Nou Camp.

Belittling their mid-table position Hibs played well. The side quickly settled into its stride with Joe Baker almost opening the scoring inside the first few minutes. The goal however was not long in coming when Baker took advantage of a mistake by goalkeeper Ramallets, and we were two up inside 20 minutes when Johnny McLeod scored with a brilliant drive from well outside the penalty area. At this point Barcelona were being jeered mercilessly by their own fans who had obviously been expecting an easy victory, and this seemed to sting them into action. A stirring fight back saw the home side pull one back just before half time, another goal shortly after the restart levelling things. If the crowd were now expecting a goal blitz by their favourites then they were to be sadly mistaken. Tommy Preston scored with a crashing drive from around 30 yards that went in off the post, Joe Baker putting us further ahead ten minutes later. Incredibly, with just six minutes remaining, mid-table Hibs were deservedly leading one of the best sides in the world, and at Barcelona's own home ground at that, but unfortunately two late goals gave the Spanish side what to my mind was an underserved share of the spoils.

As far as I was concerned it had to be the best ever performance by a Hibs team on the continent. There had been no failures. Everyone had played well, but Joe Baker, who Barcelona had apparently tried to sign a couple of years before during the club's mid-season tour of Spain, had been head and shoulders above everyone on the park, a constant thorn in the side of the Barcelona defence throughout the entire 90 minutes. Make no mistake, Hibs had fully deserved to win, but even with the draw, it was a result that resonated throughout Europe the following morning.

As I've already mentioned, it was after this game that Willie Ormond decided to take both Jim Scott and I out on the town for a couple of drinks. Once again Willie was taking on the role of the experienced elder statesman looking after the younger boys, and once again the roles were reversed later that evening when Jim and I managed only with some difficulty to escort Willie safely back to our hotel.

A few weeks later there was to be yet another dazzling performance by Hibs when Joe Baker scored nine goals against the luckless East of Scotland side Peebles Rovers, in a Scottish Cup tie at Easter Road. We were leading 6-0 before the former Hibs player Walter McWilliams pulled one back for the East of Scotland side, and 8-1 ahead at the interval, the result having been a mere formality from the start. Hibs eventually cantered to an extremely one sided 15-1 victory, the latter stages of the game spent with every player on the home side giving the ball to Baker at every opportunity as he attempted to beat brother Gerry's total of ten goals for St Mirren against Glasgow University the previous season. I was playing for the reserves in a friendly against Stirling Albion that afternoon, but can still remember being as surprised as anyone on hearing the final score-line.

The return against Barcelona at Easter Road, just over a week later would linger long in the memory of anyone who was inside the stadium that incredible evening. As expected a huge crowd of almost 50,000, which just failed to beat the record for a floodlit game in Edinburgh, crammed inside Easter Road eager to see the Barcelona superstars in the flesh.

After a disappointing start by both sides, during which time the ball was in the air more than on the ground, Joe Baker gave Hibs the lead after just 11 minutes when he flighted a header from a free kick past goalkeeper Medrano. This was merely the sign for Barcelona to step up a gear and things were looking ominous for us when the visitors went in at the interval 2-1 ahead. The Barcelona players had left the field looking composed and confident, but they found a different Hibs side in the second half.

For long periods the Spanish side could not even get out of their own half and Tommy Preston levelled the tie with a header that beat Medrano from close range with just 15 minutes left to play. Even then there was no hint of the incredible scenes that were shortly to unfold. With just six minutes remaining the referee awarded Hibs a penalty after McLeod had been brought down in the box. This was merely the sign for the irate Spanish players, including the European Footballer of the Year, Luis Suarez, to jostle and harass the German referee Malka. The game was held up for several minutes before order was eventually restored.

By this time the atmosphere inside the ground was electric, but for me there was only one man inside Easter Road who was going to take the kick. Bobby Kinloch had been bought out of the RAF earlier in the season after some useful performances in the pre-season games. Bobby was a strong, but fairly average player who worked hard, but with all due respect he was not in the same league as some of the Hibs centre-forwards I had seen. He was however, a supremely confident individual and the only player in the white-hot atmosphere of Easter Road that evening that

I would have trusted with the penalty. As I watched with bated breath from the stands, Bobby did not disappoint, smashing the ball past the goalkeeper to give Hibs the lead. The goal was to be the catalyst for some of the most amazing scenes ever witnessed on a football pitch anywhere in the world. I couldn't believe my eyes as several of the visiting players proceeded to attack the referee, pummelling him to the ground. They then turned their attentions on the police who had entered the field to assist the referee, and for a while it appeared as though some of the Hibs players were about to join the fray. Several Hibs fans attempted to join the action before they were ushered back onto the terracing. After a delay lasting several minutes the game was eventually restarted, the final proceedings playing out in a surreal atmosphere before Herr Malka blew his whistle to end the game.

At the final whistle Malka quickly made his way down the tunnel to the safety of the dressing room, closely followed by a posse of angry Barcelona players, and until the old stand was demolished several years ago, the imprint of stud marks could still be clearly seen on the referee's dressing room door after some of the angry visiting players had attempted to gain entry. The far-side linesman however was not so fortunate, and was beaten to the ground before the police eventually managed to come to his rescue. I watched from the stand, hardly able to take in the astonishing scenes that were taking place on the pitch in front of my very eyes. Incredibly, no one had been arrested or sent off. Barcelona would later play a friendly at Easter Road at their own expense by way of an apology for the incredible behaviour of some of their players that evening.

I was still in the reserves, biding my time when I was unexpectedly recalled to the first team in mid-March for a Scottish Cup tie against Celtic at Parkhead. Although the Celtic line-up still included the nucleus of the 11 that had hammered us earlier in the season at Easter Road, at that time they were a fairly ordinary side, although admittedly always difficult to beat in Glasgow. Goalless at the interval, Bobby Kinloch continued where he had left off against Barcelona by giving us the lead early in the second half. What had been a very ordinary game up until then suddenly burst into action. Playing on the left wing for the first time, I was still very raw, but knew almost immediately that I had the beating of the Scottish international defender Duncan McKay. He knew it too, and in front of an almost full house I gave the Celtic defender a hard time. McKay was obviously not overly enamoured at being given the runaround by an inexperienced youngster, particularly in front of his home crowd, and for almost the entire 90 minutes I had to endure an almost constant barrage of abuse as he tried to put me off my game.

Kinloch's goal seemed as if it would be enough to take us into the next round until Stevie Chalmers took advantage of a mistake in the Hibs penalty area, with only four minutes remaining, to earn the Glasgow side what was an undeserved replay. According to the newspaper reports later that evening I had missed a great opportunity to seal our victory with a chance that was not as easy as it looked when I ballooned the ball over the bar from six yards with the goal gaping, but overall I was pleased with my performance. With only a few minutes left to play I collided with a Celtic player and staggered off at the end suffering from treble vision and concussion, and it was only much later that I realised that there was to be a replay.

I kept my place in the side for the replay on the Wednesday at Easter Road. After the usual pre-match steak at the Scotia Hotel, I took what was by now my traditional stroll to Easter Road. It was still very early, but even then the crowds were beginning to gather in large numbers outside the ground. It would later turn out that the Hibs directors had made a huge error of judgement in failing to make the game all-ticket. Long before the start, the gates had to be closed with thousands still clamouring for entry. Scores of disappointed supporters attempted to watch the game from the roofs of the surrounding tenements. Many more, angry at being denied admission, particularly those who had made their way through from Glasgow, milled around the surrounding streets in a restless mood, one group venting their anger by overturning a parked car. Many managed to make their way into the ground after smashing through one of the large exit gates in Albion Place with the police powerless to stop them. Such was the desire to see the game that several more were arrested after climbing on to the roof of the Dunbar's lemonade factory behind one of the goals. Unfortunately, tempers became more and more frayed resulting in one instance in several of the gravestones in the nearby Eastern cemetery being overturned.

Eventually after a delay, the game got under way. By this time McKay was well aware that I had the beating of him, and I turned on the style encouraged by a huge Hibs support. Once again I had to endure an almost constant torrent of abuse from the international defender, but it was having no effect on my game. In what turned out to be another memorable evening, the first half was pretty even, but after the break there was only one team in it. Once again I had a glorious chance to open the scoring, but held the ball just a fraction too long and it was eventually cleared. A short while later I was clearly barged off the ball by McKay, well inside the penalty area, but incredibly the referee awarded an indirect free kick for obstruction *outside* the box, the kick eventually coming to nothing. It was now Hibs against goalkeeper Haffey, who was having a quite incredible game, but Celtic somehow managed to survive and there was no scoring at the end of 90 minutes. Without doubt the visitors had been lucky to survive the second half pounding, both goalkeeper Haffey and centre-half Billy McNeil outstanding in repulsing our almost non-stop attacks when we did everything but score, and it was now on to extra time. Celtic had made just the one change from the game at Parkhead when they brought in a very young John Clark in place of Bertie Peacock for what was one of the future Lisbon Lion's very first games for the club. With just 60 seconds of the first period of extra time remaining, Celtic were awarded a corner at the Dunbar end. Receiving the ball just outside the penalty area, Clark's diagonal cross-cum-shot managed to evade the despairing lunges of several Hibs defenders only to deflect off keeper Simpson's knee and into the net for the only goal of the game.

To say we were stunned after our magnificent performance would be an understatement. Unfortunately the goal seemed to completely knock the stuffing out of us after all our hard work, and the remaining 15 minutes belonged almost entirely to the visitors who manager to hold out quite comfortably until the final whistle. Although we had lost, at least I had the satisfaction of taking the current Scottish international defender to the cleaners, and I was heartened by one reporters comments the following morning:

> Young Stevenson was the star of the Hibs attack. Cool and clever from the start he used the ball with the sure control that betokens a natural footballer on the way up.

Our form since the cup victory against Peebles Rovers had been far too inconsistent, losing or drawing far more games than were won, but the brilliant form of Johnny McLeod had caught the eye of the selectors. In what would turn out to be a bittersweet international debut, Johnny was one of the very few Scottish players to perform well as England romped home to a 9-3 win at Wembley, the highest margin of victory ever between the sides. Unfortunately for Hibs, as it would turn out, McLeod's club form and his performance at Wembley that afternoon had alerted several top English sides to his obvious potential and he would soon be on his way to Arsenal.

The momentous victory against Barcelona in the Fairs Cup had paired us against the Italian side Roma in the two-legged semi-final, the first game to take place at Easter Road. John Baxter had replaced me at inside-left for the previous couple of games, defeats against Dunfermline and

Rangers, and I had not really expected to play, but was still disappointed when Hugh Shaw read out the side that would face Roma. Once again I watched from the sidelines as eighth-placed Hibs earned a well deserved 2-2 draw against a side that had topped the Italian League at one point, although they had since slipped down the table. At that time Roma were considered almost unbeatable at home, but had the worst away record of any of the sides still left in the competition. They were a formidable side nonetheless, containing several internationalists, but we fancied our chances. The extremely gifted Lojacono gave Roma a half time lead, but after the break it was all Hibs. Kicking down the famous slope Joe Baker equalised midway through the second half only for dreadful decision by the Swiss referee allowing the visitors to retake the lead from a free kick just outside the box after Sammy Baird had been harshly adjudged to have fouled inside-right Pastrin. Johnny McLeod however gave us an equaliser that was more than deserved just before the final whistle.

Once again I was fortunate enough to be included in the party that made its way to Italy for the second leg, leaving somewhat bizarrely from East Fortune Aerodrome as major work was then being carried out on the runway at Turnhouse.

In Italy both Jim Scott and myself were left out from the same 11 that had defeated Clyde 4-0 at Easter Road the previous Saturday, our places perhaps understandably taken by the far more experienced Willie Ormond and Barcelona penalty hero Bobby Kinloch. It would turn out to be Willie's last ever game for the club after a glittering career spanning 15 years, three league championship medals and six full Scotland caps. Before the game, trainer Eddie Turnbull had come up with the ruse that Baker and Kinloch should swop jerseys to confuse our opponents and the plan worked perfectly, the Italian defenders keeping a more than attentive watch on what they thought to be the dangerous Baker, allowing the real England international far more freedom than he otherwise could have expected. They only woke up to the fact that they had been tricked when they were trailing 3-1 after the real Baker had scored twice and in the end we had to settle for a credible 3-3 draw and a third game play-off.

The regulations at that time required that any play-off should take place in a neutral country, but a toss of the coin in the boardroom immediately after the game determined that the decider would again be played in Rome. It has long been accepted however that the Hibs Chairman, Harry Swan, had agreed that the game would take place in Rome in return for a substantial sum and an all-expenses-paid holiday in Italy for the players. The West German side Cologne, who had been Roma's opponents in the previous round, had also settled for Rome as the venue for the deciding game and it has to be assumed that a similar arrangement had also been in place on that occasion.

The big problem as far as Hibs were concerned was that the play-off was earmarked to take place on 27 May, almost a month after the Scottish season had ended, and in the end this would prove far too big a handicap for us to overcome.

The final league game of the domestic season had ended in a humiliating 6-1 victory for Third Lanark at Cathkin, bringing the curtain down on a campaign of mixed fortunes for a club that finally finished in seventh place, the same position as 12 months before, but one point and 40 goals worse off. For me however it was to be only the start. During the previous few months I had become something of a regular in the side, making eight appearances for the first team, scoring three goals. I had also made over 20 appearances for the reserves, but fully realised that it was only the beginning and that a lot of hard work still lay ahead.

Almost three weeks after our domestic season had ended, our preparations for the match in Italy had consisted of only one weeks training just prior to the game, a situation obviously that was far from ideal. However on a personal level not only had I been included in the party that made its way to Rome for the play-off game, I would be making my competitive European debut on the left wing in place of one of my boyhood heroes Willie Ormond. Unfortunately, Jim Scott, who had already become a great pal, was left out from the party that made its way to Italy, and although Scottie was pleased for me, I knew that his exclusion would be a tremendous disappointment for him. By now it was common knowledge that Joe Baker would be joining Torino immediately after the game and we were all determined to make his last outing in a Hibs jersey an occasion to remember, and so it turned out, but for entirely the wrong reason.

The Italian season was still well under way and considering our differing levels of fitness the game turned out to be a complete farce. Manfredini scored for the home side in the very first minute and quite simply we never recovered from the blow. The same player scored a second 20 minutes later and the writing was already on the wall. We were given a slight glimmer of hope when centre-half Losi pulled me down inside the box, but goalkeeper Panetti, who had blatantly moved early, saved Bobby Kinloch's penalty. Roma missed a penalty themselves a couple of minutes later, but by then we all knew that that there was no way back for us and were left chasing shadows for the remainder of the game. The final 6-0 score-line was the heaviest at that time to be suffered by a Scottish side in a competitive European competition.

Since joining the club I hadn't had that much to do with Harry Swan except for his warning about the dangers of the demon drink, but after the game I bumped into the chairman who heartened me somewhat after such a heavy defeat when he said, 'How are you, Eric son? Go and enjoy yourself, you have a big career in front of you.' The compliment coming from a man who had seen it all was greatly appreciated. Considering our long lay off and the consequent difference in match fitness between the sides I don't think that any of us had really expected to win in Italy and some had probably just looked forward to the holiday.

The holiday itself turned out to be a fantastic experience. Trips to the Trevi Fountain, the Coliseum and other local landmarks had all been laid on, possibly courtesy of the *Daily Express* photographer who followed us everywhere we went. An Italian family that John Fraser knew back in Edinburgh had also arranged a meal for us in a top class restaurant where the wine flowed freely. There had also been plenty of time for sunbathing, until the afternoon on a local beach when I almost burned to a cinder. Remember, I came from Bonnyrigg and we didn't normally see a lot of the sun there. I was in a great deal of pain. Eddie Turnbull may well have been a genius as far as football tactics were concerned, but he knew absolutely nothing about medical care. Eddie's remedy to the problem was to rub vinegar onto the sunburn which left me doubled up in absolute agony, almost in tears, and there was very little sleep for me that night. However, apart from the sunburn it turned out to be an unforgettable trip.

One night we were all having a quiet drink back at the hotel when John Fraser, who wasn't much of a drinker, decided that he would have an early night. As he got up to leave Turnbull barked, 'Sit on your arse, you'll leave when I say so.' Needless to say, John, just as the rest of us would have done, did as he was told. You didn't argue with Eddie.

At that time Easter Road was a happy camp with a great group of players and I was already looking forward to the new season.

CHAPTER THREE

Šekularac, Hugh Shaw's Resignation and Walter Galbraith

1961–62

THE HEAVY DEFEAT in Italy didn't prey on my mind for long during the summer months or affect my appetite for the game, and my first full season as a professional footballer just couldn't come quickly enough. As expected, Joe Baker had joined Torino during the summer. Perhaps understandably the transfer of a player who had achieved almost legendary status at Easter Road after such a short space of time had upset many of the Hibs fans who felt that the club could have done far more to keep the player in Edinburgh. In later years Joe would often relate that if Hibs had only paid him the £5 rise he was after then he would have stayed at Easter Road, but it was common knowledge amongst the players that this was only said to appease the fans. The truth is that Joe was always going to go, the money on offer in Italy making it virtually impossible for him to turn the deal down.

If losing Joe wasn't bad enough, the Hibs supporters were in for yet another shock when Johnny McLeod was allowed to join Arsenal just a few days before the start of the new season. Although the rest of the players were obviously not overly happy at losing team mates of the undoubted ability of Baker and McLeod, in all reality it was merely accepted as something that happened in the game. The pair would soon be joined on the way out of Easter Road by the illustrious Willie Ormond, the last remaining on-field link with the halcyon days at Easter Road. Willie had been unsettled at Easter Road for some time and he was allowed to join his home town side Falkirk on a free transfer as a reward for his great service during the past 15 years. I have been asked if I felt that the transfer of both McLeod and Ormond would have made it easier for me to establish myself in the first team, but I have to admit that the thought never crossed my mind for a second. I had bags of confidence in my own ability and was sure that there would be a place for me sooner or later. I also have to say that neither Johnny McLeod nor Willie Ormond ever resented the appearance of a player who could well have been a rival for their position, and both were always exceedingly helpful and encouraging, which, believe me, for a young player just making his way in the game was always greatly appreciated.

Midway through pre-season training we were joined by the future Scotland manager Ally MacLeod who had been signed from Blackburn Rovers. After service with Third Lanark and St Mirren, Ally had spent several seasons with Blackburn Rovers in the English First Division, and had been a member of the side that lost to Wolves in the 1960 FA Cup final. Ally was a real gem of a guy. He could sometimes be loud, but never in a bad way, and was a great character who liked a laugh, although invariably he would always laugh at his own jokes, and was loved by all the younger players. I always felt however that some of the older players resented him. He was a very confident lad although never big headed, and was perhaps more tactically aware than some of the more experienced players at the club at that time and possibly they were a bit jealous of him.

A memory I have of Ally is one night after a European game abroad when both Scottie and I persuaded him to come out on the town with us. Ally wasn't all that much of a drinker and at the end of the night he was absolutely paralytic and had to be smuggled into our hotel. He had been one of the first to fall foul of the recently outlawed maximum wage limit in England. According to Ally, Jack Marshall, his manager at Blackburn Rovers had always insisted that he was such a valuable member of the squad that if ever the maximum wage limit was lifted he would have absolutely no hesitation in doubling his wages. Now, after a court case during the summer, the wage structure in England had been found to be unlawful, allowing Johnny Haynes of Fulham to become the first £100 per week footballer in the country. Several of the Blackburn players including the England internationals Ronnie Clayton and Brian Douglas immediately had their wages doubled to £40 a week, but McLeod had been offered only £25. On receiving what he considered to be a derisory offer he had immediately put in a transfer request and despite a later improved offer to increase his wages to £35, Ally had agreed to join Hibs in a £6,000 deal and to his credit refused to go back on his word.

Later he would pay me a major compliment by saying that he considered me to be every bit as good a player as his former Blackburn team mate Bryan Douglas. Douglas was then the current England outside-right and would eventually go on to make 38 appearances for his country as well as 438 league appearances for Blackburn Rovers, so it was some compliment and coming from such an experienced and wholehearted player it was gratefully accepted.

In the league cup we had been drawn in the same group as St Johnstone, Partick Thistle and Celtic. In our opening game, a 1-1 draw with the Saints at MacDiarmid Park I was switched from the left wing to the right to make way for new signing MacLeod. Although Ally did well for us during his time at the club it was obvious that he was then well past his best and he could often be infuriating to play alongside. He would either have a great run ending with a 40 yard shot that tested the goalkeeper, or at other times the ball would either stick between his feet or would end up in row z. Ally made his home debut a few days later in a game against Partick Thistle when I was fortunate enough to score both our goals in a 2-1 win despite the attention of the rugged Partick full-back George Muir. George was a good lad off the field, but always tried to kick lumps out of me on it. I was usually far too quick for him however and I knew that I had had a great game that afternoon, one newspaper the next morning claiming:

> The Hibs midfield had let themselves down on the end product and it was just as well that the chances fell to young Stevenson who looked the one forward capable of hitting the target, and looks to have solved the right-wing problem.

Undefeated with two wins and two draws from the opening games, it looked as though we had done enough to qualify for the quarter-finals of the competition for the first time in eight years, but unfortunately consecutive defeats by Partick and Celtic soon put an end to that idea. Perhaps surprisingly, the group was eventually topped by a Perth side then managed by the former Rangers player Bobby Brown, but unfortunately they would be relegated at the end of the coming season.

In the Fairs Cup we had been drawn against a side called Belenenses, from Portugal. None of us knew much about them except that at that time Portuguese football was on the up. In the previous season's European Cup Final in Berne, Benfica had defeated a Barcelona side that had ended Real Madrid's run of five consecutive victories in the competition. Benfica would go on to retain the trophy at the end of the coming season, so we were taking nothing for granted. However, the Portuguese season had yet to start and we all felt, wrongly as it would turn out, that this would be to our distinct advantage. Incredibly, inside the opening 26 minutes of the first game at Easter Road we found ourselves already three goals behind, the majority of the almost 20,000 fans inside the ground not slow in registering their disproval. Somehow we managed to claw ourselves back into the game and ended the half much the better side. During this time the Portuguese goalkeeper, Pereira, had been at his very best, pulling off several saves, a couple in the breath-taking class and after the interval there was only one side in it. It was my first home European tie. The atmosphere in those games was much different than normal, and I was loving every second of it. Lining up at inside-right alongside Jim Scott on the wing, I knew that I had the beating of my immediate opponent Vicente and started to run riot. With the big crowd now roaring us on, within minutes of the restart I had laid on a cross for John Fraser to score with a header. John scored again a short while later, before Sammy Baird scored with as cheeky a penalty as you are likely to see after I had been brought down in the box by full-back Castro. On his run up, the experienced Baird briefly hesitated allowing the goalkeeper to fully commit himself before calmly rolling the ball into the other corner of the net to level the score. From then until the end it was all Hibs and we could, and should, have scored more, but I suppose in the circumstances that a draw could be considered a fairly decent result.

During the close season several players from the junior or juvenile ranks had been called up, but quite honestly, to my mind although most of them were good enough players, they were not quite good enough for the Hibs. Tony McGlyn, an inside-forward from Edinburgh Thistle made his debut against Raith Rovers on the Saturday following the Belenenses game, a 3-2 victory at Easter Road. Despite laying on a goal for me and scoring another himself, Tony would make only a handful of appearances in the coming season and would soon be on his way to Airdrie. Brian Marjoribanks, a centre-forward who had been signed from Airth Castle Rovers had also made a scoring debut this time against the Hearts and had looked fairly useful. He had been a big name in juvenile football, but unfortunately he too would make only the occasional appearance, and despite scoring three goals in just five first team starts he would be unable to stake a regular place in the first team and would soon cross the city to join Hearts. No disrespect to the boys, but the quality of the signings at this time was perhaps indicative of a club whose fortunes had deteriorated over the past few years and was now going through what was tactfully described as a transitional period.

In the return leg against Belenenses in Lisbon, manager Hugh Shaw had gambled on a defensive strategy relying on the quick break, and his plan worked perfectly. Belenenses were a good side, but we also had a lot of good players, and if we all managed to click on the same day we fancied our chances against anybody. In recent weeks John Baxter had been moved into the forward line to give us more drive up front and he turned out to be the game's best player. We went in level at the interval after John had equalised an early goal by centre-forward Matateu when he took advantage of a slip by goalkeeper Pereira. As I was leaving the field I was surprised to be given a 'roasting' by trainer Eddie Turnbull who demanded to know, in his own inimitable style, just what I thought I was f***ing playing at: 'you are meant to be playing for the team and not your f***ing self.' I felt that I had done quite well and must admit that I took the huff, sitting in the corner of the dressing room and refusing even to speak to anyone, not that this seemed to bother Turnbull in the slightest. Baxter scored again just after the break to give us the overall lead in the tie and I wrapped it up with what was reported in the press as a neat header when I dived full length to get on the end of a Jim Scott corner. Goalkeeper Pereira would later play for Portugal against England in the semi-finals of the World Cup in 1966, but he must have been a right flapper if he allowed me to score with my head, a very rare occurrence indeed.

After the game Jim Scott and I were out on the town having a few drinks when we passed John Grant, Sammy Baird and Eddie Turnbull sitting outside a bar. The impish Scottie shouted to Turnbull 'Aye, you're no shouting at him now!' I thought Eddie was going to explode, and I am sure that he would have punched us if it hadn't been for Sammy calming him down. Later that evening we were watching from our bedroom window as a taxi containing the trio turned up at the hotel. The next thing we knew we could hear Eddie arguing with the taxi driver. John Grant told us later that he and Sammy Baird had made a hasty exit from the cab leaving Turnbull to pay the fare. Eddie being Eddie refused to pay and stormed into the hotel closely followed by the irate driver who was still demanding his money. At one point Turnbull grabbed one of the large hotel ashtrays, threatening the driver while we egged him on from the safety of our room shouting, 'Hit him, Ed, hit him.' Eventually the driver, realising the hopelessness of the situation, stormed off. Eddie was some man and I don't think that many would have fancied tackling him.

Our form around that time wasn't the greatest to say the least. We had failed to register a win in the month since the Belenenses game and were then sitting just two places above the relegation zone. In a desperate attempt to freshen things up the diminutive Ian Cuthbert was among several changes made by Hugh Shaw for the game against Third Lanark at Easter Road. I had played with Ian at Edina Hearts and we were good pals. He was a very good player, had a huge heart and for someone just over five-foot tall he was reasonably good in the air. I thought that Ian had all the attributes to make it, but unfortunately he failed to get any bigger and would be handed a free transfer at the end of the season. We had played well enough against Third's, but two uncharacteristic mistakes by Ronnie Simpson eventually cost us both points, hardly an ideal result just a few days before a big European game.

Our next Fairs Cup opponents would be the Yugoslavian side Red Star Belgrade, who at that time were considered to be one of the best teams in Europe. Our recent indifferent results had seen us drop deep into the bottom end of the table and I don't think that anyone at Easter Road really fancied our chances against a side that had won the league championship six times since their formation only at the end of the war. Thirteen players, including as usual only one goalkeeper, were selected to make the trip to Belgrade. Once again my pal Scottie would have been bitterly disappointed at being left out, but in the end he would be the lucky one. A journey that would slowly descend into a nightmare began with a long delay at the airport, but that was only the start. Several other delays and a long journey by bus saw us finally arriving at our destination more than 36 hours after starting out from Edinburgh. During the trip Eddie Turnbull had warned us to watch out for the Belgrade danger man Dragoslav Šekularac, a gypsy he had played against in the 1958 World Cup finals in Sweden.

As usual Eddie would be proved right. Šekularac turned out to be a quite exceptional player, one of the best in the world. A supremely confident individual with fantastic technical ability, he could do anything with the ball and completely ran the show. In one instance I remember him flicking the ball over the head of a couple of Hibs players with his chest direct from a by-kick leaving the defenders floundering in his wake as he made his way towards goal. Later in the game he would receive a slight injury and I can still picture him walking off behind the goal before making his way to the half-way line for treatment waving to the ecstatic home fans all the way around the ground. On reaching the dugout he stood with both hands in the air to receive the tumultuous acclaim of the adoring Red Star fans. What a player.

Near the end, with Hibs trailing 4-0, Jim Easton was sent off for a fairly innocuous tackle on Šekularac. The decision surprised us all because no one had got near enough to tackle him all evening. As he was reluctantly leaving the field Easton turned to the player threatening to do him when he came to Easter Road. At that the bold Šekularac held up four fingers in one hand and a clenched fist in the other, replying in broken English 'Edinburgh 4-0 game finished!' I had been brought up on the Famous Five, but this guy was something else, a genius. Years later, I asked Eddie Turnbull who was the best player he had ever seen. Without hesitation he replied George Best. When I reminded him about Šekularac, he thought about it for a moment before answering, 'Perhaps Best just shades it.' Believe me the Yugoslav was that good.

A little earlier in the season we had played Torino at Easter Road as part of the Joe Baker transfer deal. Both Joe and Denis Law were in the Torino line-up that evening. In one instance I managed to take the ball off Denis and I remember being surprised to hear him swearing at me. Law was a truly great player, but to my mind, and probably Eddie Turnbull's as well, he was not nearly as good as Šekularac.

While we were in Yugoslavia, Ronnie Simpson was on Scotland duty at Hampden as the reserve goalkeeper for the inter-league side against the Italian League that same evening, giving Willie Muirhead a rare first team start. I can't remember us losing any particularly soft goals myself, but according to later reports, manager Hugh Shaw blamed the goalkeeper for at least three of them. I don't think that Willie ever played for the first team again. He would soon be on his way out of Easter Road, in his case, to Canada.

After the game we all sat down to the post-match meal. I had ordered a huge steak which when it arrived was extremely rare although still delicious. I was sitting next to the elegant John Grant who turned to me saying, 'Oh Eric, I don't know how you can eat that thing.' I explained, 'John, this time last year I was eating, butter and jam down the pit.' He just laughed and carried on eating.

At a heated board meeting the following midweek manager Hugh Shaw handed in his resignation, reputedly after an argument with the chairman, Harry Swan, bringing to an end an association with the club that stretched back 43 years. Hugh was a real gentleman who was never seen without a shirt and tie, but for me his resignation didn't change much at Easter Road. Except on match days and the very rare occasions that he would pop into the dressing room during the week I had very little contact with the manager except possibly a quick hello in passing. Very much a manager of the old school he didn't take the training, leaving that to Eddie Turnbull who was the main man as far as the players were concerned, and occasionally Jimmy McColl. McColl was some machine. A member of the celebrated Hibs side of the mid-'20s that had reached consecutive Scottish Cup finals, he was the first Hibs player to score 100 goals in all competitions, and with the exception of a short spell as manager of Belfast Celtic Jimmy had been at the club ever since. He would look after the kit and take charge of the reserves on match days and was a great guy who was well respected by all the players. Jimmy never criticised you regardless of how badly you had played, and was always available for a kindly word of advice. Although he never said as much, I knew that he liked me, and his support, particularly later when I was out of the side for a while, was always well received.

With Harry Swan now supposedly running the side, although in reality that role had been taken on by Eddie Turnbull and some of the more experienced players, we were turned over by Motherwell at Fir Park, the 5-1 defeat leaving us struggling near the foot of an 18-team league and in all kinds of relegation trouble.

Ian Cuthbert, who hadn't played since the defeat by Third Lanark a few weeks earlier was a surprise inclusion for the return game against Red Star at Easter Road. It would turn out to be his last appearance for the first team. In the end Šekularac didn't travel to Edinburgh, which was probably a good thing for Jim Easton as in all probability the centre-half would have spent another wasted night trying to get near enough to kick him, but I felt that it was a great pity for the Hibs fans who I am sure would have appreciated his undoubted talents. The game took place on a bitterly cold night in front of a very poor crowd who had already started to drift away long before Palensevis scored late on to give Red Star a convincing 5-0 overall lead.

Despite the demands of the now restless Hibs fans, Harry Swan had stated publicly that no new players would be signed until a new manager had been appointed, but our precarious league position made it imperative that something had to be done, and quickly. A few days later Gerry Baker, brother of Joe, was signed from Manchester City for a fee believed to be around £25,000, big money in those days for a club like Hibs. Although he failed to score himself, Gerry, who was an infectious character, brought a new energy and enterprise to the forward line and helped us to a 2-0 victory against St Johnstone at Muirton. With goals from John Fraser and yours truly, my seventh of the season so far, it was Hibs' first win for almost two months. Gerry was a great character to have around and reminded me at times of his younger brother Joe. He was a very funny guy and seldom seen without a broad smile on his face. He had this small MG car and I remember once half a dozen of us crammed inside it as we roared up the Bridges in Edinburgh singing at the top of our voices ,probably to the bemusement of the passers-by. Gerry's main weapon was his incredible speed. He was also capable of beating a man and had a great eye for a goal, but could sometimes be infuriating. He would often look the part early doors, but would fade out of games as if he couldn't be bothered. He had a similar style to his brother, but not the same attitude, and I often wonder just how good he would have been had Jock Stein got hold of him.

Gerry scored his first goal for the club, the winner as it would turn out in a 3-2 victory over his former side St Mirren at the beginning of December, but our perilous league position now made it imperative that a new manager be brought in as soon as possible. As usual several names were being bandied about in the papers as to who would replace Hugh Shaw. It later turned out that the former Rangers player Bobby Brown, who was then manager of St Johnstone, had already been interviewed as had the former Celtic defender Jock Stein who was then making quite a name for himself at Dunfermline. Eddie Turnbull was the popular choice among the players to replace Shaw and I know that Eddie himself fancied the job, so we were all surprised and possibly a little bit bemused a few weeks later to learn that the then Tranmere Rovers manager Walter Galbraith was to take over the Easter Road hot seat.

Galbraith had made something of a name for himself in England, although managing mainly the lower league clubs, Accrington Stanley, Bradford Park Avenue, New Brighton and Tranmere Rovers. Not putting too fine a point on it, he was considered somewhat of a surprise appointment and probably the less said about Walter's time at Easter Road the better. Apparently he had played alongside Ronnie Simpson at Queens Park just after the war, but very few us at Easter Road had even heard of him. A spell with Clyde followed before a move to England where he made several appearances mostly for minor league teams. As far as the players were concerned, Galbraith's appointment made little difference to the day-to-day running of the club. Like Shaw, the new manager rarely took anything to do with the training, leaving that to Eddie Turnbull as before. I suppose Walter was a nice enough man who would rarely if ever give you a rollicking, preferring to leave that side of things to Eddie, who would often lose the plot, but to be honest I didn't care too much for him. To my mind he knew absolutely nothing about the game, and my enduring memory of him is preening himself in front of the dressing room mirror as he addressed us on match days or on the rare occasions that he came downstairs in midweek. He was quite a handsome guy, very similar in looks to the film star Douglas Fairbanks Junior who was all the rage at the time, and he really fancied himself.

As often happens when a new manager comes in there was a slight, but unfortunately only temporary improvement in results. Galbraith's first game in charge was a Scottish Cup first round tie against Partick Thistle at Firhill in mid-December. Gerry Baker scored both our goals in a 2-2 draw and although we would lose the replay, overall there was a general improvement with six points taken from the following four games including a 0-0 home draw with Rangers in front of a bumper 30,000 crowd, our biggest of the season so far.

At the turn of the year I was disappointed to hear that Davie Gibson, soon to be released from the forces and then stationed at Redford Barracks in Edinburgh after his return from Berlin, had been transferred to English First Division side Leicester City. As I have already mentioned Davie was probably the best player that I played alongside at Easter Road and he had since become another great friend. He would go on to carve out a great career for himself in England, and during his nine years at Filbert Street would be capped seven times for Scotland and also play in two FA Cup finals, unfortunately losing both. I kept in touch with him over the years and he was always trying to persuade me to come down and try my luck in England as he was convinced that I would be a sensation down there, but I was a home bird and was happy in Edinburgh playing for the Hibs.

Our traditional New Year's Day game against near neighbours Hearts had originally been cancelled because of snow, but went ahead at Easter Road a few weeks later. By then my old friend Willie Bauld was nearing the end of his illustrious career at Tynecastle and was no longer considered an automatic first team choice. Turning back the years, that afternoon Bauld gave a vintage performance, laying on three of the goals and scoring the fourth himself in Hearts' 4-1 win. It would turn out to be the last goal that Bauld would score against his old adversaries during what had been a glittering career. At the other end of the spectrum, a 17-year-old Heriot's schoolboy called Alan Gordon who was just starting out on his career scored two of the Hearts goals that afternoon. Fate would dictate that Alan would score many more goals at Easter Road in the not too distant future, but by this time he would be wearing the green and white of Hibs.

Although I was still only in my first full season I was already aware that I was beginning to gain the respect of my opponents. Not only could I beat a man, but I was also a good reader of the game and was always looking for an opening. However, there were several defenders that I didn't particularly look forward to playing against although I would like to think that I usually gave as good as I got. One a bit later in my career was Jim Whyte of Aberdeen who I found to be quite a handful, but probably my most difficult opponent was Eric Caldow of Rangers and Scotland. Eric was an intelligent defender and far different from his full-back partner Bobby Shearer who would just bomb forward, although they complimented each other well and made a great defensive pairing. Caldow though was an extremely clever player, exceptionally fast, tremendous on the recovery, and although he was a good tackler, he would prefer to jockey you into a less dangerous position, sometimes by as much as 40 yards, by which time his team mates had usually come to his aid. In contrast, as I have already mentioned, I really enjoyed playing against Duncan McKay of Celtic whom I knew I usually had the beating of, so did he for that matter, and also his fellow full-back partner Jim Kennedy for the same reason.

In mid-February we managed to beat Third Lanark 2-1 at Cathkin, a result that lifted us into tenth place in the table and well clear of the danger of relegation. That afternoon I would come face to face for the first time with my immediate opponent and future team mate, Joe Davis. Fortunately I had one of these games and turned poor Joe inside out. Years later, in a newspaper interview he would pay me the huge compliment of describing me as the best player he had ever played against, and that according to Joe, also included Willie Henderson of Rangers and Celtic's Jimmy Johnstone.

One day near the end of the season before a game against Celtic at Easter Road, I was taken aside by Gerry Baker who told me that his brother Joe was waiting outside. Joe had been involved in a late night car crash in Italy only a few months before that had almost cost him his life. He was still in a hell of a mess and Gerry asked me not to mention the accident because Joe was still very self-conscious about his appearance and fairly embarrassed to be seen in public. I was not playing that afternoon and when I went to collect my tickets I just couldn't believe the state of poor Joe's face. Gone were the playboy looks that had always attracted hordes of girls wherever he went, to be replaced by badly swollen, bruised and misshapen features. Fortunately his appearance would eventually return to near normality, but it would take some time.

The arrival of Gerry Baker had instilled fresh impetus into the Easter Road attack and we managed to finish an otherwise respectable eighth in the table which was probably reasonable given the circumstances and only one place below that of the previous season. Although he had missed more than half the games, Gerry still ended the season as second-top goal scorer at Easter Road, only two behind Duncan Falconer who had scored 12. However, we were well aware that we had scored far too few goals overall whilst conceding more than most sides in the league and it was obvious that a major rebuilding programme was needed.

Willie Muirhead who had been blamed by manager Hugh Shaw for the heavy defeat in Belgrade was among the players freed, as were Bobby Nicol and John Young. Both Ally McLeod and Bobby Kinloch were retained, but had been informed that the club would not be difficult to deal with in the event of an offer.

During the season just ended Rangers had won both the League Cup by beating Hearts 3-1 after a replay, and the Scottish Cup when defeating

St Mirren 2-0, but the surprise package of the season had undoubtedly been Dundee who had won the league championship for the very first time in the club's history. Dundee were a great side packed full of fantastic players and were considered by many Dens supporters to be the best in the club's history. A pure footballing side, they had good attacking full-backs in Cox and Hamilton, particularly Hamilton who I felt was far ahead of his time in working up and down the pitch. The rugged and often rough and ready future Arsenal and Scotland centre-half Ian Ure would keep them out at the back, while target man Alan Gilzean was the main threat up front. Great in the air, Gilzean was a lethal finisher and was always hovering around the box hoping to get on the receiving end of the numerous and accurate crosses provided by the former Hibs legend Gordon Smith. Although he was then well past his best and lacking his former mobility, Smith still had his fantastic football brain that he put to great effect. Incredibly, his championship medal would be his fifth, won by three different sides, a unique feat particularly as none had been with either Rangers or Celtic.

Although they had ended the season in third place, at that time Celtic were no more than a very ordinary side, particularly compared to second placed Rangers who at times could be quite exceptional. Shearer and Caldow I have already mentioned. Both were different, and in their own way each as good as the other, but they were defensive players who rarely crossed the half-way line. At that time Jim Baxter was just approaching his peak. Signed from Raith Rovers only at the start of the previous season his incredible talents had blossomed at Ibrox. Already capped almost a dozen times for Scotland, he was now widely reckoned to be one of the best players ever produced in the country. He was a quite exceptional talent. Although he lacked a bit in pace his brilliant football brain more than made up for it. He could be arrogant on the pitch, but off the field he was a great lad, one of the boys.

At right half the Korean war veteran Harold Davis was the perfect foil for Baxter. The tough tackling, no-nonsense Davis was the direct opposite of Jim, but was no less effective. By this time my former Edina Hearts team mate John Greig had developed into one of the best defenders in the country. Not the greatest of ball players, he was nonetheless a pacey defender who would run all day, could tackle, and never knew when he was beaten. In his own way he was yet another inspirational figure at Ibrox and in later years would be voted the club's best ever player. Outside-right Willie Henderson was one of my all-time favourites. What a player! Even at 17 years of age he could hardly see, and who knows just how good he would have been had he been blessed with perfect eyesight.

Henderson and Jimmy Johnstone of Celtic were both great players, but Willie was far more direct and Ralph Brand and Jimmy Miller would almost fight each other to get on the end of his inch-perfect crosses from the right wing. Willie could also score goals himself, and with him on one wing and Davie Wilson on the other, Rangers were always a side to be reckoned with. Willie could run 20 or 30 yards at full pelt with the ball at his feet and then suddenly stop dead and change direction, leaving the defender floundering in his wake. We played together for the Scottish Juvenile select and he is still a great friend.

At that time Scotland had an abundance of good players. Charlie Cooke and George Mulhall at Aberdeen; Pat Quinn, Bert McCann and my good pal and future Easter Road team mate Willie Hunter at Motherwell; the one-club-man Davie McParland at Partick Thistle; Gordon Marshall at Hearts; and Dave Hilley, Alex Harley and Matt Gray at Third Lanark, to name but a few. Unfortunately several of them would soon take advantage of the much better money on offer down south, after the relaxing of the maximum wage limit leaving Scottish football much the poorer.

At the end of the season Hibs embarked on a five-game-tour of Czechoslovakia as a reward for our efforts during the previous campaign. As usual we gathered at the Scotia Hotel in Edinburgh on the Sunday morning before making our way to the airport. Time was getting on, but still there was no sign of manager Walter Galbraith. A late hurried phone call to his house in Willowbrae informed us that he was ill in bed and would not be coming. The only problem was that he had failed to tell the club. At that we all made a mad dash to the airport and only just managed to catch the connection to London for the first leg of the journey to Prague. Meanwhile Bobby Kinloch and goalkeeper Willie Wilson were having problems of their own, finally managing to receive their travel visas literally only minutes before boarding.

The downside of the trip however was that Eddie Turnbull would now be in charge. With his reputation as a hard task master I could hear a few groans from some of the older players who were well aware that the normal relaxing end of season holiday was now well out of the question. It was no secret that Eddie had wanted the manager's job before Galbraith's appointment and he was desperate to do well in Czechoslovakia to show the board just what they had missed. Up until that moment I'm not sure that Eddie had displayed any great signs of tactical awareness, but during the trip he came into his own, probably gaining a lot of confidence from being completely in charge and relished the opportunity of pitting his wits against continental managers. The trip got off to a bad start when the hamper containing our kit went missing at the airport. It later turned out that it had not been loaded onto the plane in Edinburgh, but luckily it arrived the following morning. Overall the tour was a great success with three victories and two draws from the five games played and it was obvious to us all that Eddie had generally outsmarted all his immediate opposites as far as tactics were concerned.

A couple of our games had been interrupted to make way for the bicycle races that were then a huge attraction in the country. The game against Vitkovik which was shown live on television, had kicked off 20 minutes late to allow a bicycle race to take place only for the game to be brought to a sudden halt after 67 minutes and Hibs leading 2-0 – when engineers started to erect a gigantic time clock on the pitch for yet another event. During another, a parachutist had landed on the pitch as the game was taking place. The quality of the opposition was reasonably good, but the refereeing often left a lot to be desired. During the game against Sokolovo, Tommy Preston had disputed one of the referee's many dubious decisions and to our utter disbelief the ref stormed up to Tommy and stamped hard on his toes. One drawback of an otherwise enjoyable trip was that there was not much to do socially. Eddie had warned us to be on our best behaviour at all times and we were only allowed to have a couple of drinks after games. Being healthy young lads a couple of us would slip the interpreter a couple of the local banknotes and he would let us know where to go for a drink, although there were no pubs as we knew them back home only hotel bars.

Part of the arrangements had meant us staying a couple of nights in the Beskydy Mountains, but not long after our arrival at the hotel some of the players complained that the place looked more like a brothel. That was enough for Harry Swan who would never accept anything but the very best for his players, and we made an unscheduled return to Ostrava in the morning.

Before a 2-2 draw with Spartak Brno, Eddie called me aside to tell me that I would be playing on the right wing. Foolishly, I mentioned that I would rather play on the left. At that Eddie informed me in his own characteristic way that left me under no illusion that if I didn't want to play on the right side then I wouldn't be 'f***ing playing at all'. I played on the right wing. You didn't argue with Eddie Turnbull. Respect, yes, but to be honest there was also more than a little bit of fear. At times he could be a very scary character. In later years a former player who will remain nameless spent some time working under Eddie the manager, and would describe arriving at Easter Road each morning like visiting the dentist.

We all knew not to cross Eddie, but away from the pitch on these trips he could often be good fun. He would keep us enthralled by tales from his navy days during the war, but I was only really interested in hearing him talk about football in the old days. Whenever he mentioned Hibs' ground-breaking tour of Brazil in 1953, Eddie would always insist that in his opinion, at that particular time, Hibs were undoubtedly the best club side in the world, and who am I to argue. He would also talk about his time with the Famous Five and it was fairly obvious that he was more than slightly envious of Gordon Smith. After watching Eddie for years from the terracing and playing alongside him in training games, I was well aware of just how good a player he was, but he would often describe, complete with his customary adjectives, how the ball would go from Ormond to him, then to Reilly, back to him then Johnstone, who would pass to Smith, when in Eddie's words, barely managing to hide his contempt, it then became the f***ing Gordon Smith show.

Unfortunately the Czechoslovakia trip didn't end too well for the stand-in manager when he contracted Gastric Flu during the final few days before our return to Edinburgh. He would eventually spend over a week in bed back home, losing more than a stone in weight.

For me though, it was all a truly wonderful experience. During my time at Easter Road the players were always treated like Kings. Nothing was too good for us. We flew everywhere, were well fed and always stayed in the best hotels. It was a far different world from what I had been used to, and I can honestly say that Hibs helped make me the person that I am today.

CHAPTER FOUR

Injury, a Freak Winter
and Relegation Dogfight
1962–63

THE SUMMER SEEMED to drag by as each new day was spent anxiously looking forward to the new season, completely unaware at the time of just how traumatic events would eventually turn out, not only for the club, but for me personally.

As usual, several new faces had joined us during the break, among them Johnny Byrne who had been signed from Walter Galbraith's former club Tranmere Rovers, Doug Logan from Queens Park, John Blair from Bradford Park Avenue, Derek Oates from Ross County, Duncan McLeod from Brora Rangers and Morris Stevenson on a free transfer from Motherwell.

Also among the new faces that first day were a couple of youngsters who would stand the club in good stead in the years ahead – Jimmy O'Rourke and Bobby Duncan. Another, Peter Cormack would later join us from Hearts. Unfortunately, with the exception of Johnny Byrne, Morris and later O'Rourke, Duncan and Cormack, none of the other newcomers would make much of an impact at Easter Road.

Nicknamed Budgie to distinguish him from the West Ham player of the same name, Byrne had been tipped as one for the future by none other than the legendary Tom Finney, but as far as I was concerned, although he was a lovely lad and I got on well enough with him, he added not a lot to the side.

Morris Stevenson however was a different kettle of fish, a quite exceptional talent who had been signed in fierce competition from Hearts, Queen of the South and the Dutch side Sparta Rotterdam. I knew him from our juvenile days and had always been impressed by his talents. He could certainly play a bit, worked hard, could pass the ball and score goals, but if he had a fault it was perhaps that he lacked that bit of guile.

For one reason or another after a bright start he would fail to make much of an impression at Easter Road and would be freed at the end of the season.

I had got on well with Morris and was sad to see him go. However he would not be out of the game long and would soon be snapped up by Morton where he would really flourish under Hal Stewart, and would come back to haunt us in the very near future. Sadly, Morris passed away during the writing of this book.

Bobby Duncan had joined the club as pretty much an average inside-forward, but had since switched to full-back and would soon develop into a fantastic defender. Unfortunately he was on the verge of international honours when he received a terrible injury playing against Celtic that put him out of the game for almost a year. Although Bobby might not agree, I don't think that he was the same player afterwards. Our other new signing Jimmy O'Rourke had been sought by a host of clubs including both Celtic and Manchester United and would soon make an earlier than expected first team debut to become the youngest player at that time to feature in a competitive European match.

At that time the traditional precursor to the new season was the annual Edinburgh Select Charities match which was then in its 19th season. Held alternately at Tynecastle and Easter Road, it normally featured six players from the home side and five from the other. I considered it a great honour to be selected along with my Easter Road team mates Jim Easton, Gerry Baker, Gerry Byrne and Ally McLeod for that year's game against Burnley at Tynecastle, where once again I found myself wearing the maroon of Hearts, this time the distinctive candy strip that was very popular with the Hearts fans at that time. At that time Burnley were one of the top sides in England with players of the calibre of the Scottish international goalkeeper Adam Blacklaw, Jimmy Adamson, Jimmy McIlroy, Ray Pointer and John Connolly. Runners up in the FA Cup the previous season and second in the league, behind Alf Ramsey's all conquering Ipswich, they were well worth their 4-2 victory in what turned out to be disappointingly drab affair. It would be the last in a series of games that had taken place annually since 1944. At one time the fixture had been capable of attracting well over 40,000 fans, but it had now lost its appeal and was capable of attracting *only* around half this number.

In his programme notes for the new season, manager Walter Galbraith had promised the fans that the forthcoming campaign would produce entertainment and good results, but unfortunately both would prove to be in extremely short supply in the months ahead. In the opening league cup fixture in a section that also comprised of Rangers, St Mirren and

Third Lanark, we went down 4-1 at Easter Road to the Ibrox side, Morris Stevenson scoring Hibs' solitary counter on his debut. Unfortunately the early defeat would turn out to be merely a portent of things to come. For a time, a 3-3 draw in Paisley, a victory over Third Lanark at Easter Road and a 0-0 draw at Ibrox looked like being enough to ensure qualification for the later stages of the competition for the first time in nine years. Sadly it was not to be and we eventually finished one point behind the section leaders Rangers.

An away defeat by newly promoted Clyde in the first game of the new campaign, a result that might well have had a major part to play in the relegation dogfight at the end of the season, was followed by a 4-0 defeat at Easter Road by local rivals Hearts. That afternoon the Gorgie side had a certain Willie Hamilton, a recent signing from Middlesbrough, dictating play from midfield as Hearts won easily enough, the heavy defeat doing little to banish the concerns of the Hibs support. Hamilton, of whom we will hear more later, would soon help his new club lift the League Cup in a controversial final against Kilmarnock at Hampden.

Another heavy defeat a few weeks later, this time 5-1 at home to Rangers, would mean us dropping into second bottom place in the table, and although it was still very early days, the signs were already beginning to look ominous. Harvey McCreadie, a free scoring centre-forward who had been signed from non-league side Mosley a few weeks earlier for the enormous sum of £1,500, had scored our solitary goal against Rangers. Unfortunately it would be one of only three he would score for the club in nine appearances.

It was obvious that Walter Galbraith really fancied Harvey, apparently even claiming in one newspaper article that he was as good in the air as the great England centre-forward Tommy Lawton, an outrageous if not highly laughable claim. Harvey was a real character, another good lad, but never a football player in his life. I don't wish to be unkind, but for me Harvey had nothing, no tricks, no heart and couldn't even head the ball. He was completely out of his depth at Easter Road and it was no surprise when he left to join non-league side Altrincham at the end of the season. Worse was to follow after the Rangers humiliation when we went down 5-0 to Dundee United at Tannadice, and even this early it was obvious that it was going to be a long hard season.

In the Fairs Cup we had been drawn against the Danish composite side Copenhagen Staevnet, a team selected from players of eight local sides. The first leg at Easter Road was won easily enough, all the goals in our 4-0 victory scored in the first half, three in a seven minute spell. It was disappointing however to hear the Hibs fans jeering us when we failed to add to the score-line after the break, although I suppose that given the recent run of poor results the reaction was perhaps understandable and could be put down to nothing more than frustration. The victory however was just the tonic that we desperately needed at that time. The Hibs side around that time was:

SIMPSON, FRASER AND MCCLELLAND, GRANT, HUGHES AND MCLEOD, SCOTT, BYRNE, BAKER, (M) STEVENSON AND (E) STEVENSON.

A few days later in a game against Raith Rovers at Easter Road, I scored my first ever penalty in senior football after a defender had punched the ball off the line. It would be the only goal in what turned out to be an extremely drab affair between the bottom two sides in the table and also the last goal that I was destined to score for quite some time. On Saturday 20 October 1962 we made our way to Paisley to face St Mirren at Love Street. Midway through the first half we were leading by a Johnny Byrne goal when we were awarded a corner. As the ball came over I can remember being tackled inside the box by the former Manchester City player John McTavish. There was nothing malicious in the tackle, but I felt my leg caught between both of John's legs as we fell and I knew instantly that it was serious. Somehow I managed to limp to the sidelines to be treated by trainer Turnbull.

Eddie had earlier shown his shortcomings as far as medical expertise was concerned during our holiday in Italy with his vinegar suggestion, and once again he demonstrated his complete lack of medical acumen, when he advised me just to stamp my foot hard on the ground a couple of times as that was sure to fix the problem. I did as he suggested and almost collapsed in agony. It was obvious that I couldn't continue. Carried to the dressing room, it was off to the Paisley Infirmary for me where the injury was later diagnosed as a broken leg. I was allowed home later that evening, but on the Monday I reported to the Western General Hospital in Edinburgh where the leg was re broken and set in plaster.

I was in hospital for about a week where I was visited by several of my team mates, but was still left with plenty of time to worry that my career could well be over, although as far as I can remember the doctors didn't seem to share my concerns. Things were vastly different in those days and I wasn't required to report to Easter Road for regular treatment or light exercises as would be the case today. I remember though that the recovery seemed to take what felt like years, although in reality it could only have been a matter of months. I would be visited regularly at home by the family doctor and was eventually able to hobble around Bonnyrigg on crutches.

During my enforced absence a lot had been happening at Easter Road. Not only did I miss the return game against Copenhagen in Denmark, a 3-2 win that gave us a comprehensive 7-2 aggregate victory, but also the visit of Barcelona who were returning at their own expense by way of an apology for the dreadful behaviour of some of their players during the Fairs Cup game at Easter Road almost two years before. That evening at Easter Road there was no sign of bad behaviour, and it was obvious from the start that the visitors had been well warned as to their conduct, apologising profusely after every foul. Regardless of their sportsmanship they still proved far too good for us, and in front of a disappointingly small crowd of around 10,000 the visitors were well worth their 3-1 victory.

Around that time a series of impressive performances for the reserves had earned the 16-year-old Peter Cormack a surprise promotion to the first team, and at the end of November he scored Hibs' solitary counter in a 2-1 defeat at Broomfield with what was described in the press as a cute header. It was difficult to believe that only a few short months before Peter had actually been on the ground staff at Tynecastle until allegedly, an incident involving a grass cutting machine and damage to the perimeter wall of the pitch had hastened the end of his time in Gorgie. Quite simply, Peter Cormack was a fantastic player. Although he was a skinny kid built like a greyhound, he was as hard as nails. A great trainer with a fabulous attitude, Peter could do everything, pass, beat a man, tackle, head the ball and had a particular talent for trapping the ball with his chest on the run. He could play wide, midfield, upfront or even in goals, and I always felt that he would have made a great sweeper. Another genuinely nice bloke, at Easter Road both Eddie Turnbull and later Big Jock really loved him. I might be wrong, but I felt that he eventually became a bit complacent at Easter Road and it was only after his move to England that he really came into his own, particularly at Liverpool where he flourished playing alongside great players like Kevin Keegan, Ian Callaghan and John Toshack. Credit must be given to the Liverpool manager Bill Shankly, who recognised that Peter's true position was a fetch and carry role in the midfield of what was unquestionably a truly fabulous side.

After his debut against Airdrie however it would be back to the reserves for Peter, though he was far too good a player to remain there for long.

Another youngster who would have a big part to play in the history of the club would also make his first team debut a few weeks later. After a 1-0 victory against Utrecht in Holland in the next round of the Fairs Cup, 16-year-old Jimmy O'Rourke replaced the injured Tommy Preston for the return leg at Easter Road. Surprised to be called from his work in the afternoon of the game, Jimmy would be even more surprised to learn that he would be playing that evening. The victim of harsh tackling throughout the game, O'Rourke, who had only turned 16 a couple of months before, making him the youngest ever player at that time to take part in a competitive European game, almost capped his debut with a goal when his cleverly lobbed header passed only narrowly over the bar. Jimmy had been chased by a number of clubs, but had been recommended to Hibs by Davie Johnstone, the same Edina Hearts trainer who had taken me to Tynecastle. Speaking to Davie at the time he enthused about O'Rourke, telling me that 'this boy can really play'. Even at such a tender age he had the legs of a much older man. As strong as an ox, he was a very good player with a good football brain and he would chase everything all day long. Quick and brave, he knew the way to goal and I always enjoyed playing alongside him. Unfortunately he would shortly receive a bad injury at Tannadice that would affect his progress quite a bit in the early days and he would have long spells out of the first team. It has to be said though that it was only after Eddie Turnbull's arrival at Hibs in the early '70s that Jimmy really came into his own, forming a prolific goalscoring partnership with Alan Gordon, and I know that Jimmy himself would be the first to admit that Turnbull made him a player.

For some reason the club found winning in Europe fairly easy, but were really struggling to make any headway in the league, although to be fair, a catalogue of injuries would not have helped. Apart from myself, Duncan Falconer, Ally McLeod and a bit later Jimmy O'Rourke would all spend a large part of the season on the treatment table.

Of the 16 games played since the beginning of the season we had managed to win only three, results that saw us dropping to third bottom place in the table and we were now staring relegation firmly in the face.

A few days before the turn of the year, the home game against Clyde only managed to pass inspection 20 minutes before the start on account of the heavy snow that had been falling all day, threatening to obliterate the lines. Watched by a crowd of only a few hundred hardy souls, brave, or foolish, enough, depending on your viewpoint, to suffer the extreme climatic conditions, the snow continued to fall even more heavily during the game. Although we were not to know it at the time, Hibs would fulfil only one more fixture between then and the beginning of March, a period of more than two months. After the game, a 2-1 defeat, the police had to be called to disperse a large crowd of dissatisfied supporters that had gathered outside the centre stand demanding change. The demonstration prompted Harry Swan, as forthright as ever, to condemn the supporters as people who just cannot take losing, adding that, 'They may as well stay away from Easter Road if that is their reaction to defeat.' Harsh words, but things would get much worse before they got any better.

My recovery seemed to take an age. Not being much of a reader, I would mostly just sit moping around the house watching TV all day long and I had plenty of time to consider the fact that my career in football could well be over almost before it had begun. Eventually, just a few days before the Clyde game, nine long, soul destroying weeks after the injury, I attended hospital to have the heavy plaster removed to be replaced by a much lighter cast. After the removal of the plaster I almost fainted when I saw the state of my leg. It was so thin and wasted that it looked as though it belonged to a prisoner of war. The lighter cast however made it much easier to get around and I could start doing light exercises as the first step towards regaining full fitness and back playing again. I was now attending the ground several times a week to take part in light exercises and also managed to take in most of the home games after which I would enjoy a couple of post-match drinks with the boys.

And still the snow continued to fall. The traditional New Year's Day game against Hearts at Tynecastle became an early casualty of the weather as did the home game against Motherwell the following day. Incredibly, like almost every other club in the country Hibs would not play another league game for over two months. It was during this period that the pools panel was first introduced, originally as a temporary measure as the pools companies, like the clubs themselves, were beginning to suffer financially due to the lack of games. The system would prove so successful that it continues to this day, my Easter Road team mate Ronnie Simpson later a member of the panel.

And still it snowed! In January Tommy Leishman was signed from Liverpool, but he would have to wait several weeks before making his debut. Tommy had been Bill Shankly's first signing as manager of Liverpool when he was transferred from St Mirren in 1959. A big strong wholehearted lad who always gave his all, he had been a member of the Paisley side that defeated Aberdeen in the 1959 Scottish Cup final, when lining up alongside his now new team mate, Gerry Baker.

At the end of January the twice postponed Scottish Cup tie against Brechin City at Glebe Park eventually received the go-ahead, Hibs' first game for almost a month. It was obvious from the start however, that the game should never have been played, the players of both sides slipping and slithering all over the place, on what was described in one newspaper as a 'porridge pitch'. But in the end, goals from John Fraser and Morris Stevenson were enough to see us safely into the next round.

Incredibly Hibs would not play again for another six weeks, but perhaps selfishly, as far as I personally was concerned, the big freeze had been a huge bonus as it had greatly reduced the number of games missed. By this point I had stepped up my training and I made my comeback against Aberdeen reserves at Pittodrie on 16 March, just under six months and 16 games since breaking my leg at Love Street. Lining up alongside me that day was my namesake Jimmy Stevenson, who would later become the brother-in-law of both Joe and Gerry Baker. We lost the game 1-0, but the result didn't concern me in the slightest. I was absolutely knackered at the final whistle, but was just delighted to be back playing again. That same afternoon at Easter Road, the first team, just back from a humiliating 5-0 Fairs Cup defeat by Valencia in Spain in midweek, were beaten 3-2 by the Dons and were now firmly stranded in second bottom place of the table and in all kinds of relegation trouble.

Despite a tremendous display by Willie Wilson who had replaced goalkeeper Ronnie Simpson after a poor performance in Spain, Hibs went down 1-0 to Dundee in the second round of the Scottish Cup at Dens Park, Dundee's goal perhaps predictably scored by Alan Gilzean. Inspired by the performance of Wilson who was taking part in his first ever Scottish Cup tie after four years at Easter Road, the Hibs defence had put up a spirited display against a very good Dundee side who just days before had reached the semi-final of the European Cup by defeating Anderlecht, who had knocked out Real Madrid in the previous round. That afternoon at Dens Park the home side had needed to be at their very best to repel the gallant efforts of Wilson and his team mates who in the end had probably been worth a replay.

The following Wednesday morning after training, Eddie Turnbull dropped a bombshell when he suddenly announced his resignation with immediate effect, stunning not only the players, but everyone associated with the club. The consecutive defeats by Aberdeen, Valencia and Dundee had probably been the final straw, but it had been obvious to the players for some time that Eddie did not get on with the manager.

Although there had been no one single bust up, there had been regular disagreements between the pair regarding training methods. Turnbull, never one to hide his feelings would often say to me, although in his own particular vernacular, that it had been clear to him from day one that Galbraith hadn't a clue about the game. I'm not sure that the younger players ever gave the manager's apparent lack of football know-how much thought, but it hadn't taken the more senior players long to suss him out and unfortunately there had been little respect shown towards him. It was no secret that Eddie had wanted the job after Hugh Shaw's resignation and that this had always been at the back of his mind. Galbraith had played little part in the day-to-day running of the club leaving that side of things to Turnbull, and the former Famous Five legend would be a huge miss. I had loved working with Eddie, but again his leaving was just one of those things that happens in football. There is absolutely no doubt however that Turnbull was well ahead of his time as a coach as he would prove in the not too distant future, both with Aberdeen and later at Hibs, and although I couldn't know it at the time, our paths were to cross again before too long.

While I was playing for the reserves on the Saturday, a 2-2 draw at Broomfield, in Edinburgh the first team were going down 2-0 to Airdrie in front of a sparse crowd of less than 4,000. With the exception of the cup victory against Brechin, it had now been eight games since Hibs had last picked up a win of any kind and we were now firmly entrenched in second bottom place in the table. With the games now starting to run out, anyone who had previously dismissed the threat of relegation, had now been forced to change their view.

The Airdrie game turned out to be yet another soulless and drab affair with the ball at times more on the terracing than on the pitch. Near the end, after the ball had yet again landed amongst the spectators, instead of returning the ball to the field as expected, one exasperated Hibs fan ran to the very top of the sparsely occupied high terracing to throw the ball over the back before turning to face the crowd with arms raised in a gesture of defiance. Arrested by the police the fan was transported to Leith Police Station to a background of booing and cat calls from his fellow supporters, but later released without charge. Described in the *Sunday Post* the following day as the 'Man Who Could Take No More' he was later contacted through a local newspaper who asked him to get in touch with the club where he would receive a free ticket for the next game. According to Chairman Harry Swan the supporter had been one of the very few people in the ground who knew exactly what he was going to do with the ball. Apparently Swan's offer was refused. A clear indication, if one was still required, that things were bad.

I arrived at Easter Road on the Wednesday to learn that I would be playing against Valencia later that evening. After the heavy 5-0 defeat in Spain there was absolutely nothing to lose and I suppose it was worth the risk of giving me a run in the first team to improve my fitness if nothing else. In a major reshuffle, new signing Willie Toner was making his Hibs debut. Signed only the previous day from Kilmarnock the former Scotland centre-half was lining up alongside fellow debutant left-back Alex Cameron as, perhaps surprisingly, we gave our visitors and eventual winners of the competition a first half pounding. Valencia had been fortunate to go in at the interval only one goal behind after Tommy Preston had opened the scoring, Gerry Baker doubling our lead early in the second half when he bulleted home a header from an O'Rourke cross. Nunez pulled one back for Valencia late on, but we well deserved the 2-1 victory and it was a pleasant change for the players to leave the field to the sound of cheers from the supporters instead of the jeers of recent months. Perhaps understandably I had tired near the end of the game and was hardly able to run at the final whistle, but I was heartened by Tommy Leishman's encouraging words as we left the field when he said that I had been just what the team had desperately needed recently, someone who could hold the ball.

The inclusion of the experienced Toner had added a bit of solidity at the back. Signed from Sheffield United in 1954 after a brief spell with Celtic, Willie had been the backbone of the Kilmarnock defence for many years, his consistent displays earning him two full Scotland caps and several appearances for the Scottish League. I had played against him at Kilmarnock and found him to be a very good player, but he had slowed down a bit and was obviously past his best. Good in the air and a very good passer of the ball for a centre-half, Willie would use his experience to jockey you into position rather than rashly jumping in, and I had always found him a difficult opponent to play against.

The defeat by Valencia left us with nothing to play for except our first division survival. The result however had restored a bit of confidence, and in the following seven or eight games only Celtic and Rangers would manage to beat us. Unfortunately during this time most of the sides immediately above us had also managed to put together a few wins and we just didn't seem able to lift ourselves away from the foot of the table.

With only four games left to play, third-bottom Clyde were four points ahead having played only one game more and were now the bookies' favourites to avoid the drop. Our next game was against Hearts at Tynecastle which in the circumstances was a daunting task. 2-0 down at half time and seemingly well out of it, we looked a beaten side until in a tremendous fight back. Two goals by Jim Scott and another from John Fraser, all incredibly scored in a six-minute spell put us in front, only for a Norrie Davidson goal 15 minutes from the end giving his side a share of the spoils. Ironically Davidson had been one of the Hearts players offered to Hibs on loan earlier in the season, but for whatever reason the offer had been rejected.

Only a few days before the Hearts game we had lost the services of the experienced Willie Toner in a freak training ground accident. We were all taking part in a midweek bounce game across the Easter Road pitch, when after scoring a goal Willie turned away in celebration and accidentally fell over the retaining wall fracturing his collar bone and severely lacerating his face. Sadly the injury would effectively all, but end his Easter Road career and he would play only one more game the following season before leaving to join second division Ayr United, eventuality ending up as manager of Dumbarton.

With the games now running out fast our next opponents would be St Mirren at Easter Road. The previous midweek Clyde had lost 2-0 at Parkhead to give us a slight hope. We were now only two points behind the Shawfield side, and although we still had the game in hand it would be a nail biting fight to the finish. At that time high flying Rangers were well clear at the top of the table, and although league cup holders Hearts were now well out of the running for the title, they were still a handy side and the draw at Tynecastle had restored a bit of self-belief. At Easter Road leading goal scorer Tommy White, brother of Tottenham's John, had given St Mirren a first half lead, but we staged another tremendous second half fight back and goals from Gerry Baker and John Baxter eventually gave us both points and a slender lifeline to survival. But the big question now was, would it be enough?

Our game in hand was against Queen of the South in Dumfries. Queen's – who included my future Easter Road team mate Neil Martin and the former Hibs player Johnny Frye in their line-up, had only been promoted to the top division that season along with Clyde. Then managed by the former Hibs and Blackpool goalkeeper George Farm, they themselves had also struggled near the foot of the table for most of the season and we were fairly confident that we could beat them even away from home. And so it was to prove.

At Palmerston two goals by Gerry Baker and another from Jim Scott gave us an unassailable half time lead. I scored the fourth myself, only my third goal of the entire campaign and the first since the penalty against Raith Rovers at the beginning of October. The victory, our biggest league win of the season and our first home and away double, was enough to lift us above Clyde on goal average. That evening in Dumfries it seemed as if we could do no wrong, dominating the game from start to finish while completely outplaying our opponents and were so much on top that Gerry Baker himself could well have scored ten.

It now all came down to the last game of the season, both at Starks Park where we were to face bottom placed Raith Rovers, and at Shawfield a few days later when Clyde would be up against champions elect Rangers. To make the nerve-tingling climax even more unbearable for the players and fans of both sides alike, if the Raith result went against us then we would then have to wait until the following Wednesday for the result at Shawfield.

It was all nail biting stuff. If we lost or drew, a share of the spoils for Clyde on the Wednesday would be enough for them to secure safety. A win for Hibs however, would leave the Shawfield side requiring a cricket score against the champions elect, an unlikely scenario, but in the end it didn't matter. On a beautiful sunny afternoon in Kirkcaldy and backed by a huge support that had made its way in those pre-Forth Road Bridge days all the way from Edinburgh, we played Raith off the park, watched by my old boss, Hugh Shaw, who was now managing the Fife club. First half goals from John Fraser, Gerry Baker and John Baxter now surely meant, barring a miracle on the Wednesday at Shawfield, that we were safe. John Baxter made sure by scoring again in the second half to give us an unassailable lead and we could all then – including the nervous supporters on the terracing – relax.

At the final whistle the relief was almost tangible, both among the players and the huge travelling Hibs support that had backed us so wonderfully. Incredibly, from hardly being able to buy a win all season we had now taken seven points from the last eight, scoring 13 goals while conceding only three. It had been an incredible roller coaster of emotions that at times had been far too close to call, but at the end of the day the 4-0 victory was immaterial when Clyde went down 3-1 to champions Rangers in midweek, the result condemning the Shawfield side to a quick return to the Second Division. The game against his former side would be Hugh Shaw's swansong, someone I had always found to be a real gentleman. After the game he would turn his back on football, ending a professional career that stretched back almost 50 years.

In many ways it had been a strange season, particularly because of the almost unique disruption caused by the severe weather. Champions Rangers had run away with the title a massive nine points ahead of their nearest challengers and had also retained the Scottish Cup. Kilmarnock, who at that time were starting to put together a decent side that would soon win the title under the leadership of the former Rangers legend Willie Waddell, were second. Partick Thistle who had been something of a surprise package finished third. Celtic were fourth and League Cup winners Hearts fifth, but perhaps the biggest surprise of all was Dundee. Champions the previous season, they could only manage to finish in ninth place.

I had played in all, but one of the last 13 games and felt that I had done fairly well, although I had never really been completely 100 per cent fit and it would take me a couple of years to get back to what I would consider to be my best. Much later I would discover that Falkirk had contacted Hibs earlier in the season with a view to buying me, probably on the prompting of Willie Ormond who was then the assistant trainer at Brockville. Apparently they had got in touch with the Hibs director Alex Pratt, who had been prepared to let me go, but I am glad to say that any further development had been dismissed out of hand, probably on the say so of Harry Swan or the then manager Hugh Shaw, both of whom I knew had a lot of time for me as a player.

No sooner had the season ended than Gerry Baker handed in a transfer request. Although he had not been at the club all that long Gerry had been unsettled at Easter Road for some time, no doubt due to our poor form, and sought a move back to England and the bigger money on offer south of the border. He would get his move eventually, but not at that precise moment.

Only 47 league goals had been scored during the season just ended, Hibs' lowest total since 1930 and a far cry from the 106 scored in the 1959–60 season. Gerry Baker had ended the campaign as our top goalscorer with 13, the next best Gerry Byrne and Jim Scott with five apiece.

As could perhaps be expected after such a dreadful season several players were released by Walter Galbraith including Brian Marjoribanks, Harvey McCreadie, Morris Stevenson and Joe Davin. Perhaps surprisingly the vastly experienced Ally McLeod who had been club captain earlier in the campaign, was also among those freed. He would soon sign for his former club Third Lanark before moving on to Ayr United where he would retire from the playing side of the game to take over as manager, the beginning of a journey that would eventually lead him all the way to Argentina. Our paths were to cross again in the not too distant future. Other frees included Doug Logan, John Blair, Ian Cuthbert and Malcolm Bogie. Malcolm was something of an enigma. A team mate of Joe Baker's in the Scottish Schoolboy side that played the English Schoolboys at Goodison in 1955, he had been at Easter Road since signing from Balgreen Rovers as a 17-year-old, but had been unable to secure a regular first team place, managing only three league appearances during his time with Hibs. An immensely talented individual, Malcolm was one of those players who could beat three men in a room, but his main problem was that he would go back and try to beat them again invariably only to lose the ball. He was an extremely gifted player, but unfortunately had no finish. After leaving Easter Road he would join second division Grimsby Town before a short spell with non-league Aldershot, eventually returning to Scotland to play for Hawick Royal Albert and Gala Fairydean in the East of Scotland league.

Meanwhile in England, my good pal Davie Gibson had reached Wembley with Leicester City only to lose 3-1 to Manchester United in that year's FA Cup Final. Unfortunately, it was to be the first of two losing FA Cup Final appearances at the national stadium.

Lawrie Reilly, my first great hero in action, against Queen of the South at Easter Road. Bobby Johnstone centre, Gordon Smith in the distance.

Lawrie Reilly in his pub the Bowlers Rest in Leith serving team mate Willie Ormond c.1950s.

Left: Chairman Harry Swan at his house in Alnwickhill Road in Edinburgh.

Right: The well respected manager Hugh Shaw. The players didn't see much of Hugh except on a Saturday.

Eric Stevenson playing for the Scottish Juvenile side
against Ireland at Muirton Park.

Early days at Easter Road. Check out the snazzy haircut.

The legendary Joe Baker in action against Queen of the South at Easter Road.

Left: John Grant, who was a big help to me in the early days and also welcomed me with open arms into the drinking school.

At Turnhouse Airport after the team's return from the great result in Barcelona 1960–61. Back Row left to right: Trainer Turnbull, manager Shaw, Stevenson, (J) Macleod, Scott, Fraser, McLelland, Baxter and Ormond. Front row: Simpson, Easton, Preston, (J) Baker and Grant.

Pre season trial match at Easter Road c. 1961–62. Back Row left to right: Fraser, Grant, Simpson, Baxter, Easton, Baird. Front Row: Bogie, Stevenson, Kinloch, Preston and (A) MacLeod.

East of Scotland Shield final at Tynecastle March 1962. Back Row: MacLeod, Easton, Preston, Simpson, McLelland and Fraser. Front Row: Scott, (G) Baker, Grant, Stevenson and Bogie. Hibs won 3-1 and I scored.

On the beach in Italy where I almost burnt to a cinder. That's me standing on the left of the photo.

Davie Gibson, perhaps the best player that I played alongside.

The future Scotland manager Ally MacLeod who took me to Ayr late in my career.

Hibernian season 1964–65. Back row left to right: (E) Stevenson, (D) Hogg, Simpson, Allan, Duncan, Whiteford, Fraser, Hamilton. Middle row: Gartshore, McNeill, Martin, Leishman, Reilly, Wilson, Baxter, Wilkinson, McNamee, Easton, Stein (manager). Front Row: (J) Stevenson (trainer), Quinn, O'Rourke, Johnny Grant, Cormack, (J) Stevenson, Vincent, Scott, Cullerton, Stanton, Tom McNiven (physio).

Action from the Summer Cup final at Pittodrie, 1964.

CHAPTER FIVE

Exit Harry Swan
and Enter the Big Man
1963–64

DURING THE SUMMER, Harry Swan had sold his shares in the club to William Harrower, a well known Edinburgh bookmaker who owned several dozen betting shops and numerous other properties around the city. After almost 30 years at the helm, including the successful post-war period when Hibs had been widely recognised as the best side in the country, Harry had possibly become disillusioned after the disastrous events of the previous season. He would not be lost to the game however, and would remain a lifetime director at Hibs, a fitting reward for his past services to the club. The change in ownership would make little if any difference to the players or the day-to-day running of the club. In my three years at Easter Road I had rarely spoken to any of the directors or had any kind of contact with them. With their starched shirts, stiff collars and ties, to me men like Harry Swan and Tom Hartland belonged to a bygone age. The players, particularly the younger ones, were possibly in awe of them, and we tried to keep well out of their way, particularly Swan who was undoubtedly the main man at Easter Road. Like the previous chairman, we would rarely see much of Harrower, except possibly on the odd occasion when he would pop into the dressing room after a game to hand the players a few quid to have a drink.

One change that was to have a major impact on the players however was the appointment of Tom McNiven as trainer. Tom, a qualified physiotherapist, was one of the nicest guys you could ever wish to meet, and although he had played at Junior level with Stonehouse Violet he wasn't really a football man. His main sporting interest was athletics and apparently he had been an amateur sprinter of some repute in his younger days. Previously trainer at Third Lanark he had agreed to take up a similar post with Morton when he learned of Hibs interest, and fortunately for a generation of Hibs players the Greenock side did not to stand in the way of his move to Easter Road. Before his arrival, training had mainly consisted of the time honoured running, either around the track or repeatedly up and down the huge main terracing, all requiring little in the way of intellectual expertise. Now, under Tom's watchful eye we would spend ages warming up before even starting the training sessions, which were now usually much more varied and interesting.

After the debacle of the previous season it was evident that a major rebuilding programme was needed at Easter Road. During the summer the prolific goalscorer Neil Martin had been signed from Queen of the South and he was among the players taking part in the time honoured trek around Queens Park on the first day of pre-season training, that had been endured by generations of Hibs players before him. I knew Neil from when he used to train at Easter Road in the evenings as a part timer with Alloa and we were friends socially, his home in Tranent not all that far from Bonnyrigg. At Palmerston he had fallen out with manager George Farm over travelling arrangements that had resulted in him missing a cup game at Palmerston, but as far as I was concerned Queen's loss was our great gain. It may come as a surprise to some, but if I was asked to select my best ever Hibs XI I would pick Neil before Joe Baker, although I have to say that a place would have to be found somewhere for Joe. Baker was probably a better football player than Neil, but Neil was the better goalscorer. I always enjoyed playing alongside the Tranent man and think that he would say the same about me. If I gave him the ball I knew that nine times out of ten I would get it back which was not always the case with Joe. Martin could hold the ball up, was strong, particularly in the box, had a huge heart and was always prepared to go in where it hurt. No matter how I sent the ball over Neil would always be lurking around the penalty area somewhere ready to pounce. He was one of the best headers of the ball that I had ever seen, and although he couldn't place the ball like Willie Bauld, he could really leap and connected the ball with great power. Among the newcomers that first day was a shy inside-forward named Pat Stanton who was destined in the not too distant future to become a Hibs legend. I already knew the 18-year-old Stanton from his time with the local Bonnyrigg Rose where he had been farmed out by Hibs the previous season, and could tell immediately that he was going to be something very special. Pat was another who could not be held back for too long and he would make his first team debut within a matter of months.

In our opening league cup game against St Mirren at Easter Road, Neil Martin scored his first goal for the club with what was soon to become a trademark header to give us a share of the points, and even this early he was beginning to look a real prospect.

Considering the trials and tribulations of the previous season, it was something of a surprise when we managed to take nine points from a possible ten from our next five games against Dundee United, Aberdeen and St Mirren to qualify for the later stages of the league cup for the first time in ten years. Our 4-2 victory at Tannadice however came at a heavy price when young Jimmy O'Rourke was carried off with a suspected broken leg. Not yet turned 17, since making his debut against Utrecht the previous season Jimmy had already firmly established himself as a first team regular and looked every inch an exciting prospect. His injury later turned out to be the equally serious torn ligaments and would prove a severe set-back to his fledgling career. Out of football for almost a year, it would perhaps take him much longer to recover mentally, and he would have great difficulty in regaining a regular first team place for some time to come.

Neil Martin however was already beginning to repay his transfer fee. Settling into a prolific partnership with Gerry Baker, the pair had already scored five goals apiece in the league cup section games. I myself had managed to chip in with three, including a double, one from the penalty spot in our win against Dundee United at Tannadice, the press reports the following day describing our performance that evening as 'devastating form that had not been seen since the days of the Famous Five'.

After the great result at Tannadice we were brought crashing back to earth the following week, at Tynecastle of all places, when we went down 4-2 in front of a crowd of well over 30,000, Edinburgh's biggest of the season so far. We had started the game well, but soon had our backs to the wall, the recently reliable defence looking likely to crumble every time Hearts had the ball and we were perhaps fortunate to go in at half time only 2-1 behind. Hearts scored again soon after the restart to make it 3-1 and we seemed well out of it until Gerry Baker popped up with his second of the afternoon to give us a chance before Davidson wrapped it up for Hearts near the end. I always enjoyed playing at Tynecastle, but it was obvious that I was not a huge favourite of the Hearts fans, particularly those in the enclosure where all you could see were maroon and white scarves. The jeers would start as soon as my name was read out before the game and would continue throughout the entire 90 minutes every time I got the ball, and it would appear that they had never quite forgiven me for signing for their great rivals. In truth I loved the barracking, which you could make out quite clearly, and it always made me more determined than ever to do well. That day I was lining up in direct opposition to my former Edina Hearts team mate Chris Shevlane and although we lost

,I felt that I had done well against him all afternoon. Chris was a very clever player who would try not to dive in, but he was mostly left footed, so I would always try to go around him on his weaker side and usually succeeded.

In the first leg of the League Cup quarter-final a 3-3 draw at Dens against a very good Dundee side had given us a great chance of reaching the semis with the return in Edinburgh still to come. We were now a vastly different side from that of the previous season and at Easter Road we put on what one reporter later described as 'a vintage performance'. Gerry Baker had been injured early in the second half, but despite being effectively down to ten men we were by far the better side. I managed to score two of our goals, one from a fierce drive from just outside the box, the other with what was later described as a powerful header. Baker before his injury scored the other and I was heartened to read in the following day's *Evening News* that 'Once again Hibs had given the fans full value for their money, and the word is spreading round Scotland that they are once again a big attraction'.

The following Saturday I once again managed to score twice, both from the penalty spot, in a 2-2 home draw with Falkirk before facing Dundee in the return leg of the league cup. I was now finding the net fairly regularly and after just nine games had already doubled my total from the previous season.

In the return game at Easter Road Dundee were seen off easily enough, the 2-0 victory sealed just after the restart when Gerry Baker scored our second from a seemingly impossible angle near the bye-line. We were now through to the semi-finals of the competition, a feat not achieved at Easter Road since the halcyon days of the Famous Five.

By now the press were firmly behind us, most predicting that we could go all the way and actually win the cup. This confidence however was to prove our death knell as we struggled in the games leading up to the semi-final. A 5-0 humiliation at Ibrox was by far the worst of three consecutive defeats that saw us tumbling down the league from a relatively safe position and once again deep into relegation trouble. That afternoon in Glasgow, in front of a huge home support, Willie Henderson had been in absolutely fantastic form giving poor Joe McClelland a terrible roasting. Indeed, Rangers were so much on top throughout the entire 90 minutes that I was a virtual spectator out wide on the left, unable to even get a touch of the ball as the home side kept coming at us in waves. If truth be told Rangers were so dominant that afternoon that they could well have scored far more and the final whistle couldn't come quickly enough for us.

For some reason, after our bright start, once again we were really struggling. In an attempt to remedy the situation Walter Galbraith had made an audacious bid to sign both the Hearts left-back Davie Holt and inside-forward Willie Hamilton, but the approach had been dismissed out of hand by the Gorgie side. He then turned his attention to England, but with no suitable candidates to be found, I suppose that the manager was left with no other alternative, but to turn to some of the younger players on the books, and on the Saturday teenagers Billy Simpson and Pat Stanton, who had both impressed since joining the club only at the start of the season made their first team debuts against Motherwell at Fir Park. It was immediately obvious to anyone who knew the game that Pat Stanton was going to be a player. Although he was yet to fully develop, potentially this boy had everything. A clever player in the mould of Davie Gibson, he could read the game, was brilliant defensively, great in the air and could also score goals. Although he wasn't the fastest he was no slouch either. To my mind his best position was sweeper, but unlike players like Willie Miller and Alan Hansen, Pat could play anywhere. His best years at Easter Road though would be in the midfield of Eddie Turnbull's great side of the early '70s and his only fault in my opinion, if you could call it a fault, was that that he never fully realised just how good a player he really was. A very quiet lad, he had a great dry sense of humour, but also a hard streak as we witnessed one day during training when both he and Jim Scott almost came to blows after a mistimed tackle during a bounce game.

Joining Pat at Fir Park that afternoon was the former Scottish Schoolboy international Jimmy Stevenson and full-back Billy Simpson, both signed from Edina Hibs. I thought that Billy was going to be some player. He certainly looked the part. He could tackle and was good in the air. Defensively he wasn't the greatest and he couldn't overlap like Bobby Duncan, but he had great potential and to my mind there was something there to work with. His best spell was during the 1965–66 season when he was a near regular, but apart from a short period 18 months or so later, for some reason he seemed to lose his way at Easter Road and would later join Falkirk before moving on to Albion Rovers, Alloa and finally Cowdenbeath.

Lining up at inside-right that afternoon, in direct opposition to the experienced former Scottish international Bert McCann, Stanton looked a natural, scoring one of Hibs goals in a 4-3 defeat, the future Celtic and Hibs player Joe McBride scoring a hat trick for the Steelmen. Stanton had done more than enough to suggest that Hibs had unearthed yet another gem and enough to keep his place in the side that would face Morton in the semi-final of the league cup at Ibrox in midweek. After almost 20 years as a professional, the Motherwell game would turn out to be the last that the former Scottish international Willie Toner would play in the top league, before a move to Second Division Ayr United.

I'm still not sure if we took Second Division Morton far too easily in the semi-final, but we didn't really get into the game. The eventual 1-1 score-line in no way reflected the enormous pressure that we had been put under throughout the entire 90 minutes by the Second Division side, and only a tremendous rearguard performance by the defence had allowed us a second chance in the replay. After only three minutes the vastly experienced Ronnie Simpson had made an uncharacteristic mistake allowing Alan McGraw to open the scoring. But thereafter the goalkeeper was in outstanding form, two saves in particular from McGraw in the stupendous class. However we were outfought throughout by a lower league side, who wanted it far more than us and in the end they should have won without the need for any replay. For obvious reasons Morris Stevenson had been determined to do well against his former team mates and he had a particularly good game as did top goal scorer Alan McGraw. The young Stanton did little wrong, although he passed up a great chance to score what would have been the winner, but it was asking far too much of the inexperienced youngster to influence the course of the game. Neil Martin, who scored our equaliser in the first half later broke his wrist, and although he managed to complete the entire 90 minutes the injury would keep him out of the side for several weeks.

A few days later the former Motherwell player Pat Quinn was signed from Blackpool for a fee said at that time to be the biggest ever paid by a Scottish club. The former Scottish international, who along with our own Johnny MacLeod had been one of the better Scottish players in the 9-3 debacle against England at Wembley in 1961, was better known as a member of the celebrated 'Ancell Babes' at Motherwell during the late '50s and early '60s when lining up alongside the likes of Ian St John, Bert McCann and the Edinburgh-born Willie Hunter. Pat was a very clever player with a real football brain who liked to control the game from the middle of the park. You would rarely see him breaking through to have a shot, but would spray passes about, similar in style to Alec Edwards at Easter Road a few years later. At that time he was in his late twenties and had been around the block, but he would take time to settle at Easter Road, eventually going on to give the club several years of sterling service before leaving to join East Fife in 1969.

Pat made his debut a few days later against Dunfermline in Fife, which would turn out to be yet another defeat. With Bobby Duncan making only his second first team appearance at right-back, Quinn showed several neat touches, but appeared to lack match fitness. We had most of the pressure, but with a very young Alex Edwards pulling the strings for Dunfermline in midfield we somehow found ourselves two behind at the interval. Edwards himself had opened the scoring after a great 30 yard thunderbolt by George Miller had come crashing back off the bar, and from then on there was no way back. Full-back John Lunn, whose life unfortunately would soon be cut short by illness, scored a third in the second half, the final result condemning us once again to second bottom place in the table.

We had now gone five games without a win and were languishing deep in the-relegation mire, hardly an ideal preparation for the cup replay with Morton. With Quinn in as a straight replacement for the injured Neil Martin the second game lacked the excitement of the first, and for a while it looked as if neither side would score. In the end it all came down to two penalty decisions, one given, the other turned down. Perhaps predictably, Alan McGraw who would go on to score an incredible 62 goals in all competitions that season, opened the scoring, this time from the spot with just over an hour played. Try as we might, we just could not force a breakthrough until, with just ten minutes left to play, we were sure that we had been thrown a lifeline when Pat Quinn was brought crashing down in the box. Referee Bobby Davidson however saw it differently and it was a sad journey home to Bonnyrigg later that evening. Both the Morton goals over the two games had been scored by Alan McGraw who would later become a team mate at Easter Road and is still a great friend. Perhaps he was not the greatest of football players, but was a fantastic competitor, an even more fantastic goalscorer and yet another great guy.

The Hibs team at Ibrox that evening was (Quinn for Martin the only change from the first game):

SIMPSON, FRASER AND MCCLELLAND, GRANT, EASTON AND BAXTER,
SCOTT, QUINN, BAKER, STANTON AND STEVENSON.

A 4-0 home defeat by Dundee on the Saturday did nothing to ease our relegation worries. Goalless at the interval, in the second half Alan Gilzean ran riot scoring all four of his sides goals, mostly from crosses supplied by the veteran Gordon Smith on the right wing. By this time Gordon was well past his best, but he was still a very tricky individual and his inch perfect crosses would help Gilzean score 33 goals from only 30 league appearances before his transfer to Tottenham Hotspur a few months later. Smith was still a much revered figure in the game and according to Pat Stanton, during a break in play he turned to see Gordon smiling at him, the lifelong Hibs fan's legs immediately turning to jelly. It would turn out to be Smith's last ever appearance as a player at Easter Road.

In yet another attempt to freshen things up, Walter Galbraith had flown to Ireland to sign John Park from Linfield immediately after Northern Ireland's 2-1 victory against Scotland at Windsor Park. The international defender had been attracting the attention of several Scottish clubs including Celtic and Dundee, but Hibs' decisive move paid dividends and Parke made a memorable debut in a 4-1 win against St Johnstone. It was our first win in well over a month and one that now lifted us to third bottom of the table. John lost no time in demonstrating that he could be yet another very good signing, and his performance against St Johnstone was described in one newspaper as: 'as fine a display of defensive work seen at Easter Road for a very long time.'

The victory however would prove to be yet another false dawn with only seven points collected from the following 11 games. Meanwhile, Willie Hamilton had been signed from Hearts just in time to make his debut in a 2-1 defeat by Partick Thistle. Although Hearts had rejected an earlier bid from Hibs for the enigmatic player, it was clear that Willie was desperately unhappy at Tynecastle and Hearts eventually, but reluctantly had accepted an increased offer from Hibs. I had admired Willie as an opponent, but it was only now when playing alongside him that I truly appreciated just how good he really was. A brilliant ball player with bags of natural ability, Willie was as mad as a brush, but in a nice way. But what a player, a genius. Pat Stanton tells the story that not long after he had joined Celtic, the players were discussing the best players they had played with, when Pat mentioned Willie Hamilton. The rest of the Celtic players all thought he was joking until Jock Stein stepped forward to confirm Pat's opinion – believe me Willie was that good. Often described as a flawed genius, I have to say that during his time at Easter Road, he never missed training and always did all that was asked of him, particularly after the arrival of Jock Stein. Jock knew how to get the best from Willie and if truth be told I think that he was frightened to death of Jock.

Within weeks Gerry Baker would get his wish for a move to England, when he joined Ipswich Town. Both Hibs and second division Bury had already agreed a fee when the First Division side came in with an improved offer and Baker joined the former Hibs player Doug Moran at Portman Road. Unfortunately, Ipswich would be relegated at the end of the season after finishing rock bottom of the table. As far as I was concerned Gerry was always chasing the money and he rarely stayed with any side for long. Later he would sign for Coventry City before moving on to Brentford, Margate, Nuneaton Town and finally Bedworth United.

In the traditional New Year's Day derby we managed to pick up a desperately needed point after a 1-1 draw with Hearts at Easter Road.

However I was as surprised as the fans at the inclusion of the five foot nothing Johnny Grant who had been signed from Kilwinning Rangers just a few weeks before. That afternoon Johnny was absolutely incredible, beating player after player as if they weren't there as he skipped down the wing, and I can still remember thinking to myself, where did we get this guy from? He was an absolute revelation, and reminded me of Jimmy Johnstone or Willie Henderson although he didn't have quite the same heart or drive. Unfortunately, after a bright start Johnny seemed to lack the appetite to take the kicks and bruises that are part and parcel of the professional game and he soon dropped out of the picture. He was a nice wee guy though. Released at the end of the following season he would have short spells with Raith Rovers and Ayr United before emigrating to play in South Africa with Durban City, and I later heard that he did quite well for himself in business over there.

The following week we came up against a Rangers side at the top of their form, and in the end we did well to limit the defeat to just a solitary goal. In a game that sometimes bordered on the nasty, Neil Martin and wee Johnny Grant came in for some extreme attention from the Rangers defence, although in saying that I suppose you could say much the same for Willie Henderson. In the first half I felt my groin go, but didn't think too much about it at the time. Although I wasn't all that keen, at half time I was persuaded to have an injection that dulled the pain and I managed to last the entire 90 minutes. The following week, in a game against Aberdeen, I felt the groin go again and although I didn't know it at the time I would not play again for several months, and it would take me well over a year to regain full fitness. This time though I would be in the more than capable hands of Tom McNiven although I am sorry to say that the injury resulted in me having a rare disagreement with the Hibs trainer. Although the injury was mostly treated at Easter Road by Tom in his own tender and caring way, I still continued to visit Archie Campbell at his clinic in Dalkeith as I had done for several years, and it would be fair to say that Tom wasn't too happy when he found out. Archie was a well-known local physiotherapist who had treated many of the top sportsmen throughout the years including Willie Bauld, Gordon Smith, Eddie Turnbull and Willie Ormond, as well as myself. Archie's method of treatment was totally different to Tom's. He believed in getting deep and forcibly into the trouble with his educated hands, while Tom's philosophy was to take it much easier, but consequently, longer.

At that time the club was having a terrible time with injuries which may have had something to do with our extremely concerning league position. Toner had been out with his dislocated shoulder, Leishman and

O'Rourke both had torn ligaments. Neil Martin had missed several games with his broken wrist soon after recovering from a broken collarbone and new signing John Parke now required a cartilage operation after being carried off during a 5-3 defeat at Airdrie, a game incidentally that had seen Neil Martin sent off for fighting. Now, apart from my own injury there was even more concern for the manager when Jim Easton was carried off with a broken leg in a game against East Stirling. Joe McClelland, John Fraser and John Grant had also all been out at some time or other during the season, and because of our perilous league position Walter Galbraith turned to Cowdenbeath to sign centre-forward Stan Vincent. A prolific goal scorer for the Fife club, Stan was seen as the answer to our problems and he joined us just in time for a trip to Cannes on the French Riviera where we were to take on the local second division side for the Cannes Sports Festival Trophy.

The trip proved to be a welcome distraction from the worries of relegation and we enjoyed our few days in the sun which was more than can be said for the game itself. After a slow start we gradually managed to claw ourselves back from two goals behind, thanks to a double by Neil Martin, and another, the winner as it would turn out and his first goal for the club, with a brilliant header near the end by Stan Vincent. When the local side realised they were facing defeat, what had up until then been at times a nasty and ill-tempered affair threatened to really get out of hand and develop into a full scale brawl as they started to kick and punch anything that moved, and on one occasion had even threatened to assault the referee. The behaviour of the Cannes players disgusted even their own fans who began to turn on them, and in the circumstances the cup was presented to captain John Fraser in the safety of the dressing room.

Because of the injury I hadn't really expected to take part in the game, but the evening before I had again fallen out briefly with Tom McNiven. A few of us, including the stylish John Grant, had taken a stroll along a harbour that was packed full of luxurious yachts. Nicknamed 'The Duke' by the rest of the players, the always elegantly dressed John Grant had a thing about himself. Suddenly, striding aboard one of the huge yachts, John stood there looking around like the lord of the manor saying, 'This is the life, eh Stevie – do I not look the part?' At that, I kicked the gangway into the water and we all legged it, leaving poor John stranded on board the yacht. Forced to make a jump for it, he twisted his ankle on landing and we did not look forward to telling Tom McNiven how it had happened when we got back to the hotel. As usual on these trips abroad, one drink led to a few more and we were late arriving back at the hotel, very late. In the morning we were reprimanded by Walter Galbraith and

I later accused Tom McNiven of grassing on us to the boss, only to be informed that the noise we had made coming in would probably have wakened the entire resort. The upshot was that John and I were told by an angry Galbraith that both of us would be playing that afternoon 100 per cent fit or not.

After the game, a few of us had decided to visit a local night spot to unwind. The club was packed with beautiful girls and while we were sitting quietly discussing the game, we happened to see one of the local punters smooching on the dance floor with this lovely looking woman. Suddenly all hell broke loose when the punter punched the woman full in the face, sending her crashing to the floor. For obvious reasons we were reluctant to get caught up in the middle of a brawl and made a quick exit. We only found out later that the girl had actually been a man, her/his dancing partner taking immediate exception after allowing himself an over intimate inspection.

Victories over St Johnstone and St Mirren, followed by a 5-2 win against second bottom Queen of the South, the prolific Neil Martin scoring four against his former side, lifted us to 11th place in the table, our highest position since the beginning of September seven months before. With safety from relegation now seemingly all, but assured, manager Walter Galbraith tendered his resignation with immediate effect. Things had obviously not been all that great during the manager's 28 months in charge at Easter Road and his resignation didn't come as a huge shock. Many of us were of the opinion that he had probably been pushed. Sadly, Walter had never been overly popular with the players. Rarely seen on the training ground, it was now fairly obvious to us all that his football knowledge had been extremely limited to say the least. According to the man himself, he had been keen to resign for some time, but had waited until the club was in a secure position in the table. Stating a preference to return to coaching south of the border, he would later spend a season as manager of third division Southport before returning to manage Berwick Rangers. It has to be said in Galbraith's favour however, that apart from some of the signings made in the early part of his tenure at Easter Road, many of them frankly downright awful, he had since shown a great eye for a player with the acquisition of Neil Martin, John Parke, Pat Quinn and Willie Hamilton. He had also brought the promising youngsters Jimmy O'Rourke, Pat Stanton, Billy Simpson, Bobby Duncan and Peter Cormack through the ranks.

It was no big secret as to the favourite to take over from Galbraith. But despite the predictable rumours that Eddie Turnbull could be making a return to Easter Road, just a few weeks before Jock Stein had confirmed that he would be leaving Dunfermline at the end of the season. Stein had been prevented from taking over from Hugh Shaw in 1961, after Dunfermline had refused to release him, and although he now stated that he had no particular job in mind, it was obvious that he had already been contacted by Willie Harrower regarding the Easter Road job.

The official announcement that Jock Stein would be taking over as manager at Easter Road came as no big surprise to the players, and although I can't remember him introducing himself to us on his first day, I suppose he must have done. Stein was big man in every sense of the word, and although at that time he didn't have quite the reputation he would later have at Celtic, he certainly had a presence about him. He was very charismatic and when he walked into the dressing room everything went quiet. I don't think that he was overly popular with some of the older players, but I suppose we were all in awe of him in some way and a little bit unsure. He could be gruff, didn't suffer fools gladly and at times I thought that he looked more like a member of the Glasgow mafia, but as far as football was concerned he was quite exceptional. Technically he was out of this world and would explain exactly what he wanted from the players. Eddie Turnbull was possibly, only possibly, a much better coach, but he lacked the man management skills of Stein. Although he could be a bit dour at times, Jock was also capable of having a laugh with us, something that couldn't really be said for Eddie. I think that Stein was aware of Tom McNiven's limitations regarding football and he would get him to do the warm up, leaving Jimmy Stevenson who had come from Dunfermline with him to take the actual training itself, although everything would almost certainly have been organised by Stein in advance. Most of the football talk would also be between the pair and I don't think that this went down particularly well with Tom.

The new manager made an almost immediate impact at Easter Road and there was a fresh sense of anticipation and excitement around the place. The training was far more intense than before and much different from what we had been used to, but enjoyable. Trainer Jimmy Stevenson however I found to be quite a dour man. He knew the game and like Stein would not suffer fools gladly, but he was not much of a mixer and rarely got involved in any of the mickey taking which is usually a big part of the game. Nicknamed Doberman by joker Jimmy O'Rourke after the character in the Sergeant Bilko programme that was then very big on television, he was not nearly as popular as Tom McNiven who was loved by everybody.

I was not that far away from a return to full fitness when Jock Stein arrived at Easter Road, but to his credit, he took me aside one day to tell me that he was leaving me out of the side. He explained that while I wasn't being dropped and I could play if I wanted to, I clearly wasn't fully fit. He went on to say that I was still a big part of his plans and wouldn't lose any money including bonuses' by not playing. I had been a first team regular for a couple of seasons now and had built up a fair bit of a reputation. Not many managers would have left me out, so I suppose that Stein's decision took a fair amount of courage. He was an exceptional man manager however, knowing exactly how to get the best from his players. He even had Willie Hamilton playing out of his skin and training like a bear. Although he still liked a drink, I am convinced that Hammy was genuinely terrified of Stein and managed to put more effort into hiding his off-field habits. They did have one big fall out however, after which Hammy was told not to report back to Easter Road until he was called for. The result was an immediate transfer request, but things were eventually straightened out between the pair and Willie started to play the best football of his career.

Stein's first game in charge was against Airdrie at Easter Road on 4 April 1964. Willie Wilson was recalled to the first team in place of the injured Ronnie Simpson, while Tommy Preston and Stan Vincent were left out of the side altogether. There were no goals at half time and I watched from the stand as the new manager showed his tactical acumen by switching all the forwards around to almost instant improvement, Jim Scott scoring Hibs' first and Martin the other in a 2-1 victory. One of Stein's many changes had been to recall Tommy Leishman at centre-half, but with Stanton, Hughes, Grant and Falconer all sharing the position over the past few weeks it was obvious that a centre-half was a priority. With this in mind Stein returned to his former club Celtic in midweek to sign John McNamee. McNamee was an uncompromising player with a towering presence and he didn't take long to achieve almost legendary status among the Hibs fans, particularly with his habit of venturing into the opposing penalty area at corners. John had made his debut for Celtic at Parkhead in 1961 deputising for the injured Billy McNeill against Hibs in immediate opposition to Joe Baker, but had spent most of the time since then languishing in the reserves. He made his debut in a 5-2 victory against East Stirling in the penultimate game of the season, and although he was badly at fault for the first Shire goal, when he was caught out trying to beat an opponent, he did more than enough to suggest that he would be yet another sound acquisition.

What had been another disappointing league campaign finally came to an end with a 1-1 draw at Tannadice. John Baxter was sent off after only 18 minutes, but McNamee started to repay his transfer fee when he scored our equalising goal shortly after United had squandered the chance to go two ahead from the spot.

At the end of what had been at times a long and arduous season, the long serving John Grant, Joe McClelland and Tommy Preston were all handed free transfers. Tommy, who had taken over as temporary trainer after Turnbull's surprise resignation, had apparently been told at the time that he would be offered the position permanently when he retired from playing. He would soon join St Mirren as a first team player with the added responsibility of coaching the youngsters in the evenings. However, disillusioned, after an argument with the chairman, he would soon leave without even playing a game for the Love Street side. The long serving John Fraser had also been called into the manager's office that morning expecting to be released, but was taken aback when offered the club captaincy for the coming season.

We had eventually managed to finish the campaign in mid-table, which I suppose was reasonable considering our earlier trials and tribulations. Rangers had won their second consecutive league title and their first treble since 1948-49 when defeating a very good Dundee side 3-1 in the Scottish Cup Final and Second Division Morton 5-0 in the League Cup Final. Kilmarnock had finished in second place two points ahead of both Celtic and Hearts while Steins former side Dunfermline had finished fifth. At Easter Road both Willie Hamilton and Neil Martin had earlier asked to be put on the transfer list, Willie after his fall out with the manager. Neil had ended the season as Hibs' top scorer with just under 40 goals in all games, which in the circumstances was nothing short of phenomenal. He had been selected for the Scottish League side against the Football League and also for the Scotland under-23 side against France, and had perhaps been another player to be swayed by the stories of the big money that was to be made south of the border.

Stein meanwhile had fallen out with Ronnie Simpson for some reason, reportedly going as far as to tell the player that he would never play for Hibs again, and he too found himself on the open to transfer list. The veteran goalkeeper would soon be offered the player-manager's job at Berwick Rangers, but before that could happen, he would be approached by Celtic to coach the young goalkeepers at Parkhead, and the rest, as they say is history.

But first there was the Summer Cup, a tournament that had mainly been the brainchild of the Hearts chairman Nicol Kilgour. It was somewhat of a surprise as had the Gorgie side finished top of their qualifying group, they would have been unable to fulfil the remaining fixtures as they had already agreed to take part in an end-of-season tour of North America.

Without the participation of both Rangers and Celtic, Hibs kicked off a regional section that comprised of neighbours Hearts, Dunfermline and Falkirk with a 3-2 defeat at Tynecastle. A 1-1 draw with Dunfermline followed by a 4-2 defeat at Brockville left us bottom of the group table and seemingly well out of the running to qualify for the later stages. Before the return game with Hearts at Easter Road I asked Jock Stein if I could play on the Saturday. I suppose that with qualification looking highly unlikely it was a chance to give me a run out. Except for one reserve team outing, I had not played since a 5-1 defeat by Queens Park Rangers in a friendly in London just a few days after arriving back from Cannes, and it would be my first appearance during the new manager's reign at Easter Road. With a very young side containing six players under the age of 21, we staged an unlikely fight back after a shaky start to shatter Hearts' unbeaten record in the competition, Stan Vincent scoring the only goal of the game just 90 seconds after the interval. I would not play again that season, but another 1-1 draw with Dunfermline and a 4-0 victory against Falkirk at Easter Road handed us the unlikely scenario of a play-off game against a Fife side that had managed to draw 0-0 with Hearts in the final game of the section. The game at neutral Tynecastle ended in a 3-1 win for Hibs, Jim Scott scoring twice before Stan Vincent settled things with a third goal late on. In a thrilling semi-final first leg against Kilmarnock at Rugby Park, a hard fought, but slender 4-3 defeat made us slight favourites to go forward to the final after the return game at Easter Road, and so it would prove with what turned out to be a rather one sided 3-0 win. The scene was now set for a meeting with Aberdeen in the home and away final, but before the games could take place a typhoid scare in the Grampian area meant the final being postponed until the following season.

I am often asked how Jock Stein had managed to turn around a relegation haunted side in such a short period of time, but the answer is simple. He played the players in a formation that suited them and their individual strengths. Out went the traditional 2-3-5 to be replaced by a 4-3-3 system that, in the months ahead, would eventually see Pat Stanton as sweeper, Willie Hamilton, Pat Quinn and John Baxter in midfield and Jim Scott and Neil Martin up front with Peter Cormack occupying a floating role.

CHAPTER SIX

The Summer Cup, Real Madrid and Dreams of the 'Double'

1964–65

IN ONLY A few short months, Jock Stein had completely revitalised a side that at one stage had looked odds-on favourites for the drop. There was now a new sense of vitality and optimism around the club. Of the 12 games that had been played during this time, seven had been won and two drawn, and whilst hardly championship form it was more than enough to suggest that we were now heading in the right direction. We were all hugely optimistic at the approach of the new campaign, but for me personally it would turn out to be yet another season of frustration. Although I was now physically fit enough to play if selected, I knew that it would take me much longer to get over the injury mentally.

As usual several new faces had joined us in the summer, all from the minor ranks. Goalkeeper Thomson Allan had been signed from my side old Edina Hearts and would figure in the first team before too long. Bernard Cullerton a tricky outside-left from St Bernard's would make 20 appearances for the reserves, scoring six goals, but unfortunately he would be released at the end of the season. Bernard was not a bad player, but without wishing to be unkind I don't think that he had the ability to play in the first team at this level. Outside-left George McNeill had been signed from Tranent Juniors on the recommendation of Neil Martin, but unfortunately the lightning-fast George was yet another who would fail to make much of an impact on the first team. While he would be a regular in the reserves during his almost four years at Easter Road, George would make only one first team appearance, a 3-0 home win against St Johnstone in 1965 before moving on to Morton, then to Stirling Albion, before finding his true vocation. Blessed with an almost unbelievable turn of speed, in 1969 he would be a surprise entry for the famous Powderhall Sprint reaching the semi-finals. He would win the event the following year, but because he had played professional football he was barred from competing in amateur competitions. In 1972 he would become the world professional sprint champion and was described by the prominent former runner Chris Brasher, who had been pacemaker for Roger Bannister when he famously broke the four-minute mile in 1954, as the greatest natural born sprinter he had ever seen in this country. Later, in 1981, during one of his many trips to Australia, George would win the famous Stawell Gift Competition, then said to be the richest professional race in the world to collect an estimated 50,000 dollars in prize money.

In winning the Powderhall Sprint and the Stawell Gift, George became the only man in history to win both of the most famous professional sprint races in the world, so who said he made the wrong decision in giving up football to concentrate solely on running?

A very funny guy with a wicked sense of humour, he is now an extremely successful after dinner speaker. One of his stories concerns the day he was listed as a substitute for Hibs famous home victory against Napoli in the Fairs Cup in 1967. I had taken a slight knock during the game and for a while it looked as if I was struggling to continue. Sensing that this was his big chance to make a name for himself, George started to limber up. Eventually he was summoned by manager Bob Shankly, only to be asked to go and get Shankly's matches from the dressing room. While there is not a grain of truth in the story, it is nevertheless extremely funny when George tells it.

Still on the subject of Tranent. Just before the start of the new season Neil Martin turned up at my house one day, driving a brand new car. Not many footballers had cars in those days and it created quite a stir ,especially when he arrived in it for training at Easter Road a few days later. I'm still not sure if it was common knowledge among the rest of the lads, but Neil told me that the car had been a present from the club. He was such a big player for us at that time, that no doubt the generous gift had been a sweetener intended to persuade him to withdraw his transfer request. I bore him no animosity, at least he had had the courage to ask for more money.

The new season opened with the first leg of the Summer Cup Final against Aberdeen that had earlier been postponed because of the typhoid scare. I wasn't selected for the game at Pittodrie, a 3-2 win for the home side, but was at the match. We could perhaps have considered ourselves fortunate at going in at half time only 2-1 behind as Aberdeen had been by far the better of the two sides, but in the second half we mounted a great comeback. After a 25 yard thunderbolt from Stan Vincent had twice been cleared from the line, Jim Scott scored his second of the game to level things. Ernie Winchester scored what was probably a deserved winner for Aberdeen near the end, but the narrow defeat had now given us a real chance of winning the trophy back in Edinburgh. In the return at Easter Road in midweek, I replaced the injured Jimmy O'Rourke in a game that had everything in 90 minutes of intense drama and excitement. There were no goals at the interval, but midway through the second half Stan Vincent put us ahead to level the aggregate scores, and it was on to extra time. With just seven minutes of the extra 30 remaining, I received a pass from Willie Hamilton to thunder an unstoppable drive past goalkeeper Ogston and that looked like being enough to give us the cup. However with just seconds remaining a miss-hit header by Charlie Cooke deceived everyone including goalkeeper Willie Wilson who was horrified to watch helplessly as the ball squirmed over the line to force a third game play-off. Later a toss of a coin in the boardroom dictated that a third and deciding game would take place back at Pittodrie.

Meanwhile we had kicked off our league cup campaign with a fine win against Third Lanark during which I had another great tussle with left-back Joe Davis. I managed to score in our 3-0 victory so you could probably say that once again I had the upper hand over Joe. Further home and away wins against both Thirds and Clyde however meant nothing when we could only manage to take one point from four against Dunfermline to finish second in the group to a Fife side who obviously would have been delighted to get one over their former manager.

Although we had failed to qualify for the later stages of the league cup we were still confident that we could beat Aberdeen in the Summer Cup third game play-off at Pittodrie. The game was only a few minutes old when the mercurial Willie Hamilton opened the scoring, and although Ernie Winchester equalised midway through the half, in reality we were never in any real danger of losing the game. Inspired by man-of-the-match Hamilton pulling the strings from midfield, we hit the bar on at least three occasions, and could even afford the luxury of a missed Pat Stanton penalty after both Jim Scott and Peter Cormack had scored to give us a comfortable victory and the cup. After the presentation of the trophy, John McNamee hoisted captain John Fraser onto his shoulders and followed by the rest of the players we proceeded on a lap of honour around Pittodrie. Our big mistake was to make our way towards the home end first where we were pelted by stones and jeers from the few remaining Aberdeen fans before making a hasty retreat.

In only a few short months Jock Stein had completely turned the club around and had now collected his first silverware as a manager since Dunfermline's Scottish Cup victory over Celtic in 1961. It was also Hibs first silverware since the League Championship win in 1952. Although the Summer Cup could hardly be considered a major trophy, make no mistake we were absolutely delighted at the victory and we all had a great night at the Beach Ballroom in Aberdeen that evening before making our bleary eyed way back to Edinburgh in the morning. Perhaps the luckiest man on the field had been full-back John Parke. Now fully recovered from his cartilage operation at the end of the previous season, John had collected a winner's medal after his very first appearance in the competition.

The teams for the third game play-off:

HIBS: WILSON FRASER AND PARKE, STANTON MCNAMEE AND J STEVENSON, CORMACK HAMILTON SCOTT MARTIN AND E STEVENSON.

ABERDEEN: OGSTON BENNETT AND SHEWAN, COOKE COUTTS AND SMITH, KERRIGAN BURNS FRASER WINCHESTER AND MCINTOSH.

A few days later we were once again brought crashing back to earth when we went down 5-3 to our Edinburgh rivals Hearts at Easter Road. In what most of the newspapers later described as a thrilling game, we were two behind at the interval, although Hammy had struck the underside of the bar in the closing minutes. In the second half Jim Scott scored to get us back into the game, but in the end it seemed as though every time we scored Hearts would score again, and in the end the Gorgie side were well worth the victory. Although they were not the side of the halcyon days at Tynecastle during the late '50s and early '60s, the 'maroons' were still a more than reasonable side. By now Jim Cruickshank had taken over from Gordon Marshall in goal, after the latter's move to Newcastle United. Jim was a very good goalkeeper. One of the Hearts lads that we would often meet in town after a game for a few drinks, he was only one of many good players on Hearts books at that time. My former Edina Hearts team mate Chris Shevlane was another. A regular first choice at right-back, he formed a great defensive partnership with the former Queens Park player Davie Holt. A solid defender with a fair bit of pace, Holt's speciality was his slide tackle and you knew you had been tackled if you were caught by the rugged left-back. At the heart of the defence there was Alan Anderson who had surely been the bargain of the season when he was signed from second division Scunthorpe United for the princely sum of £2,000 just over 12 months before. Alan would go on to serve the club with distinction for many years. He was a big man in every sense of the word, but I have to say that I did sometimes get the better of him. He was another that we would often meet out on the town after games and on the occasions that I had played well against him, he would tell me light-heartedly to stay out of his fucking way. Perhaps the main man at Tynecastle at that particular time though was Willie Wallace, who was destined to soon achieve immortality as a member of the Celtic European Cup winning side of 1967. An extremely dangerous and determined competitor, Wallace was as strong as an ox, had a great football brain, could hold the ball and score goals. He could also bring others into the game and was a perfect foil for his inside-forward partner, Alan Gordon, a player who would become a great favourite with the Hibs fans a few years later.

With no European football in Edinburgh that season it had been Jock Stein's idea that Hibs should attempt to bring the great Real Madrid to Easter Road for a challenge match. It would be a great financial gamble, but in the end it was felt that even a slight loss would be more than compensated by the prestige that the five times European Cup winners would bring to the city. Although they were not the legendary Real Madrid of old they still presented a formidable challenge and had reached the European Cup Final at the end of the previous season only to lose to Inter Milan. It was well known that Real Madrid didn't approach any game in a friendly manner and the fixture would give Jock Stein the perfect opportunity to gauge himself tactically against what was still one of the best teams in the world. One of Real's many demands apart from their huge financial guarantee, was that the Hibs players should wear no white. Chairman Harrower suggested that red shorts could be worn instead, but this was completely ignored by Jock Stein who ordered that the players should wear green shorts.

With Real wearing their famous all white strip, Hibs took the field wearing all green except for the traditional white sleeves and collars. Before the game Jock Stein had gone over the tactics on the blackboard, but things turned out even better than even he could have imagined. I had played in the previous half dozen or so games and had half expected to play, but my place in the side was taken by Pat Quinn who was recalled to play in a deep lying role in midfield alongside Willie Hamilton. Once again I have to say that 'Big Jock' got his tactics just right. That evening 'Hammy' was a revelation, outshining even the aging, but still brilliant Ferenc Puskás, and it was possibly his best ever game in a green and white jersey. Straight from the first whistle Hibs refused to allow their more illustrious visitors to settle. Young Peter Cormack, who had turned 18 only a few days before, put the Easter Road side ahead after just 13 minutes with a brilliant drive. In the second half a Pat Quinn free kick was deflected into the net by a defender to give Hibs a more than deserved

2-0 victory. Friendly or not, it was a famous victory that reverberated throughout the land, the *Evening News* reporting somewhat exaggeratedly that it was perhaps Edinburgh's finest ever 90 minutes. I watched from the stand as the Hibs players took a well-earned lap of honour before almost 30,000 ecstatic fans at the final whistle, but it might surprise you that I was not overly disappointed at having missed the match. Of course I always wanted to play in every game, but I can honestly say that the fact that it was Real Madrid did not bother me in the slightest. It was only a friendly, and friendly matches, with the possible exception of the Edinburgh Select fixture and games against the Hearts in the East of Scotland Shield – I always desperately wanted to beat the Hearts – I never took friendly games particularly seriously.

At the end of the game there was the now well known incident when Jock Stein bumped into the journalist John Rafferty in the tunnel. For days in his column in *The Scotsman* Rafferty had been scathing regarding our chances against the Spanish giants, stating that it was the craziest thing he had ever heard for Hibs to even contemplate playing a team of Real's stature, and he was convinced that we would be soundly thrashed. Stein almost physically marched him into the home dressing room to apologise to the players, but to give the embarrassed Rafferty his due, he was man enough to do so. The Hibs side that momentous evening was:

WILSON FRASER AND PARKE,
STANTON MCNAMEE AND BAXTER,
CORMACK HAMILTON SCOTT QUINN AND MARTIN.

The inclusion of Pat Quinn against Real had probably worked out even better than Jock Stein himself had expected and he had possibly now discovered what he felt to be his strongest starting 11. The result was that although I was now fully fit, once again I found myself on the side-lines, and would make only the occasional first team outing during the following few months usually filling in only because of injury. With the exception of the opening fixture against Aberdeen in the Summer Cup at Pittodrie, I had played in most of the games so far and it was really disappointing to be back in the reserves. However the first team just kept on winning, proving that Stein was probably right to leave me out. You couldn't blame manager, in those days you rarely changed a winning side if you could help it. I had confidence in my own ability however and knew that I would be back sooner or later and would just have to buckle down and be patient.

As I settled down to reserve team football, the first team were embarking on a great run that would eventually see them missing out only narrowly on a possible league and cup double. At that time both Rangers and Celtic were having ordinary seasons by their own high standards and it was left to Kilmarnock, Hearts, Dunfermline and ourselves to challenge for the title.

As I was reporting to Easter Road for a reserve game against Rangers in what would eventually turn out to be a comprehensive 5-0 victory, perhaps unsurprisingly the same 11 that had defeated Real Madrid in midweek were making their way through to Glasgow for the first meeting of the season with the Ibrox side. With Quinn and Hamilton again occupying the midfield positions, Rangers opened the scoring after just ten minutes. Not long after a crude tackle by Bobby Shearer on Neil Martin a good three yards inside the box was totally ignored by the referee, so no surprise there then, Jim Scott booked for appealing over-zealously. The inevitable was only delayed however and a great shot by Cormack drew Hibs level just before half time. Rangers scored again a few minutes after the break, but further goals from Cormack and Hamilton gave Hibs the lead, Quinn putting the result beyond doubt a few minutes from the end.

At that time the brilliant form of my pal Jim Scott was beginning to attract the attention of several of the top sides in England and a bid in the region of £40,000 from Wolves for the player eventually proved successful. I had become great friends with Jim and was sad to see him go. He himself was obviously delighted to be given the opportunity to test himself against the best defenders in the country, but just as he and his wife Ann were about to board the Midlands-bound train at the Waverley Station in Edinburgh, he was informed that for some unknown reason the move was off, and it was a bitterly disappointed Scott who rejoined his Easter Road team mates for training the following morning.

It was also around this time that Jim Easton was allowed to join Dundee. Since the signing of John McNamee, Jim had found great difficulty in securing a first team place. I had always thought that he was going to be great player, but a bad leg break against Airdrie followed by another against East Stirling just 17 months later proved a huge setback to his Easter Road career. As a youngster Eddie Turnbull had really rated the player. He had a great physique, was a good tackler and good in the air. He possibly lacked a bit in a one-to-one situation, but he would go on to serve Dundee well for many seasons, before moving to Queen of the South, finally ending his career with the American side Miami Toros.

Our reserve side was also going well and we were just seven points behind league leaders Dunfermline, but had played five games less. There were some very good players in the side including several with first team experience in Billy Simpson, Jimmy Stevenson, Tommy Leishman and Jimmy O'Rourke. The usual line-up would be along the lines of:

REILLY, SIMPSON AND GARTSHORE, (J) STEVENSON WHITEFORD AND
LEISHMAN,
GRANT, HOGG MCNEILL O'ROURKE AND MYSELF, (SOMETIMES
CULLERTON).

By now John Parke had fully recovered from his cartilage operation the previous season and was back to his best. After an absence of almost a year he had been selected for the Northern Ireland squad that was due to face Switzerland at the beginning of November, but before the game could take place Hibs had somewhat surprisingly accepted a bid from Sunderland for the international defender.

The move had come right out of the blue, probably surprising even John himself. Stein however was not long in signing a replacement, and that same day both Parke and left-back Joe Davis, who had just joined us from Third Lanark were photographed together at Easter Road. The highly rated Davis, a hard tackler and very different to the cool ball playing Parke, was absolutely delighted to be playing full time football for the first time in his career and pleased to meet up again with his former Cathkin trainer Tom McNiven. The astute Stein, who was probably unsure if Parke's legs would be capable of standing up to the rigours of the Scottish game after three operations, had allowed the defender to go for a fee believed to be around £40,000. Davis, on the other hand, who would go on to give Hibs several years of sterling service had been signed for much less and it would turn out to be yet another outstanding piece of business for the club.

Joe made his Hibs debut in a convincing 5-0 win against his former side Third Lanark at Easter Road on the Saturday and looked a very good signing. I had scored in our 3-1 victory in the corresponding reserve fixture at Cathkin the previous evening, but both Joe and I were destined to form an extremely productive partnership in the very near future. Unfortunately, only days after making his debut he would go down with appendicitis, but incredibly he would miss only three games before his return in a 2-1 victory against Partick Thistle a few weeks later. In total Davis would go on to play an incredible 273 consecutive first team games for Hibs, many of them as captain, before his move to English Second Division side Carlisle United in 1969.

During Joe's enforced absence the team had suffered a setback in its quest to win the championship for the first time since 1952 when they could only manage to draw 2-2 with Dundee after a 1-0 defeat by Dunfermline the previous week. We had now dropped to third place in the table, six points behind leaders Hearts, although we still had a game in hand. Apart from that temporary set-back however things were going well. Only four points had been dropped from the previous ten games since a defeat by Kilmarnock at Easter Road almost three months before with the great win against Real Madrid sandwiched in between. During all this time I had only managed to feature in the first team twice, both times only because of injury, and while I was extremely disappointed at being unable to regain a regular first team place, I really could have had no complaints as the side had kept on winning. To give the manager his due he always kept me in the picture, but understandably his main priority would always have been the first team.

A 4-3 victory at home against Clyde extended our good run before the traditional New Year's Day fixture against league leaders Hearts at Tynecastle. In preparation for a game that was now far more important than normal because of our respective league positions at the top of the table, it had been decided that we should stay overnight at our usual meeting place in Great King Street. Just before midnight Chairman Harrower came in with a case of champagne for us to 'Toast the Bells' before we were packed off to bed. Some players refused the offer, although not me personally I hasten to add as I had already been told that I would not be playing the following day.

Sometime later, it must have been around two or three in the morning, I was wakened by trainer Tom McNiven who asked me to accompany him downstairs. In the lounge we found Willie Hamilton still drinking away quite merrily on his own. I helped Tom to get Hammy under the shower in an effort to sober him up before packing him off to bed.

In the morning he still looked rough, but that didn't prevent the mercurial Hamilton from having the game of his life, scoring Hibs goal in the 1-0 victory. In an absorbing fast and furious game at Tynecastle played in front of more than 38,000 fans, there were several near things at either end until the game was settled by a quite sensational goal from Hammy. With just 20 minutes remaining and the game still goalless, Hearts centre-half Alan Anderson fouled Neil Martin just outside the penalty area. Hamilton took a quick free kick to Quinn who returned the ball to him. The Hibs inside-left, complete with his trademark sweat soaked shirt, managed to evade a challenge from an opponent that sent him wide. At first it looked as if the opportunity had gone, but incredibly from a seemingly impossible angle near the bye line Willie proceeded to unleash an unstoppable shot past goalkeeper Cruickshank from all of

15 yards and into the far top corner off the net, the goal enough to give us the points. Before the game Willie had been left under no illusion at just what myself and the rest of his team mates thought about his highly unprofessional early morning behaviour, leaving him in no doubt that he was well out of order, especially before a game against Hearts of all teams. We were having a few drinks back at the hotel after the game when the bold Hammy let everybody know just what he thought about our pre-match criticism by telling us: 'Aye, your no shouting at me now. I've just won everybody their bonus money.' That was Hammy for you. He was some guy and had the manager been present then I'm sure he would just have shaken his head.

Although he was a quite exceptional talent with the touch of a ballet dancer, Willie could sometimes be frustrating to play alongside. Often he would fail to give you the ball back when you were in a far better position and would sometimes just let fly from 25 or 30 yards. To be fair he was a great striker of the ball and on the rare occasions that it did come off it would be tremendous.

At that time it was the habit of Scottish teams to play on consecutive afternoons during the New Year period, something that wouldn't even be considered nowadays, and 24 hours after our great win at Tynecastle Neil Martin scored four in Hibs 6-0 victory against the unfortunate Falkirk in Edinburgh. I think it would be fair to say that at that time, despite the magical talents of Willie Hamilton, there was absolutely no doubt that Neil Martin was the main man at Easter Road. His goals against Falkirk meant that Neil had now scored 14 from 19 league games while forming a prolific partnership with centre-forward Jim Scott who himself had scored 12 including four from the penalty spot. Jim had been signed from Bo'ness United in 1958 as an outside-right and had been an established first team regular since 1962. Although he had played through the middle before he was normally to be found on the wing, and it was really Jock Stein who had realised that centre-forward was his best position. Extremely tricky on the ball, Scottie could look timid at times, but that was just his style, you would not last long in England if you were timid, and although he was not the greatest of tacklers, he could hold the ball up, and more importantly like all good centre-forwards, knew exactly where the goals were.

The emphatic victory over Falkirk had put us level on points with second placed Kilmarnock, although we still had that game in hand, but a point dropped at Aberdeen and both against Dundee United the following week saw us drop into third place although still well in the running for the title. I had replaced the injured Neil Martin for the game against United, but the eventual 4-3 defeat was particularly disappointing as it had been our recent home form that was causing all the problems. That afternoon the Dane Finn Dossing had been a particular thorn in our side, scoring a hat trick as United cruised to a 4-0 interval lead. Indeed United had been so impressive that even the Hibs fans had cheered them from the field at half time, but what a turn around after the break. Our position looked hopeless until two goals by Cormack and another from the penalty spot by Quinn gave us fresh hope as we went all out for the equaliser, but unfortunately United just managed to hold out to take both points.

At the end of the month Rangers were the visitors to Easter Road. Neil Martin had now recovered from his injury and once again I had to be content with a seat in the stand. With my old pal Willie Henderson making a return to the Rangers side after several weeks out through injury, both teams took to a snow covered pitch wearing black armbands in a mark of respect for the former Prime Minister Winston Churchill who had died earlier in the week. Rangers were possibly the bookies favourites, but a Neil Martin goal in the first half was enough to give us the points and a famous victory, Hibs first league double over Rangers for 62 years. Not since the championship winning season of 1902–03 when the home side had won 1-0 at Easter Road and 5-2 at Ibrox had the feat been achieved, and not even by the celebrated Easter Road side of the immediate post-war years. Even better, both our nearest challengers Hearts and Kilmarnock had lost that afternoon and we now had second place all to ourselves.

We now trailed league leaders Hearts by only three points, but still had two games in hand and things were starting to look very interesting. At that time Celtic had been underperforming for several years, their last trophy success as far back as 1957 when they had famously defeated Rangers 7-1 in the League Cup final at Hampden. In direct contrast Rangers had been by far the most dominant side in the country. In the 20 years or so since the war the championship had been spread around several of the so called provincial clubs, but recently only Dundee had managed to interrupt a run of four consecutive titles for the Ibrox side who had also won both the Scottish and League Cups three times during this time. Celtic on the other hand, except for that league cup win against Rangers had not won the Scottish Cup since 1951 and the league title since as far back as 1938.

Although they had undoubtedly missed the talents of both Willie Henderson and Jim Baxter for a large part of the season through injury, Rangers still presented a considerable challenge and one that put Hibs great win into perspective.

The exhilaration of the landmark victory would be tempered later that evening by the breaking news that manager Jock Stein had agreed to join Celtic at the end of the season. Stein had achieved so much in such a short space of time that the shattering news was barely conceivable and it badly affected everyone connected with the club. It is difficult now to convey to anyone not around at the time just how devastating the news was. We were clearly heading in the right direction, everyone convinced that major honours were just around the corner, and the breaking news of Stein's impending departure came as a gigantic hammer blow to all of us.

As a welcome diversion from the demands of the championship race, in the first round of the Scottish Cup we had been drawn against lowly ES Clydebank and as far as we were concerned a fairly easy passage into the next round. Clydebank had a chequered history. Formed only at the outbreak of war in 1914, a Clydebank side had been members of the Scottish League until financial difficulties had forced them to resign completely from the second division in 1931 after they had finished second bottom. By coincidence the following season East Stirlingshire, who would have an indirect part to play in the formation of the new Clydebank, would be promoted into the top league for the first time in its history. In 1964 the entrepreneurial bothers Charlie and Jack Steedman had purchased East Stirlingshire Football Club. The 'Shire' had ended the previous season rock bottom of the Scottish first division and the Steedman brothers decided to amalgamate East Stirling with Clydebank Juniors, a team that had no connection with the aforementioned Clydebank and move lock stock and barrel to Clydebank. Now renamed ES Clydebank, the new team took its place in the second division in time for the start of the 1964–65 season, eventually ending in fifth place.

The game against Hibs would be their first ever Scottish Cup tie, but the second division side surprised everyone inside Easter Road by earning a deserved draw against their more illustrious opponents. During the 90 minutes, try as they might Hibs just could not find a way past their courageous opponents until Neil Martin scored with a header midway through the second half. The lead lasted all of five minutes when a Bankie's side that included the future Scotland manager Andy Roxburgh in their line-up, scored a more than merited equaliser and it was now on to Kilbowie on the Wednesday evening for the replay.

The replay turned out to be yet another hard fought affair and Hibs had to be at their very best against plucky opponents. I again watched from the side-lines as we were given a real fright in the first half when the home side were well on top. Worse still, at one point the game had been so one sided that the home fans had started the traditional 'easy, easy' chants. In the end it was probably only our superior stamina that told, and goals from Hamilton and Cormack in the second half allowed both the players and fans to breathe a huge sigh of relief on the long journey back to the capital later that evening.

In the second round an easy 5-1 win against Partick Thistle at Easter Road set up a third meeting of the season with Rangers. Hibs were now bidding to defeat the Glasgow side for a historic third time in the same season, something that no Easter Road side had ever achieved before. Rangers welcomed back Jim Baxter after his leg break against Rapid Vienna in Austria earlier in the season and in front of a huge 47,363 crowd, which was Edinburgh's biggest for many years, the scene was set for another thrilling encounter. Willie Hamilton opened the scoring for Hibs after just four minutes when Ritchie could only parry a back header from John Fraser, but we then had had to survive a period of sustained pressure that ended in Hynd equalising with a tremendous drive from 25 yards. It was now all to play for. In the second half of a pulsating game there were near things at either end until with just two minutes remaining and the fans on both sides starting to make arrangements for the replay in Glasgow, Hamilton got the slightest of touches to a shot from John Fraser that already looked over the line to send Hibs into the semi-finals and hand Rangers their first cup defeat in 22 games.

The jubilation of the momentous win had still not subsided on the Monday morning when everyone at Easter Road – players, backroom staff and supporters alike – were absolutely stunned with the devastating breaking news that Jock Stein had now agreed to join Celtic, not at the end of the season as originally planned, but with immediate effect. Captain John Fraser later told us that he had been called up to the managers office that morning to be given the news. According to Stein it had always been his ambition to manage Celtic and concerned that they would not wait for him until the end of the season he had decided, although very reluctantly, that he would be leaving immediately. Stein had been at Easter Road for just under a year, but in that time had worked wonders in transforming a relegation haunted side into one that was capable of challenging for honours and it's fair to say that as well as being shattered at the news, both the players and the fans also felt more than a little let down. The manager's record of 25 wins and six draws from 37 games was, considering the circumstances in which he had arrived, nothing short of phenomenal and he would be an extremely difficult, if not impossible act to follow.

Although it had already been announced that the then Dundee manager Bob Shankly would be replacing Stein at the end of the season, the newspapers were still taking bets on a potential successor to Stein. The well-known Glasgow bookmakers John Banks had already installed Eddie Turnbull as the 6-4 odds on favourite, with both the Clyde manager John Prentice and former player Sammy Baird at 5-1, but in the end it was the 54-year-old Shankly, a close friend of Stein's who had been recommended for the position by the outgoing manager, who became the fifth Easter Road boss since the end of the war. One of several brothers to play professionally, Bob was a couple of years older than the perhaps more famous Bill who was then manager of Liverpool, but he himself also had an impressive pedigree in the game. The former Alloa player had won a Scottish League cap with Falkirk in 1938 before taking over as manager at Brockville. A short stint in charge of Third Lanark followed before a move to Dundee in 1959. There, with the assistance of the evergreen Gordon Smith and the former Hibs player Sammy Kean who was now trainer at Dens, Shankly had led the club to its first ever league championship in 1962 and the semi-finals of the European Cup the following year, with what was generally regarded to be the best ever side in the 69-year history of the club. They had also reached the final of the Scottish Cup in 1964 only to lose 3-1 to Rangers at Hampden.

It was obvious that Shankly had been well aware of Stein's imminent departure as he had watched his soon to be new charges defeat Rangers from the Easter Road stand while his current side Dundee had been facing St Mirren in a league game at Dens Park that same afternoon. It would later turn out that Shankly had been disillusioned at Dundee for some time and had lost his enthusiasm for the game after being repeatedly forced to sell top players like Alan Gilzean to Spurs and Ian Ure to Arsenal. Now of the opinion that any Dundee player would be sold if the offer was good enough he had recently revealed in a newspaper interview:

> It was the nursing of players to greatness during my 36 years in the game that had given me the greatest pleasure, but being a football manager is like creating a cudgel to beat your own back. If I had the qualifications for some other position I would give up the game tomorrow!

Shankly would obviously have harboured regrets about leaving Dundee after six mainly successful years, but would be taking over a club that was in the last four of the Scottish Cup and within touching distance of the league championship. The new manager was as different as chalk and cheese to the previous boss. Stein had been a hands on tracksuit manager who liked nothing better than to be out on the training ground with the players working on his tactics during the week, a system incidentally that had proved extremely successful without me. Shankly on the other hand was a fairly dour though likable character from the old school who preferred to leave that side of things to Jimmy Stevenson who had remained behind after Stein's departure for Parkhead and Tom McNiven. He had gained a great reputation for unearthing young talent, but rarely took anything to do with the actual training itself, usually looking on from the side as we were put through our paces. Unlike Stein, and later Eddie Turnbull for that matter, Shankly was anything but a strict disciplinarian. Rarely seen without a shirt and tie, to me he looked more like chief executive than a football manager.

The same 11 players that had defeated Rangers took the field for Shankly's first game in charge, a 2-0 home victory against Motherwell on Wednesday 10 March 1965. The report in the following days *Evening News* suggesting that the players had 'turned on the style to impress the new manager with a scintillating display of vintage football.' With Pat Quinn and Willie Hamilton again providing the ammunition from midfield, Jim Scott and Neil Martin had proved a constant threat in front of goal and Hibs could well have scored more. With no substitutes in those days and no reserve game that afternoon, once again I had to be content to watch the proceedings from a seat in the stand, little realising that things were about to change for me under the new manager.

In a move that would soon have repercussions back in Edinburgh, that same week Eddie Turnbull had started out on a managerial journey that would eventually lead him back to Easter Road when his new side Aberdeen had defeated Rangers 2-0 at Pittodrie.

While obviously all managers want to win games – winning was Stein's priority above all else – I always felt that Bob Shankly wanted more to entertain, and he changed big Jock's customary and highly successful 4-3-3 system to a more flexible 4-2-4 which fortunately meant a place in the side for me wide on the left.

A few weeks later second placed Hibs made their way through to Glasgow to face Jock Stein's Celtic in a game that had already been postponed twice, first by fog and again because of wind damage to the Parkhead lights. A magnificent fighting display gave us our first league win in the east of the city for nine years and Neil Martin his third hat trick of the season. After scoring his third goal, Neil, one of the many Hibs players who had been bitterly disappointed at Stein's earlier than planned abdication to Glasgow, made a bee line towards the Celtic dugout to give an impassive Stein the famous V-sign accompanied by the words 'F*** you,' a comment that apparently drew no response from the stony faced Celtic manager. The best goal of the evening however, and one as good as you are ever likely to see, was reserved for my direct opponent that evening, full-back John Young who headed spectacularly past John Fallon in trying to clear a cross.

I think it's fair to say that Stein's premature departure had left an air of despondency hanging over Easter Road and the cup semi-final against Dunfermline at Tynecastle a few days later turned out to be a huge anti-climax after the highs of the previous round against Rangers. The same 11 that had defeated Celtic in midweek started well enough against the Fifers, but after a promising start we never even looked like scoring apart from a disallowed goal by Willie Hamilton who was clearly well offside, and the 2-0 defeat was the end of our hopes of winning the magical double. In the end it had all come down to a disappointing few days. During this time our dreams of Scottish Cup glory had evaporated, and although we managed to defeat Dunfermline 1-0 at Easter Road in a league game on the Wednesday, a 2-1 defeat at Dens Park followed by a heavy 4-0 home defeat by Celtic that allowed the Parkhead side to gain revenge for the recent defeat in Glasgow, meant that with just two games remaining any hopes of the elusive double had crumbled to dust.

In many ways it had been a strange season, with neither of the Old Firm managing to finish in the top four for the first time since the league began in 1890. We ourselves eventually had to settle for fourth place, four points behind Kilmarnock who had won the title only on goal average from Hearts in an exciting climax to the season at Tynecastle, and three behind third placed Dunfermline. Hearts would later be the main mover in a successful bid to change the archaic goal average to goal difference. Had goal difference been in place then Hearts would have won the league for the first time since 1960. Somewhat ironically had the original goal average still been place in 1986 then Hearts would have ended the season as champions instead of Celtic.

Jock Stein's Celtic would go on to defeat Dunfermline in the cup final, and it would be only the start. It was the dawn of a new era at Parkhead and the start of the most successful period in the clubs history as they proceeded not only to collect a then record nine consecutive league titles, but also become the first British side to win the coveted European Cup by defeating Inter Milan in Lisbon in 1967.

Jim Baxter's move to Sunderland at the end of the season would signal the end of Rangers recent near domination of the Scottish game, a decline that coincided with Celtic's resurgence under Jock Stein. For all his talent Baxter's off field behaviour had caused manager Scott Symon many sleepless nights and had probably also frightened off some of the bigger clubs in the country to deny him the chance of displaying his undoubted talents on a far bigger stage.

As far as Hibs were concerned we had again qualified for the semi-finals of the Summer Cup from a regional league again consisting of Hearts, Dunfermline and Falkirk. Unfortunately we would stumble against Motherwell, losing 6-2 at Fir Park after a 2-0 win in Edinburgh.

Once again Neil Martin had ended the season not only as Hibs top goal scorer, but the top marksman in the entire country profiting from a prolific partnership with Jim Scott, and I was pleased for my good pal when he became the first Hibs player to be selected at full international level since Johnny McLeod against Czechoslovakia in 1961 when he was chosen for Scotland's 1-1 draw with Poland in a World Cup Qualifier in Chorzow. Neil would win his second cap seven days later while lining up alongside his team mate Willie Hamilton in Scotland's 2-1 victory over Finland in Helsinki in the same competition.

An invitation to take part in an end of season International Tournament in New York had been rejected by the club in favour a three week tour of Canada and the United States where we were to play eight games in a hectic 17 days.

Our opening game was a 2-1 victory against the English first division side Nottingham Forest who were just ending their own American tour, but the remaining games were all mainly against inferior amateur sides. We eventually ended the trip without losing a game, scoring the grand total of 72 goals for the loss of just six although the quality of the opposition obviously has to be taken into account. Our next game against the British Columbia All Stars ended in a 9-2 victory with full-back Joe Davis scoring his first goal for the club, ominously from the penalty spot. After five straight wins, Bob Shankly took several of the more senior players aside including myself, to tell us that if we defeated Toronto Italia who were reckoned to be reasonable side, then we wouldn't have to take part in our next game and could just sit back and enjoy the holiday. This was just the incentive we needed and we managed to beat Toronto quite comfortably by a 4-0 margin.

Our schedule could be quite tight with on one occasion three games in three days, and after our victory against Toronto, Neil Martin, Willie Hamilton and myself who had all been excused duty against the Ottawa All-Stars, travelled to the game by taxi after downing a good few beers. During the journey the taxi driver happened to mention that there was a silver salver on offer for the game's man-of-the-match. I thought no more about it until we arrived at the ground to find that Willie Hamilton was nowhere to be seen. The next thing we knew the bold Willie was taking the field with the team and he had had far more to drink than us. The upshot was that Hammy spent the bulk of the game refusing to even pass the ball, scoring seven consecutive goals in a 15-1 victory to be awarded the man-of-the-match trophy. The rest is a well known story. With his holdall far too small for the silver salver, Willie promptly bent it in two for the journey home. On the whole the tour had been extremely relaxed, the games played in a friendly and cordial atmosphere and usually watched by reasonably large crowds of expat Scots.

Our penultimate game was against Montreal Italia in the local stadium which by all accounts had a bad reputation for trouble and was avoided by many of the touring sides. We took the field to find dozens of armed police surrounding the pitch which was thought to be a bit strange, but things were about to get much worse. Played in a somewhat surreal atmosphere, events eventually took a turn for the worse late in the second half when Jim Scott was sent off for the first time in his career when he retaliated after being punched full in the face. To our amazement his opponent, who had been putting it about all afternoon, was not even booked.

Near the end of the game we were alarmed to see that a large number of the Italian fans had left their seats and were now surrounding the perimeter of the pitch shouting and screaming abuse, which believe me was a very frightening experience particularly for myself playing out wide on the wing. This didn't seem to bother big John McNamee as much as it did the rest of us and at the final whistle John just strutted through the aggressive throng with his chest in the air.

Not being nearly as brave as Big Mac, I decided that the safest place would be tucked in nicely behind him as we left the field and I looked behind a few seconds later to discover that the whole team had taken my cue and there was not an inch of daylight to be found between us, all tucked safely in behind the big man. John was some guy. He didn't have a great sense of humour and was normally someone you didn't take liberties with. I don't know if it was the drink, but during an earlier part of the trip, myself and my room mate Jim Scott had decided to invite McNamee and another couple of the players back to our room. We ordered large steaks, all the trimmings and a case of Budweiser from room service. McNamee couldn't believe his eyes when the huge steaks arrived and I told him that it was all included in the bill and that Hibs would pick up the tab, which off course was total nonsense. The next I heard was that John and his roommate had ordered steaks nearly every day.

The upshot was that when it came to collect our spending money at the end of the week McNamee was absolutely furious to discover just how much he owed the club. For some reason John didn't seem to think this was as funny as the rest of us, and he chased me through the hotel, making it extremely obvious that he was not in a humorous mood, while calling me all the names under the sun, some I had never even heard of. I genuinely think that he would have killed me if he had caught up with me, and it was sometime before he calmed down and eventually saw the funny side of it. There were some serious moments though. One evening after a game, some of us were having a drink in our room when Neil Martin and Jim Scott started arguing about who was the better goalscorer. A few too many drinks had been consumed and what had started out as banter started to get really heated and almost leading to blows. I was asked to decide who was the best, but diplomatically I managed to cool things down before things really got out of hand.

CHAPTER SEVEN

A Stroll at Tynecastle
and Semi-Final Disappointment
1965–66

THE RESURGENCE UNDER Jock Stein of a side struggling to avoid relegation into one potentially capable of winning the title in just under a year had been incredible, but the general consensus was that even without Stein we could only get better. At that time the side had a great balance of youth and experience, and although I was still only 23, I was considered to be almost a veteran.

Both John Murphy and John Blackley were still on the ground staff and were joined at Easter Road during the summer by Bobby Hogg a centre-forward from Sauchie, inside-forward Colin Grant from Scottish Junior Cup winners Linlithgow Rose, and Colin Stein a former full-back from Armadale Thistle who had since been converted into a free scoring centre-forward.

Under Bob Shankly we were now playing in a system that suited me perfectly and I was delighted if not a little relieved to be back in the side. I knew that Big Jock had rated me, but for most of his time at Easter Road I had not been fully fit and really could have had few complaints about being left out of the side.

An opening day defeat in the league cup at Brockville would turn out to be Willie Hamilton's last game in a green and white jersey, a move that was always going to happen. Willie had been unhappy at Easter Road for some time seeking a move back to England and the much bigger money on offer, and had already posted several transfer demands. It was only now that we discovered that several earlier bids by Aston Villa for the unsettled player had been rejected, but now, probably accepting that it would be futile in trying to keep an unhappy player at Easter Road, Villa's perseverance had finally paid off. During his time at Easter Road Willie had made almost 90 appearances in all games, scoring 39 goals including the seven against the Ottawa All-Stars in Canada, and now the enigmatic player was finally on his way to Villa Park for a fee reckoned to be around the £25,000 mark. The game at Brockville-had also been the former Hibs and Dundee trainer Sammy Kean's first outing as manager of Falkirk and he took the opportunity to meet up again with his former boss at Dundee Bob Shankly.

Understandably the Hibs fans were not pleased at losing a player of Hamilton's undoubted talents, and although I was not happy to see him go, I merely accepted his moving as just something that happened in the game. I will always have fond memories of watching Willie walking along Albion Road in the morning before training gulping down a bottle of milk, wondering just what he had been up to, and his premature death a few years later would be a tragic end for such a talented player.

In the midweek game against St Mirren at Easter Road, Willie Wilson was recalled to the side in place of young Jack Reilly who had performed poorly in the 3-1 defeat at Brockville, but it would turn out to be anything but a happy return for the goalkeeper. Willie was as brave, or as daft, as they come and midway through the first half he was carried off after being injured pulling off a daring save at the feet of an opponent. In those pre-substitute days, Peter Cormack took over between the posts and performed as if he had played there all his life pulling off several fine saves, one in particular from centre-forward Redpath in the exceptional class, and managed to keep a clean sheet for the rest of the game. Although still slightly concussed, Wilson returned to take his place on the right wing at the start of the second half sporting a huge skull cap that covered a nasty head wound. I scored the only goal of the game with an angled shot from a cross field pass by Pat Quinn who had been recalled into the side to replace Willie Hamilton, but Wilson was the real hero of the game. Egged on by an enthusiastic home crowd, he repeatedly caused havoc in the St Mirren defence with his often unorthodox wing play, and on one occasion even almost managed to score himself. Late in the game I failed to get on the end of one of his thundering cross field passes that was a full 20 yards in front of me that even George McNeill couldn't have got anywhere near, and I could hear Willie shouting across, 'Stevie get your f***ing finger out,' although when I glared back I could see that he was laughing. Later in the dressing room some of the players joked that I should start taking lessons on wing play from Willie – at least I hoped they were joking!

Just the solitary opening day defeat by Falkirk allowed us to finish top of the league cup section to qualify for the later stages of the competition for the second time in three seasons, an ideal preparation before facing Valencia in the Fairs Cup at Easter Road.

At that time I felt that I was playing the best football of my career and was being tipped for a place in the Scotland under-23 side. There were also rumours going around that I was also being watched by Liverpool, but if that was indeed the case then I had been told nothing about it by the club. In any event I was very happy at Easter Road especially now that I was back in the first team. It was a was great life for a young lad and being a footballer also opened many doors in the city with numerous invites to functions and immediate entry to many of the dance halls in the city without queuing.

After recent victories against both Real Madrid and Barcelona it was evident that Valencia would be difficult opponents, but in the end our 2-0 win in Edinburgh was far easier than the score-line would suggest. Perhaps surprisingly I was the only one of the current line-up who had faced the Spanish side just over two seasons before, although Jimmy O'Rourke was still at the club, but at that time featuring mainly in the reserves.

A Jim Scott header gave us the lead after just four minutes and the fans settled back waiting for a goal avalanche that failed to materialise. Sustained pressure in the visitors penalty area produced several near things, but desperate defending, good goalkeeping and I have to say incredibly poor refereeing when we were denied at least three blatant penalties, prevented us from increasing our lead. Somewhat bizarrely, at half time our captain John Baxter had been called to the referee's room where he was told bluntly that we were to cut out the shouting to each another, a directive that we couldn't quite believe. Needless to say the instructions were ignored, and although it took us to the final minute of the game to score what could well have been an important second goal when John McNamee bulleted a header into the net from close range from a Cormack cross, the two goal victory was no more than we deserved. It had been Big John's third goal of the season after only eight games, an extremely impressive statistic for a centre-half, but the big question now was – would it be enough in Spain? The game had also allowed Bob Shankly to become the only manager in the country to have managed a side in all four of the European competitions – the European Cup, Cup Winners Cup, Fairs Cup and also the Friendship Cup, an ill-fated tournament that had taken place in the early years of the decade.

In the quarter final of the league cup we had been handed a potentially easy draw – with a game against second division Alloa, but after our struggle against Clydebank the previous season we were taking nothing for granted. In the first game at Recreation Park however, the tie to all intents and purpose was already as good as over as early as the first minute when Pat Quinn opened the scoring. Despite several brilliant saves by goalkeeper Hodge, a spectacular header by Neil Martin midway through the first half meant, that with due respect to plucky Alloa who never stopped battling away, we were already confident that we had done enough to take us through to the semi-final. In the return leg at Easter Road a Jim Scott goal, this time after three minutes, saw any lingering hope of a remarkable comeback by the second division side completely disappear, before the roof finally caved in on plucky Alloa. Eight ahead at the interval we eventually cantered to a 11-2 victory, but in all honesty it was all too easy and could well have been 20. Jim Scott and Neil Martin took the goal scoring honours with four apiece with Pat Quinn and myself also managing to get in on the act. Joe Davis scored our seventh goal from the penalty spot, McNamee later missing from a similar award. In recent seasons Jim Scott, Neil Martin, Peter Cormack and myself had all failed from the spot, Cormack's poor effort against Kilmarnock a few days before, our fourth miss in five attempts. Now, McNamee's failure left the newspapers headlines proclaiming 'Wanted, a penalty kick expert at Easter Road'. Although we didn't know it at the time, we already had one in our midst and the clinical finish by Joe Davis would now see him handed the job permanently.

Sandwiched between both league cup ties we had faced Hearts at Tynecastle in the first derby of the season. An announcement over the tannoy just before the start that the popular Neil Martin would miss the game because of injury drew groans of disappointment from the large number of Hibs fans inside the ground. His replacement Jimmy O'Rourke had originally made plans to spend the Edinburgh holiday in Blackpool with friends before being hurriedly recalled the previous day. It would be Jimmy's first start of the season, but what a start! With many fans still making their way into the stadium O'Rourke celebrated his 19th birthday by opening the scoring after only two minutes when he blasted a shot past Jim Cruickshank from close range. Two minutes later I added a second from a narrow angle after my first shot had rebounded from the keeper, and further goals by both O'Rourke and myself gave us what was an already unassailable 4-0 lead after just ten minutes. I heard later that the shopkeepers in Gorgie had profited from the early scoring burst when many of the latecomers had not even bothered to gain entry to the ground after discovering the score. For the first 20 minutes or so we had been unplayable when Hearts just didn't know what had hit them. Although they later put up some semblance of a fight, in all reality they were gone – finished. I have to confess that although it was not really in my nature, I started to take my foot off the peddle, showboating a wee bit to the obvious fury of my Hearts 'friends' in the enclosure, as did some of my team mates, and it was only after the game that we realised just what a chance we had missed to set up a record score. Pat Stanton, Jimmy O'Rourke and myself were all huge Hibs fans and were all obviously highly delighted at the victory, but in hindsight we should have kept going and who knows just what the final score might have been, possibly even overtaking the famous 7-0 victory at Tynecastle a few years later.

We had now gone ten games without defeat since the opening day reverse at Falkirk, scoring 30 goals while conceding just seven and were brimming with confidence. The *Evening News* later that night agreed:

> Hibs are playing better football now than they did under Jock Stein. Stein picked them-up and put them back on the rails, but Bob Shankly's influence has moulded them into an effective and consistent goal scoring machine.

Neil Martin was back in the side the following week against Falkirk, and while Jimmy O'Rourke was managing to get on the score sheet in the reserves 4-2 defeat at Brockville, Neil justified his recall by scoring four in a 5-1 whitewash of the 'Bairns' at Easter Road. It was no real surprise when Martin opened the scoring inside the first few minutes, and although we were surprised when Falkirk equalised midway through the half, our fighting spirit kicked in and what eventually turned out to be an easy victory saw us sitting at the top of the league table just ahead of second placed Celtic.

After the injury disappointments of the previous few seasons at that time I was really enjoying my football. Although I say it myself I considered myself to be a real football player with a good football brain. I could read the game, beat a man and make room for myself. If I received the ball in a tight space I was more than capable of getting out of it, and although I was mainly all left foot I could also hit the ball with my right and was equally comfortable on both sides of the park. Although not the greatest in the air and perhaps not as quick as some, I could nevertheless cover the ground with the ball at my feet as fast as I could without it. With my slight build, I wasn't the greatest of tacklers, but as Eddie Turnbull once told me, players like myself didn't really need to tackle. But more than anything, I loved playing in the big games at Parkhead, Ibrox and Tynecastle. In those games, particularly against Celtic and Rangers you tended not to get as much of the ball as usual and I could sometimes be a wee bit selfish, but I always tried to make sure that my opposite number knew that he had been in a game. Overall I think that the supporters appreciated my style of play, with the possible exception of my 'fans' in the Tynecastle enclosure, who always gave me a hard time.

In the league cup semi-final we had been drawn against Celtic, the game to be played at Ibrox. At that time we were playing well and with our unbeaten run now extended to 13 games we feared no one and we made our way to Glasgow in confident mood.

That evening at Ibrox, Joe McBride opened the scoring for Celtic after just eight minutes from a position that looked at least a couple of yards offside, a fact that I believe was confirmed on TV later that evening, before Neil Martin equalised with a great header from a perfectly flighted Jim Scott cross. The same player put us in front after an hour when he rifled home my cutback from the left and we were well worth out lead. At that point the team was playing well and the goal looked like being enough to take us into the final when Celtic scored a cruel equaliser in the very last seconds of the regulation 90 minutes to set up extra time. After Neil Martin's second goal we had really started to turn on the style and were playing some magnificent football, although a Celtic side that always played right to the final whistle were always going to be a threat. With just seconds remaining Tommy Gemmell was allowed to charge down the wing unchallenged. His shot-cum-cross bounced off the chest of Willie Wilson only to fall perfectly at the feet of Bobby Lennox who wasted no time in firing the ball past the goalkeeper.

To my mind we had been much the better side and had fully deserved to have reached the final. I have to admit though that occasionally I didn't have quite the same conviction as players like Jimmy O'Rourke or later Alex Cropley who would chase anything, and possibly several of our players also had the same attitude in the later stages feeling that perhaps the game was already won. The equaliser came as a cruel blow and although there were several near things at either end in extra time, there was to be no more scoring and 22 players who had given their all were given a great reception by the fans as they left the field at the end. The final result was a cruel disappointment for all of us, but mainly for Pat Stanton, John McNamee and our goal scorer Neil Martin who had all been particularly outstanding.

There was a major controversy at the end of our game against Motherwell at Easter Road on the Saturday when referee Smail chalked off what looked like a perfectly good goal. With the sides level at two each, the official blew for time up just as a Jim Scott header from a corner was literally crossing the line. It was a quite incredible decision that stunned the players and infuriated the fans. For me it was an unbelievably over fussy judgement and one that just wouldn't happen nowadays. Jim Scott agreed and was booked for his protests. The final score-line however had now extended our long unbeaten run to 15 games. Motherwell had taken the lead early on, but shortly after, the tenacious Cormack had chased what seemed to be a lost cause. Managing to catch a ball on the byline that seemed certain to go out of play, Peter's cut back caught out the Motherwell defence who could do nothing to stop the unmarked Neil Martin from scoring from close range. Our other goal was scored from the penalty spot by Joe Davis with what would become his customary ease after a visiting player had handled in the box, and only a quite incredible decision by the referee had robbed us of a deserved victory.

In what would turn out to be an important few weeks for the club, in the return leg of the Fairs Cup against Valencia in Spain we went down 2-0 despite a heroic display by goalkeeper Willie Wilson. That evening Willie was in absolutely tremendous form, denying the home side on numerous occasions and it took a quite brilliant free kick from Waldo to pierce our defensive barrier. In what was said to have been one of the best games seen at the Mestalla stadium for many years, once again we seemed to have done enough until Valencia equalised from the penalty spot near the end after Simpson had brought down Guilliot inside the box. Later a toss of a coin would determine that the third game play-off would take place back in Spain.

On the Saturday our long domestic run finally came to an end with a 2-1 defeat at home to Rangers. I had equalised a first half goal by Alex Willoughby with what the Sunday papers later described as a spectacular equaliser after, I had 'ghosted in' to flick a Jim Scott shot that Ritchie appeared to have covered over the goalkeepers head and into the net. Willoughby however scored his own second and what would prove to be the winner a few minutes from the end with a great drive from just outside the penalty box. Although the defence had performed well, I have to confess that they had been let down by the forwards who missed several decent chances to secure the victory, including a couple of uncharacteristic misses by Neil Martin. Neil had only recently had a request for a move turned down and was then rumoured to be the target of transfer speculation from several sides in England.

It had now been decided that the replayed league cup semi-final against Celtic would again take place at Ibrox despite protests by both sides who felt that the winners of the other semi-final between Rangers and St Mirren would be gaining a psychological advantage by playing their game at the national stadium.

Unfortunately, for us the replay was effectively as good as over almost before it began with Celtic taking a commanding 2-0 lead inside the opening 20 minutes, and despite sterling performances from Pat Stanton and to a lesser extent John McNamee early in the game, we were never really in the hunt. When you played against either Celtic or Rangers with a big crowd behind them, particularly in cup games, once they got on top they would just keep coming at you in waves and this game was no different. After scoring the vital opening goal they never looked back, and we were never really in the hunt during the entire 90 minutes. There was little danger of an upset after McBride had opened the scoring early on, but any hopes of a comeback disappeared completely midway through the second half. With Celtic leading 3-0, John McNamee was sent off by referee Bobby Davidson for complaining too heatedly after being booked for a foul on John Hughes out near the left touchline. McNamee was adamant that he hadn't even touched the Celtic player, a fact seemingly born out on TV later that evening, and for a while refused to leave the field. You took on the big man at your peril and for a second I thought he was going to attack the referee until he was finally ushered away by Pat Stanton, kicking out at the dugout as he went down the tunnel.

With the game already all, but over Celtic scored a fourth a few minutes from time. Once again our previously high scoring forward line had been found wanting. We were all aware that not only had we let ourselves down, but also the huge number of Hibs fans that had made their way through from Edinburgh for the game, and we couldn't get off the field quickly enough at the final whistle. McNamee was it tears in the dressing room and I understand that he later went into the Celtic dressing room to apologise for his actions. His apologies however would not prevent him from later being suspended for 21 days at a disciplinary hearing, a sentence that would convince the big man that he was now a marked man by referees. To be fair to John, probably only because of his size, he would often receive a warning from some officials after committing the simplest of fouls while most others would escape Scot free and there were many in the game who agreed with him.

The Celtic game would also be Neil Martin's last for the club. Neil had never hidden his desire for a move to England, particularly after the recent transfer of Willie Hamilton. Several requests had already been turned down, but now it seemed that the club had had enough and he was allowed to join Sunderland for a fee in the region of £45,000. As I've already stated, I usually took players leaving in my stride and as something that had always happened in the game, but I have to confess that I was really sorry to see Neil go. Apart from the fact that he was a proven match winner, I had become extremely friendly with him both on and off the field. Although both Neil and Willie Hamilton had been unsettled at Easter Road for some time, it was no secret that like many others before them, their heads had probably been turned during the Scotland get togethers by the tales of the big money that was to be made down south.

While Martin was making a scoring debut in Sunderland's 3-1 away defeat at Sheffield Wednesday on the Saturday, we were continuing our impressive league form with a 2-0 win at St Mirren. With Jimmy O'Rourke replacing Martin at inside-left there were very few attempts on goal from either side in a desperately dull and drab game until Joe Davis opened the scoring from the penalty spot after I had been tripped in the box. It was to be the start of a very productive partnership. During the next four seasons or so Joe would score 47 goals for the club in all games, a phenomenal record for a full-back. Almost all would come from the penalty spot and a headline that would serve the newspapers well in the coming years: 'Davis scores from the spot after Stevenson had been brought down in the box,' was born. Contrary to popular belief I have never taken a dive. My style of play with close ball control inside the box lent itself to my being tripped, but I have never consciously gone down without being touched. I would push the ball past players and I was not going to jump out of the way if they wanted to tackle me, making it extremely difficult for defenders not to bring me down. At that time players like Ian Sneddon and Chris Shevlane at Hearts, Tommy Miller at Dundee United and John Greig at Rangers were hard men, who although they were good pals of mine would not have hesitated for a second in putting you up in the air, but they would not have been long in letting you know if they thought that you had dived. Despite my protestations of innocence, my reputation often went against me particularly in one game against Kilmarnock when defender Andy King really caught me, almost breaking my leg. I was rolling about in agony on the ground, but referee 'Tiny' Wharton simply shouted for me to get up, making the diving motion with his hands. I rarely if ever got anything from big Wharton. To my mind Wharton was all about himself. He was a big heavy man who was often 50 yards behind play, and I was convinced that he would regularly allow himself to be influenced by the crowd particularly in games at Ibrox or Parkhead.

Our new penalty taker Joe Davis was an extremely confident lad, who could also be a bit cocky at times. He travelled through from Glasgow every day with Pat Quinn, John Baxter, Jimmy Stevenson and occasionally John McNamee. In the dressing room they could be quite loud although they were friendly enough with the rest of the lads, but would usually keep themselves very much to themselves, with the exception of John McNamee, who for whatever reason would often tell us that he was going to kill those bastards, and I think that they kept out of his way as much as possible. I don't know why, but it seemed to me that McNamee never got on particularly well with Pat Quinn. Pat could be a bit funny, fairly serious with not a lot of humour, although I got on well enough with him. McNamee however was some lad. On the field he was good at everything. Almost unbeatable in the air, he could read the game, tackle and pass the ball. He had the physique of a Greek God and I think that many of our opponents were literally frightened of him. He didn't mix much with the rest of us although he was popular enough, and while far from being shy and retiring he was fairly quiet. Believe me nobody *ever* took the mickey out of big John, and you would be taking your life in your hands if you even argued with him. One time we were training near Aberlady Bay in East Lothian when we decided to have a muck about game of rounders. During the game big John claimed to have bowled out Jimmy Stevenson. Jimmy however refused to go. One thing led to another and eventually John had to be held back from punching Jim. As I've said, he was some guy.

The secret behind Joe Davis's success from the penalty spot was his technique. Instead of smashing the ball as hard as possible as many would do, Joe would simply pass the ball into the net at pace with the inside of his foot. Sometime later he would be asked to write an article for a football annual describing his penalty technique for which he was to be paid, prompting Pat Quinn to pipe up that he should be giving half the money to me for earning the penalties in the first place.

The third game play off with Valencia was always going to be incredibly difficult. Watched by a huge crowd of almost 60,000, the entire 90 minutes was played during a relentless downpour. We got off to the worst possible start conceding an early goal when Minoz scored from a position that looked well offside. Despite our appeals the goal was allowed to stand by the French referee and it then became an uphill battle. We had several chances to equalise when we were well on top, particularly in the second half, but when Minoz scored his second of the evening the game was effectively all, but over. Late on Jim Scott hit the post before goalkeeper Zamora produced a couple of good saves, one when he managed to push a great McNamee header over the bar. A third goal by Guillot just before the end was immaterial, but over the piece I don't think that it was a disgrace in losing to such a talented side.

Hamilton Academicals had been promoted from the second division only at the end of the previous season, and were already finding the going tough. Unfortunately, for them things were about to get much worse. On Saturday 6 November 1965, Accies made their first visit to Easter Road on league business since 1953 and they just didn't know what had hit them as we chalked up a comfortable 11-1 win. It was, and still is at the time of writing, Hibs record victory in a league match at Easter Road and just failed to beat Celtic's 11-0 home win against Dundee over 70 years before. Driving forward from midfield it was all too easy and I managed to score my first ever hat trick in senior football. Lining up against us that day was the former Hibs player Johnny Frye who had left the club shortly before I joined and another good pal of mine, the ex-Hearts player Andy Bowman. Andy was then nearing the end of his career and I would go past him for fun in midfield and all I could hear behind me was Andy shouting, 'You little bastard.' I really enjoyed that game. That side could score goals with even full-back Joe Davis getting in on the act and unusually this time it was not from the penalty spot. Accies had started brightly enough creating a couple of good chances before the roof fell in and it soon looked as if we could score every time we went up the park. In truth Hamilton were out of their depth in this league and would be relegated at the end of the season. Davie Hogg who was making his first appearance of the season also managed to get in on the act by scoring our last goal and his first for the club two minutes from time. Davie had joined Hibs in 1963 from Tynecastle Boys Club and was an exceptional talent. He was pacey, a great striker of the ball and could beat a man. His main problem was that he was as blind as a bat. Another great lad, he was full of mischief, too much at times for Jock Stein's liking, who once called Dave's father down to Easter Road to complain about his sons antics. Davie had made his debut against Dundee United a couple of seasons before, but like many others before him had found great difficulty in establishing himself in the first team. Unfortunately after only a dozen or so appearances at Easter Road he would join Dundee United where he would become a regular before moving on to Dumbarton, Berwick Rangers, Hamilton and finally Alloa.

In midweek I made my way through to Glasgow with goalkeeper Willie Wilson and the then Berwick Rangers manager Jock Wallace to watch Neil Martin in action for Scotland against Italy in a World Cup Qualifying match at Hampden. Jock was driving and I remember that we were just talking about football in general, when Wallace, a gruff character who never minced his words, suddenly said in his own inimitable style 'Stevie, you need a kick up the fucking arse. The potential you have is incredible, but you have too much nonsense in your head and would rather be out socialising. You have everything, so get the finger out, you still have time.' Listening from the back seat I was completely taken aback by his sudden outburst and could only reply, 'I know Jock, I will have to get a grip,' only to add a few seconds later, 'Let's stop at Whitburn for a couple of pints.'

At that Jock could only shake his head bemoaning, 'You haven't been listening to a fucking word I've said have you?'

With Neil Martin lining up at inside-left between the Tottenham centre-forward Alan Gilzean and John Hughes of Celtic, Scotland recorded one of the most important and famous results in their recent history when defeating the much fancied Italy. With the game still goalless and only two minutes remaining on the clock, right-back John Greig made a last desperate charge up the field. Receiving a pass through the middle from his Rangers team mate Jim Baxter, without breaking his stride, Greig proceeded to rifle the ball past goalkeeper Negri for the only goal of the game, to give Scotland a real chance of qualifying for the World Cup Finals in England the following year. Unfortunately it would turn out to be Neil's last ever cap, and an injury plagued Scotland side featuring centre-half Ron Yeats at centre-forward would eventually lose 3-0 in Italy to deny them qualification for the finals.

It was around that time that Bob Shankly returned to his former club Dundee to sign Alan Cousin. Now nearing the veteran stage of his career, Alan had recently lost his place at Dens Park, but would turn out to be another very good signing for us. Obviously he was then past his best, but he was a nice lad, quiet and fairly reserved. A schoolteacher at Alloa Academy during the week Alan was part time and we would only see him on a Saturday. A league winner with Dundee and twice capped for Scotland at inter league level, he was still a very good player and excellent in the air, although he fell far short of Neil Martin in that respect. He was a brainy player who could spray balls about, score goals and had a great double shuffle. One vivid memory I have of Alan however is one day when sitting in the coach outside East End Park after a bad defeat by Dunfermline. I was soon joined by Pat Stanton who was as down as me after the disappointing result, when we spotted Alan who would not be travelling back to Edinburgh with us, talking and laughing with a couple of friends, leaving Pat to retort, 'It's easy to see that Alan's got another job. It's not funny, this is our livelihood.'

Alan scored his first goal for the club a few weeks later in a 3-0 home win against St Johnstone. Once again I had been having slight problems with my groin and had been replaced in the side by the 18-year-old speed merchant George McNeill who was making his first team debut. George almost capped his baptism with a goal direct from a corner in the first half, whether he meant it or not is open to debate, but he later almost did it again the ball this time hitting the crossbar before being cleared. Unfortunately it would turn out to be George's only first team appearance at Easter Road, before he eventually embarked on a more lucrative career in professional athletics.

Because of the recurring groin strain I would also miss the New Year's Day derby against Hearts at Easter Road, which would also be the official opening of the covered enclosure behind the bottom goal, the fans, in what was an exceptionally good turn out, considering the foul weather making good use of the new cover. I watched what was probably the best game between the sides for many years from the stand as two first half goals by Peter Cormack appeared to put us on east street. Willie Wallace scored for Hearts a full two minutes into first half injury time, a lengthy extension which was something of a rarity at that time. The goal appeared to give our opponents a huge psychological lift and another goal by Kerrigan early in the second half brought a fighting Hearts side right back into it. On the hour mark Willie Wallace scored the winner with a shot that came of the knee of John McNamee to deprive Hibs of their first win at Easter Road on New Year's Day for 18 years. Worse still, a great header from Cormack in the dying seconds struck the bar and out of play to deny us at least the draw that would have been more than deserved.

After a disappointing 1-0 defeat at Kilmarnock the following day, Bob Shankly reshuffled the side in a bid to get us back to winning ways in a home game against Morton. Out went John Baxter to be replaced by Alan Cousin at left half. At that time we had several good young players on the books who were all, but ready to make a breakthrough into the first team, and the 18-year-old Colin Stein made his debut in the middle of the attack replacing Jim Scott at who reverted back to the right wing. I had now recovered from the groin strain, and I took over at outside-left from the in form Peter Cormack who moved inside. Stein, who had been Bob Shankly's first signing for Hibs, had a magnificent debut. For a young player making his first start he was an absolute revelation with not even the hint of nerves, his all action style and never say die attitude really exciting the fans. He was up against a tough opponent that day in centre-half John Madsen, and although he failed to score himself in our 4-2 win, some Hibs fans were already hailing him as the new Lawrie Reilly or Joe Baker. Although they were quite preposterous claims after just one outing, he had certainly shown enough to suggest that he had a big future in the game. Originally a full-back at Armadale, the same side that had produced the Hibs players Johnny McLeod and Joe Baker, Colin had been played at up front in a friendly game to discover that he was a natural goal scorer and very difficult to knock of the ball. With his non-stop energetic and aggressive style he chased everything, even lost causes, and after just one game he had already become a huge favourite with the fans who always appreciated effort. He worked hard, was fearless and could tackle, and although he lacked a bit at times due to his inexperience, his performance had suggested even this early that he was soon going to be a permanent fixture in the first team. He scored his first goals for the club, the opener in the very first minute at Brockville the following week, a ground incidentally that I always disliked playing on, and although we eventually lost 3-2, Colin's performance seemed to confirm that Hibs had unearthed yet another genuine prospect.

In a 4-3 win against Third Lanark in the Scottish Cup, a game that we seemed determined to throw away despite taking an early 2-0 lead, it was left to Joe Davis to score the winner late in the game to set up a meeting with rivals Hearts at Tynecastle in the next round. It would be the first meeting of the sides in the competition since Joe Baker had famously scored all four Hibs goals in the 4-3 victory at Tynecastle in 1958.

By now I had fully recovered from my groin strain only to go down with a virus that swept through the club during the week, and was desperately disappointed to miss the cup tie. The game had been postponed on the Saturday on account of a heavy overnight fall of snow that covered the Tynecastle pitch several inches deep, but an unexpected thaw allowed it to go ahead on the Monday evening. John McNamee, who had been dropped for the Rangers game the previous week after posting a transfer request, was reinstated in a Hibs side that also gave debuts to goalkeeper Thomson Allan who replaced the injured Willie Wilson, and Colin Grant who replaced Colin Stein who had also complained of feeling unwell. Hibs started well and received a gigantic boost after only six minutes, when we were awarded a penalty after Chris Shevlane had taken the feet from young Colin Grant inside the box. The usually reliable Davis however swept the ball wide of the upright, his first miss of the season from the spot after five earlier successes. Still it was all Hibs, and we deservedly took the lead midway through the half when McNamee scored after a melee in the box following an O'Rourke corner. In the second half Hearts went all out for the equaliser and were pressing when Jim Scott almost uprooted the right hand post with what the papers later described as an 'electrifying' shot, only for Colin Grant lying handy in a great position to blast the rebound well over the bar from close range. It was a miss that was to prove costly. Less than a minute later Hearts were level when Traynor scored from a Polland cross that Thomson Allan might well have intercepted. Hearts had their tails up now and a late Higgins goal from a pass by Wallace denied Hibs the draw that their performance had probably deserved. Both Thomson Allan and Colin Grant had done well in their first starts, although the goalkeeper may well have been a bit slow in cutting out Polland's cross for Hearts opener, but both had shown great promise in what had undoubtedly been a highly charged atmosphere and a difficult baptism for an inexperienced youngster. In the second half Hearts had been the more determined and the win had now extended their unbeaten run to 15 games. For us, there was now nothing left to play for except a possible European place.

Only one point was dropped from the following half a dozen games to keep us well in the running, but our fine run came to an abrupt end when an Alex Ferguson goal gave Dunfermline the points in a narrow 3-2 victory when he swept an Alex Edwards pass past goalkeeper Thomson Allan.

Draws with both Dundee and Celtic cemented our position in mid-table, but perhaps the highlight of the remaining few games was a 5-4 defeat by Dundee United at Tannadice. Played in a torrential downpour and on a pitch that only just received the go ahead 20 minutes before kick-off, both sides still managed to serve up a thriller, the result in doubt almost to the end. A Cormack goal soon after the restart made the score 3-2 for United before Davis levelled things with a goal that unusually for him was not from the penalty spot when his 35 yard shot that was dummied by Cormack deceived the goalkeeper. It required all our fighting qualities against a very good United side who retook the lead only for Davis to again level the game at 4-4 this time from the spot. The winner when it came however was shrouded in controversy. United had been awarded a penalty when Joe Davis had punched clear on the goal line. Thomson Allan saved Mitchell's kick only for referee Webster to order a retake claiming that the goalkeeper had moved, a decision that dumbfounded everyone in the ground including apparently the reporters in the press box, but regardless, this time Mitchell made no mistake from the retaken kick. Earlier, McNamee had been booked following a jostle with Finn Dossing as United prepared to take the penalty, a booking that took him over the limit and another probable suspension. Interviewed after the game McNamee told the waiting reporters that while he was happy at Easter Road he may well have to move as he was convinced that he was becoming the victim of a witch hunt in Scotland.

A 1-0 defeat at Easter Road by Eddie Turnbull's Aberdeen brought the curtain down on what had been yet another extremely disappointing season. The only goal of a dull and drab 90 minutes that had been played in scorching summer sunshine was scored late in the game, but by then I am sure that neither the players nor the fans were all that bothered.

In the end we could only manage to finish in sixth place, two places below that of the previous season and level on points with Hearts although with a better goal average. Celtic were league champions, two points clear of second placed Rangers, their first title since 1954 and the first of what would eventually turn out to be a record breaking nine consecutive successes. In a great start to the season we had gone on a great 15 game unbeaten run and had also reached the semi-final of a cup playing at times some exceptional football, but once again inconsistency had cost us dearly and a place in the following seasons Fairs Cup. The loss of Neil Martin and to a lesser extent Willie Hamilton hadn't helped. After Neil's move to England we appeared to lack confidence, and what had at one time been a free scoring side now found goals extremely difficult to come by. With Bob Shankly's desire to play open attractive, and above all entertaining football, we possibly had too many players who wanted to play pretty football and sometimes lacked the required mental and physical toughness.

An indication of just where our problems lay was the fact that despite featuring in well under half the fixtures, Neil Martin had still ended the season as our top goal scorer with 18 in all games, one ahead of Peter Cormack. I myself had chipped in with 13, which was my best total to date. In the four months leading up to the turn of the year, we had scored 81 goals in all games, a total obviously boosted by the Alloa and Hamilton results, but in the remaining four months of the season we had managed just 37, which perhaps says it all.

Twenty three players had been used during the season, five more than the previous year, only Pat Stanton and Joe Davis managing to play in every game, Joe continuing his incredible consecutive run. On the positive side several talented young players had made a breakthrough into the first team. The encouraging performances of Colin Stein, Colin Grant and Thomson Allan, plus the likes of Davie Hogg, George McNeill and Bobby Duncan ensured that the club could look forward to the future with confidence.

At the end of the season the long serving John Baxter would be only player to be freed, his release coming as something of a surprise as he had been a regular for most of the campaign. The popular player with the thunderball shot would soon be signed by Falkirk before finally ending a playing career that stretched back to 1955 with second division Clydebank. Sadly John was another who passed away during the writing of this book.

During the summer both Jim Scott and Pat Stanton had made their first appearance for the full international side in Scotland's game against Holland at Hampden. Both players did well, Scott having a great header well saved by goalkeeper Graafland shortly after Stanton had cleared a shot off the line from the then fairly unknown Piet Keizer, but the 3-0 home defeat was met by a withering barrage of criticism from an insular press who were completely unaware that Holland were then in the throes of developing into the great side of the late sixties and early seventies. A few weeks later there would be even more international recognition for the club when Peter Cormack also won his first full cap when lining up in Scotland's 1-1 draw with Brazil at Hampden. Peter did little harm to his growing reputation in one of the South American sides warm up games for the forthcoming World Cup Finals in England, a tournament sadly for which Scotland had only just failed to qualify.

CHAPTER EIGHT

An Epic Battle at Dunfermline and a North American Tour
1966–67

BOB SHANKLY WOULD have been well aware of just where our deficiencies of the previous season lay, and he wasted no time in signing the prolific goal scorer Alan McGraw from Morton, for a bargain fee of around £10,000. Alan had scored 87 league goals at Cappielow in just a few seasons including the remarkable total of 62 in all games during Morton's promotion season in 1962-63, a total that also included the winning goal in Morton's league cup semi-final victory against Hibs and would prove to be yet another good signing. Perhaps not the greatest of football players, don't ask him to beat two or three players from midfield like Joe Baker, but Alan's phenomenal scoring record proved that he certainly knew the way to goal. Originally a centre-half with Renfrew Juniors, he had since discovered a flair for scoring goals instead of preventing them. He worked hard, had a good attitude, and although he was no Neil Martin he was extremely good in the air and was another player who was good to play alongside.

Another newcomer that season was the 16-year-old Peter Marinello who had been signed from Salvesen Boys Club during the summer. Peter would join John Murphy on the ground staff, a position that had only recently been vacated by John Blackley who had now stepped up as a full time professional.

McGraw wasted no time in opening his account, scoring the opener in his very first start, a 3-2 victory against Joe Baker's Nottingham Forest in a pre-season friendly at Easter Road. As could be expected, Joe received a warm reception from the fans on his first appearance back at Easter Road since the Torino game several years before and he responded by scoring both his sides goals. Later that evening Joe and several of his team mates celebrated with some of the Hibs players at the Saxe Coburg Hotel in

Stockbridge. In the intervening years Joe had never changed a bit from the friendly outgoing guy I had known earlier and remained that way until his premature death from a heart attack while playing golf in 2003 aged only 63. He had been the first real celebrity that I came across in the game and I remember the days when we would train at Aberlady, the good looking Joe always surrounded by hordes of girls, although if truth be known he would probably have been more interested in going out for a few pints with the lads than in the girls.

In a league cup section comprising of Rangers, Kilmarnock and Stirling Albion we got off to a disappointing start at Ibrox. Rangers, fielding their two recent big money signings Alex Smith from Dunfermline and Dave Smith from Aberdeen, collected both points when George McLean scored the only goal in the last few minutes of the game. At the beginning of the season Scotland had finally come into line with England in allowing the use of a substitute, but only in event of injury. That afternoon at Ibrox Jimmy O'Rourke had become Hibs first official substitute in a domestic game although not called upon.

Alan McGraw opened his competitive account for the club against Kilmarnock in midweek when his two headed goals gave us a 2-1 victory in Edinburgh. A few days later at Annfield a spirited Stirling Albion who had lost 8-0 to Rangers at Ibrox in midweek stunned us by coming back from 2-0 behind until two second half goals by Peter Cormack eventually gave us victory, and after three games we were now lying handy just a single point behind section leaders Rangers. Both sides had taken the field wearing black armbands as a mark of respect for the Hibs director and former owner Harry Swan, who had passed away the previous day after a short illness. Swan had been a larger than life character who had led the club from near oblivion in the early 1930s to the very forefront of the Scottish game, and his passing was the end of a golden era, not only for Hibs, but for Scottish football. Later at his funeral at Warriston Crematorium all the current players and staff mingled with players of yesteryear, dignitaries from all over the world of football and the ordinary man in the street, all wishing to pay their respects in their own particular way. Swan's passing meant that now only Jimmy McColl and treasurer Kenny McIntyre remained from the halcyon post-war days. At that time Jimmy McColl had been at Easter Road for over 43 years first as a player, first team trainer under Hugh Shaw, and now in charge of the reserves on a Saturday. McIntyre, who had been with the club for the past 37 years as treasurer and finally director, was a lovely fairly gentle man who along with secretary Wilma would look after the finances and attend to the wages. He would often pop into the Scotia Hotel for a quiet drink after the games and I was always kidding him that my wages had been short that week, his reply invariably – 'Oh Eric you're an awful man.'

A great win against Rangers in the return game at Easter Road now saw us leading the section, with a great chance to qualify for the quarter-finals. 2-1 behind with just ten minutes remaining goals by McNamee and McGraw added to the one scored in the first half by Jim Scott gave us a victory that few would have thought possible earlier in the game. That afternoon I was up against a very good opponent in the Dane Kai Johansen who had been signed from Morton the previous season. Johansen was an extremely hard opponent, but fair and wouldn't try to kick you as some did. That afternoon I gave him a torrid time, and I think it would be fair to say that I usually more than held my own against the Rangers defender. That afternoon at Easter Road there had not been a failure in the side so I was surprised to be singled out by one reporter. According to Alec Young writing in Monday's *Daily Mail*:

Eric Stevenson may be a surprise choice on the left wing when the Scottish League side to meet the League of Ireland next week is announced tomorrow. Stevenson can earn his cap as a reward for the way he helped to destroy a legend on Saturday the legend of an Ibrox defensive superiority that began in the 1940s with players such as George Young, Willie Woodburn and 'Tiger' Shaw.

In the end, Young's generous prediction would fail to materialise, and although I would obviously have been delighted to have been selected for either the inter-league or full Scottish sides, I can say in all honesty that missing out on a cap never really bothered me. I was having a ball just being a professional football player and each game couldn't come quickly enough.

With the victory against Rangers behind us we made our way to Kilmarnock at the penultimate stage of the section in good spirits and brimming with confidence. Unfortunately an unbelievably incompetent one sided performance by referee Crawley from Glasgow did nothing to help our cause. Our problems started early when goalkeeper Thomson Allan dropped a simple cross to give McIlroy the easiest of chances to open the scoring. The first real moment of controversy came not long after when the referee awarded Kilmarnock the softest penalty you are ever likely to see when Pat Stanton was harshly adjudged to have elbowed Tommy McLean off the ball. Justice was done however when Thomson Allan saved the spot kick. The main talking point of the entire evening however came a few minutes later when we were awarded a free kick just outside the Kilmarnock box. As usual in those circumstances John McNamee made his way into the opposing penalty area closely followed by the Kilmarnock centre-forward Bertelsen. There was the usual jostling in the area when Bertelsen suddenly appeared to fall to the ground without seemingly being touched. To the amazement of almost everyone in the ground the referee immediately ordered the Hibs player off despite McNamee protesting furiously that he had not even touched the Kilmarnock player. Incredibly, Crawley would later admit that he had not seen the incident himself, but had relied solely on the word of his linesman who many felt was in a far worse position than the referee, the alleged incident no clearer when shown on TV later that evening. John's protests however were to no avail and he reluctantly made his way to the pavilion. Just before half time Kilmarnock were awarded yet another penalty that was once again saved by Thomson Allan only for Gerry Queen to score from the rebound, and the game was effectively as good as over. Kilmarnock scored a third a few minutes after the restart, but by that time it was all immaterial. The next morning, even the newspapers were scathing at Crawley's inept handling of the game, but the damage had already been done and even a comprehensive 3-0 victory against Stirling Albion on the Saturday would mean nothing when Rangers defeated Kilmarnock 1-0 to top the section on goal average. I believe that Hibs later sent an official letter of complaint to the Scottish League regarding Crawley's inept handling of the Kilmarnock game, as did the home side, but I suppose as could well be expected nothing more would be heard of the matter. McNamee himself later appealed the decision, but this also would make no difference and the centre-half's forthcoming savage 28 day suspension suggested that he was indeed a marked man in Scotland and only strengthened his determination for a move.

In one of the most exciting and fiercely fought games seen at Easter Road for many years, a 3-1 victory over Hearts gave us our first home success against our great rivals for many seasons. Joe Davis made amends for his earlier penalty miss in the cup tie at Tynecastle when he opened the scoring from the spot before Alan McGraw gave us a deserved two goal half time lead. Jim Scott added a third nine minutes from time, before Don Kerrigan scored a consolation goal for Hearts in the very last minute of the game. In what had been at times an overly tough encounter, on several occasions the game had threatened to get out of hand, mainly because of the weak handling of referee Bobby Davidson who consistently failed to clamp down on several of what could kindly be described as overzealous tackles, the majority of which I have to say coming from our opponents.

After our derby victory we were in a fairly confident mood as we made our way to Fife for the first meeting of the season against a Dunfermline side that had lost 5-3 at Parkhead the previous week. Our self-belief seemed to be justified when goals by Peter Cormack and Jim Scott gave us the comfortable interval lead that our at times dazzling play had deserved. With just over 20 minutes of the game remaining further goals from both myself and Alan McGraw had given us an unassailable 4-0 lead – or so we all thought. The home side managed to pull one back, but even when Delaney scored a second there still seemed nothing to worry about, an attitude that quickly changed when Dunfermline scored a third a few minutes later. McGraw reaffirmed our superiority with a fifth goal that would now surely put the game beyond doubt only for Robertson to again reduce the deficit before a certain Alex Ferguson – I wonder whatever happened to him? – scored with a header to level the game at five each. By this time we were all over the place and incredibly in the very last seconds Dunfermline appeared to have scored again, when McNamee cleared a ball from under the crossbar that many thought had already crossed the line. The ball was swept up field and with the referee about to blow for full time, Jim Scott took advantage of a quickly taken free kick to score the winner after his first shot had come back off the keeper. By then I'm sure that most of the Hibs fans in the 11,000 crowd would have required medical attention to calm their nerves, and it was a mightily relieved Easter Road support that made their way back to the capital over the recently opened Forth Road Bridge after the game, and us players to face a heated inquest at Easter road on the Monday morning.

Our good run continued the following week against Partick Thistle, but this time we managed to avoid giving away any silly goals. I felt slightly sorry for the former Rangers goalkeeper George Niven as we cantered to an easy 7-0 victory, but the result was enough to see us at the top of the table joint equal with Celtic.

John McNamee meanwhile had started his 28 days suspension after his alleged indiscretions at Kilmarnock, a suspension that couldn't have come at a worse time for us with a game against high flying Celtic due to take place a few days later. McNamee's suspension had been the heaviest handed out at the disciplinary meeting and only confirmed what many were already thinking that John was being made an example of, the draconian suspension having no little part to play in the giant defenders move to England a few weeks later.

At that time both ourselves and Celtic were the top scoring sides in the entire country. Both were also neck in neck in the table and something just had to give. In the end it proved to be yet another incredible afternoon with the players of both sides giving their all. We were obviously minus the suspended McNamee and how we missed the big man. Celtic scorned a couple of early chances before Cormack opened the scoring after ten minutes. With Alan Cousin standing in for McNamee, McBride and Chalmers gave the visitors the lead only for Davis to level things with his customary penalty after a 'certain' Hibs player had been nudged off the ball inside the area by McNeill. In what turned out to be an absorbing encounter, further goals by McBride gave Celtic a 4-2 half time lead, the future Hibs player scoring his own fourth and his sides fifth goal just after half time, before Alan McGraw gave the final score-line a degree of respectability when he scored our third in the very last minute of the game. At the time the heavy defeat was obviously a huge disappointment for us all, but looking back I don't think that there was any disgrace in losing to a side of Celtic's unquestionable quality.

It was around this time that Stan Vincent was allowed to join Falkirk, the former Hibs player scoring his sides solitary goal in our 3-1 home victory against the 'Bairns' a few weeks later. Stan was a great wee guy, a real comedian, and if he was playing today he would find a place in any team. Perhaps he was not the greatest of football players, but he worked hard, could score goals, rumble up defences and for his size was very good in the air. I always felt that he was unlucky to be at Easter road at a time when Hibs had so many good forwards in Jim Scott, Neil Martin and Peter Cormack, with Colin Stein, Davie Hogg and Colin Grant also knocking on the first team door.

A few weeks later Pat Quinn became Hibs first ever substitute in a competitive game, when he replaced the injured Joe Davis near the end of what could only be described as a calamity at Shawfield, Clyde eventually running out easy 5-1 winners. We were missing flu victim Pat Stanton, and at that time the Shawfield side had a few very talented players including Harry Hood who had just been signed from Sunderland and would soon join Celtic, but that can be no excuse for our absolutely abysmal performance. For the entire 90 minutes we were second to every ball as Hood pulled the strings from midfield, his powerful shooting a constant threat to Willie Wilson in the Hibs goal, and in the end we were perhaps lucky to get away so lightly. At that time substitutes were only allowed in the case of injury, but it was not unknown for managers to abuse the system by letting players know that they were to go down injured, but I am sure that this would have been abhorrent to the gentlemanly Bob Shankly. Regardless, from topping the table only a few weeks before, the embarrassing defeat had now seen us slip to seventh place.

After yet another defeat, this time at Dundee the following week, I was left out of the side to face Rangers at Easter Road although I was listed as substitute. I felt that I had been no worse than anybody else in what had been another extremely poor performance at Dens Park, the entire defence in particular nervous throughout. I was far from happy and immediately asked for a transfer. With Pat Quinn taking my place, a goal by Jimmy O'Rourke had put us ahead just before half time, only for two second half strikes by Jim Forrest giving Rangers a merited lead and the points. The defeat meant that we had now dropped to tenth place, a quite alarming slump in only a few weeks.

I was recalled for a game against Stirling Albion in Edinburgh. At that time Albion were captained by the former Rangers and Scotland player Eric Caldow. Over the years I had often struggled against Caldow, but as if to show the manager that he had been wrong in dropping me, I celebrated my return by scoring twice in what eventually turned out to be an easy 6-0 home victory. The only disappointment would be a rare miss from the penalty spot by Joe Davis, an award this time that I am pleased to say I had no part in. The *Pink News* later that evening was generous in its praise when stating: 'Stevenson's performance surely confirmed that he would never be dropped again.' It was a tremendous compliment, one that meant a lot to me at the time, but unfortunately would turn out to be somewhat presumptuous.

A half decent run had seen us winning four of our next five games, but once again a lack of consistency was to be our undoing. This was never more clearly demonstrated than when we went down to a heavy 5-2 defeat at the hands of St Johnstone at Easter Road the afternoon before Christmas. Heavy snow in the morning had left the playing surface in a treacherous state, the slippery underfoot conditions making good football all, but impossible. The much smaller and nimble footed St Johnstone players however seemed to adapt to the treacherous conditions much better than us, and while players like John McNamee were slipping and sliding all over the place, our more sure footed opponents were racing to a an emphatic and well-earned victory. The final whistle was greeted with jeers of derision from the small band of Hibs supporters who had braved the dreadful conditions until the very end, many of whom I'm sure would much rather have been out last minute Christmas shopping. The treacherous pitch could in no way be used as an excuse for the embarrassing defeat as it had been the same for both sides, but nevertheless the humiliating rout had left us stranded in mid-table. It would turn out to be John McNamee's last ever game for the club. In midweek an offer from Newcastle United for the rugged defender would be accepted and the big man would be on his way south and well away from what had at times been the overzealous attentions of the Scottish officials.

While the unquestionable and at times sublime skills of the outra-geously talented Willie Hamilton had been sorely missed, perhaps a far greater loss to the side had been the free scoring Neil Martin, but I think it would be fair to say that in his own way the rugged McNamee would possibly turn out to be just as big a miss. As well as a rock in the heart of the defence, 'Big Mac' had also proved a constant threat in the opposing penalty area, scoring many important goals, and although he could mix it when necessary and could be very aggressive, he didn't need to be dirty. His huge bulk could certainly be intimidating, but he was hard, but fair, similar to John Greig of Rangers, although he wasn't one to take liberties with and I think that many of his opponents had been literally frightened of him.

Just as before the transfer of John Parke to Sunderland, which had not taken place until a suitable replacement had been found, the transfer of McNamee was put on hold until a successor could be secured. His replacement would turn out to be non other than the Danish international John Madsen who joined us from Morton for less than half of what Hibs had received for McNamee, which at the end of the day represented another great bit of business by the club.

As McNamee was making his debut against Spurs at White Hart Lane in direct opposition to the former Dundee player Alan Gilzean, John Madsen would himself be facing a tough baptism against the rugged heavyweight and often uncompromising David Marshall in our 1-0 victory over the recently promoted Airdrie on a snow swept Broomfield. He acquitted himself well however and it seemed as if Bob Shankly had made yet another shrewd acquisition. Madsen was a completely different type of player to McNamee. Although not as commanding, he was more mobile, quicker on the recovery and used the ball better. He was good in the air and could tackle, but he would not go through a player as some centre-half's including McNamee would do, and I always felt that perhaps his style was more suited to that of a wing half.

On New Year's Day we had to settle for just a solitary point against Hearts at Tynecastle, in what was the first goalless league game between the sides for 33 years. We had been much the better side throughout and only a quite incredible performance by goalkeeper Jim Cruickshank had stood between us and what would have been a convincing victory. That afternoon Jim had defied everything that we could throw at him, several of his saves in the miraculous class. Not only did he stop a Joe Davis penalty after I had been brought down in the box by Alan McDonald who was playing in his first Edinburgh derby, but a double rebound. I can remember driving into the penalty area with Shevlane on one side of me and McDonald on the other. I could see the tackle coming, but wasn't just going to jump out of the way and consequently was sent crashing to the ground. It was as definite a penalty as you are ever likely to see, although Shevlane and McDonald both thought differently, as I was roughly manhandled back to my feet. As was my normal habit after we had been awarded a penalty I turned my back as the kick was being taken to make my way back to the half-way line, only to see the hordes of marooned bedecked supporters in the 31,000 crowd dancing with delight after Cruickshank had had not only saved Davis's otherwise well taken penalty, but also the follow up, first from Davis himself then McGraw. As Davis passed me on the way back upfield I couldn't resist remarking 'Oh Joe how could you, anybody, but them?' At that Joe just shrugged his shoulders. He was a very confident guy who had already been successful with eight conversions from the spot that season, but it would have made absolutely no difference to him if he had scored eight out of eight or missed the lot, he would still have been first in line, volunteering to take the next one.

After just a few games on Tyneside, John McNamee had already become a huge favourite with the Newcastle fans. Back in Edinburgh, we had taken seven points from eight in John Madsen's first four games with only the draw against Hearts, while conceding just the one goal. Madsen had lost no time in settling into the side and although it was a bit premature, some newspapers were already predicting that the Hibs fans would soon forget all about McNamee.

A 2-0 home victory over Brechin City was enough to see us into the next round of the Scottish Cup. That same afternoon at Berwick, the wee Rangers had recorded what is still considered to be the greatest victory in the club's history when Sammy Reid scored the only goal of the game in the second half to stun not only the large travelling Glasgow Rangers support, but the entire country. It was the first time that the Ibrox side had made an exit from the completion at the first round stage for 30 years and the first ever time they had lost to a second division side in the cup. The result would have far reaching ramifications at Ibrox that would eventually lead to the sacking of manager Scott Symon. Both George McLean and Jim Forrest were made the scapegoats for the humiliating defeat and within weeks they would be transferred, McLean to Dundee and Forrest to Preston North End, their departure leaving the way clear for a debut for a very young Sandy Jardine and the signing of Alex Ferguson, a £65,000 record buy from Dunfermline._

The draw had paired us with Berwick in the next round the game to take place at Easter Road, but regardless of our opponent's fantastic giant-killing act, the well known Glasgow bookmakers John Banks had installed Berwick as 20,000-1 outsiders to win the cup. At 5-1 we were now second favourites behind Celtic. After their incredible feat in the previous round our game against Berwick had generated colossal interest not only locally, but throughout the country and at kick off around 30,000 were packed tightly inside Easter Road on a cold and overcast winter's afternoon. We started the game much the better side, but Berwick weathered the early storm and were convinced that they had taken the lead after goalkeeper Thomson Allan had cleared a ball that many in the crowd thought had already crossed the line. Although we had the bulk of the play you have to give credit to Berwick for their battling display. They were a typical Jock Wallace side, everything based on energy. They chased everything but were never really in the hunt, although I myself had a quiet game when tightly marked by right-back Gordon Haig, a player I knew well. No disrespect to Gordon, but he would 'kick his granny' and that afternoon I didn't see much of the ball. Every time I managed to go past him he would bring me down and Jock Wallace later told me that Haig's instructions had been – 'If Stevie goes for a piss at half time, you go with him.' Because of Berwick's at times over physical defensive play, for long periods we had managed to create little in the way of danger ourselves, but just a few minutes before half time Jim Scott scored with a shot from around 20 yards. I felt player-manager Wallace should have saved it, but he went down like a carthorse. The second half continued much the same as the first with little goalmouth action, but we had the opportunity to finish the tie near the end when Scott was brought down in the box. Probably because Joe Davis had missed from the spot against Brechin City in the previous round, Jim took the kick himself, but this time Wallace was his equal and was down well to save. There was to be no more scoring and we were through to face Aberdeen in the next round. At the final whistle, the Berwick players were rightly applauded from the field by both sets of supporters after their valiant efforts.

In the next round, a real blood and thunder cup tie against Aberdeen at Easter Road, I scored possibly the best goal of my career to give us an early lead. Receiving a one-two from Pat Quinn just inside the box I hesitated only briefly before crashing a thunderous first time left foot drive past Bobby Clark and into the top left hand corner of the net. It was my first ever goal in the Scottish Cup and one that looked like being enough until Jimmy Smith scored what on the balance of play was probably a deserved equaliser just minutes from the end. In a hectic 90 minutes that as far as I was concerned was poorly refereed by my old pal 'Tiny' Wharton who once again gave me nothing, the game was at times allowed to degenerate into a kicking match. The following day most of the Sunday newspapers also commented on the at times over physical play and the referee's total lack of control in Hibs grim relentless struggle against a no nonsense Aberdeen side who seemed determined to stop us at all costs. In the opinion of many of the observers Wharton had failed completely to protect the ball players. As already mentioned for some reason he had absolutely no time for me probably because of the unfair reputation I had earned for diving, and I would be wasting my time in even complaining after I had been kicked, something unfortunately that happened with monotonous regularity. Incredibly, after the violent play that had gone unpunished beforehand, Wharton threatened to send me off for swearing after I was on the receiving end of yet another over robust tackle.

Unfortunately for the large number of Hibs fans who made their way to Aberdeen for the replay on the Wednesday evening, we just didn't turn up. A whirlwind start by the home side meant that the game was as good as over after just 15 minutes when Jim Storrie, a recent signing from Middlesbrough, added a second goal to the one scored after only three minutes by Ernie Winchester. Played during a horrendous thunderstorm that never relented for a second and watched by a 44,000 crowd which at that time was Aberdeen's record attendance for a midweek game, the gates were closed ten minutes before start with hundreds more locked outside, the kick-off held up for several minutes. The home side had set their stall out early, and before many had managed to even gain a vantage point Aberdeen took the lead. Years later, Eddie Turnbull would tell me that he had instructed the recalled Ernie Winchester, or 'The Gun' as he was affectionately known for obvious reasons, to batter Madsen in the opening minutes with or without the ball. This Ernie duly proceeded to do, leaving Madsen in a crumpled heap on the running track, the incident incidentally completely ignored by my good friend referee Wharton. The tackle appeared to unsettle Madsen who had been such an inspirational figure for us since his signing, and without his influence in defence in was no surprise when Aberdeen scored a third early in the second half to seal a comprehensive and ultimately well-deserved victory. It was only our second defeat in 15 games and the heaviest since the 5-2 reverse against St Johnstone on Christmas Eve. At that time Eddie Turnbull was beginning to put together an extremely formidable side at Pittodrie and after the first game at Easter Road he had apparently told the well-known *Evening News* reporter Stewart Brown that he would be wasting his time in even coming up to Aberdeen for the replay as Hibs didn't have a chance, and as usual Turnbull had been proved right.

Despite a narrow 1-0 defeat by second placed Rangers who had struggled at home against what was reported in the press at the time to be one of the poorest Hibs sides to visit the stadium for many years, with just seven games remaining we were still in with a great chance of securing a Fairs Cup place.

The loss at Ibrox however was followed by a highly embarrassing 1-0 home defeat at the hands of a Stirling Albion side that would finish the season third from bottom of the table. Worse still, it was Albion's second victory at Easter Road in consecutive seasons. An extremely poor crowd of well under 5,000 had even bothered to turn up, most of them probably well aware of what was about to unfold considering our recent end of the season experiences.

Despite the consecutive defeats we still clung on grimly to fourth place in the table which should have been more than enough to qualify for the Fairs Cup, but with only a few games left to play it was imperative that we collected both points against relegation haunted St Mirren at Easter Road. With Colin Grant back in a reshuffled forward line in place of Jim Scott, the best we could manage was a disappointing 1-1 draw, our goal somewhat predictably scored by Joe Davis from the spot after Cormack had earlier missed from a similar award.

At that time both Clyde and Eddie Turnbull's Aberdeen were going well and were now our nearest rivals for a European place. However, despite wins against both Ayr United and St Johnstone, a final day home defeat by an Airdrie side that had only been promoted to the top division at the beginning of the season, meant that we could only manage to finish in fifth place, level on points with Aberdeen, but with a far inferior goal average.

Yet again a total lack of consistency had proved our undoing, and despite at times playing some tremendous football, we had perhaps been far too soft, on several occasions losing games that we had been more than capable of winning.

Pat Quinn had been recalled to the side in November and had been a revelation, playing some of the best football of his career. In John Madsen we had found a more than reliable replacement for John McNamee and already he had become a huge favourite with the fans. Peter Cormack finished the season as joint top scorer along with Joe Davis, both with 13 league goals and incredibly for a full-back Joe would have been well out on his own had he not asked to be relieved of the spot kick duties earlier in the season. He had however continued his incredible run of consecutive games and he and fellow full-back partner Bobby Duncan had been the only ones not to have missed a single game.

Both Jimmy Stevenson and left-back George Gartshore were among the free transfers announced by Bob Shankly at the end of the season. My namesake Jimmy had been tipped by many to have had a big future ahead of him when he signed from my old side Edina Hearts in 1962, and although he had managed to make several appearances in the league side he had failed to establish himself as a regular and would soon sign for English Fourth Division side Southend United. George Gartshore was a more than reliable defender who had also been at Easter Road since signing from Edina Hearts in 1962, but unfortunately had not managed to make a single appearance in the first team due no doubt to the amazing consistency of Joe Davis.

Meanwhile, probably because of our successful trip to North America a couple of years before, Hibs had been invited to take part in an end of season North American League Tournament involving sides from as far apart as Brazil, Uruguay, Italy, Holland, Northern Ireland and Eire as well as both Scotland and England. The North American League had only recently been recognised by FIFA and the tournament was an endeavour to raise awareness of the game among the locals. In a competition that would go some way in making up for us missing out on a place in the Fairs Cup, each side would take the name of their host city throughout the competition. Based in Toronto for the duration, Hibs would take the name of the Canadian city. Lasting almost seven weeks, the trip would turn out to be arduous, but enjoyable, although ultimately for most of us, particularly the married guys, just a bit too long. Sixteen players had been selected for the tour, but unfortunately Colin Stein would miss out on what would undoubtedly have been the trip of a lifetime for a young lad from Philipstoun when he came down with Chicken Pox. Colin's misfortune however would be a stroke of luck for young John Murphy who was drafted into the side as a last minute replacement.

Wearing new lightweight strips designed to combat the oppressive heat, our opening game was a 1-1 draw against the Uruguayan side Cerro from Montevideo. The match kicked off in the gigantic 70,000 seated Yankee Stadium in New York in front of what was reported at the time to be a 25,000 crowd, but we found out later that the attendance would probably have been only half that number. The facilities at the stadium however were terrific with every player designated his own individual bath. The pitch however left a lot to desired, very tight with little room on the wings to take corners and with the remnants of a Baseball mound at one end. Cerro however were a decent side and it took us until the second half to assert ourselves when Alan McGraw scored with a header. After a second half mix up over substitutions it was only as we were lining up after Alan's goal that the referee noticed that our opponents had played for at least a quarter of an hour with 12 men. The new lightweight strips had not really helped in the humid atmosphere and for the last quarter of an hour some of us were struggling for breath.

Our first home game was against Eddie Turnbull's Aberdeen who happened to be staying in the same hotel as us and it took place in front of a respectable crowd of around 10,000, many of them ex-pats who gave both sides tremendous backing. Pat Quinn continued his impressive end of season form, but despite his promptings from midfield we found ourselves two down early in the second half. We managed to stage a fighting comeback and I reduced the deficit when scoring from close range after a Peter Cormack cut back and although we kept up the pressure for the rest of the game, we just couldn't find an equaliser. Although we had lost at least it gave us a great opportunity to catch up with some of the Aberdeen players in the bar after the game, although knowing Eddie Turnbull it would probably have been an early curfew for them while all the Hibs players went out on the town. A major downside of the trip however had been the standard of refereeing that often left a lot to be desired, although I suppose it has to be taken into consideration that the game at that level was still relatively new in the country at that time.

Just days after our first victory of the tournament, an impressive 2-0 win against the Dutch side ADO who had defeated Sunderland 6-1 in the previous game, we faced Wolves in Toronto. Early in the second half Joe Davis equalised an earlier Derek Dougan goal from the penalty spot. The big talking point however came midway through the second half when the Wolves winger David Wagstaffe punched Jim Scott in the face in an off-the-ball altercation. At first the referee appeared to send Wagstaffe off, only for Derek Dougan to step in, insisting that if Wagstaffe went, then the rest of the team would join him in the dressing room. This seemed to confuse the referee who eventually changed his mind and merely booked the Wolves player, a quite incredible decision! To make matters worse Dougan himself scored the winner a few minutes from the end after intercepting a poor cross field pass by John Madsen.

Colin Stein meanwhile had recovered from his illness and had now flown out to join us. Colin made his first appearance in a 2-2 draw against fellow Scots side Dundee United, but it was during our next game, against the Italian side Cagliari in Toronto, that we would encounter even more astonishing scenes. Peter Cormack scored in the very first minute of the game to give us the lead. Midway through the half the Italian full-back was sent off after first head, butting Jim Scott then felling the Hibs player with a punch. Not long after the sides were level when the Italian player was joined in the dressing room by Cormack who had retaliated after just the latest of a series of dreadful tackles.

With tempers still at fever pitch, Cagliari equalised shortly after the restart, but with only seven minutes remaining there was great controversy when a quickly taken free kick by Pat Quinn allowed Colin Grant to score what would turn out to be the winner. The Cagliari players immediately surrounded the referee gesturing and pushing, protesting that the free kick should never have been given. Courageously the referee refused to change his decision and after instructions from their manager, the entire Cagliari side walked from the field. At that, some of the spectators among the 15,000 crowd who were all mostly of Italian extraction entered the fray attempting to assault the referee and only the timely interception of the police managed to save the official from what could have been a far more serious situation.

After a long delay, the Cagliari players still refused to return to the field and ultimately we were awarded the points. Things had been so bad that we were locked in the dressing room for some time afterwards until it was felt safe for us to emerge. Bob Shankly would later state that it had been the most disgraceful exhibition that he had ever witnessed in all his years in the game, the incident later leading to Cagliari, who had staged a similar walk off if their previous game against Cerro, having three of their players suspended indefinitely from the tournament. Discussing the incident after the game, our trainer Tom McNiven was also of the opinion that Cagliari had been the most ferocious and violent side he had ever witnessed. While we were locked in the dressing room, my pal Scottie who was still raging, revealed that he had been just about to belt his attacker when the referee intervened by sending his assailant off. Later that evening Jim and I caught the hotel lift on our way out for a few drinks in town and who was already inside, but Jim's attacker, a huge black guy who must have been six foot five inches tall and just as wide. I whispered to Scottie that this was his big chance to punch him, but for some reason he declined, and we both poured from the lift laughing our heads off.

Our game against Sunderland in Vancouver which was shown live on television, gave us the opportunity to catch up with our former team mates Neil Martin and John Parke and also Jim Baxter who had joined Sunderland a couple of seasons before. In what turned out to be our first home win of the tournament, the game played in conditions that were much nearer to that of back home, Neil Martin gave Sunderland an early lead. In what was later claimed to be the best game yet in the entire tournament, I managed to equalise before a rare Pat Quinn goal, his first for the club in over 20 months, gave us the lead, Jim Scott later adding a third. George Mulhall pulled one back for Sunderland, but I managed to put the result beyond doubt 15 minutes from the end. Both teams were in the bar after the game enjoying a well-earned refreshment when a replay of the game came on TV. I had played particularly well against my former team mate John Parke in scoring two goals and was pointing that out loudly to everyone when laughingly John jumped to his feet shouting, 'Turn that f***ing thing off.'

We drew 1-1 against the Brazilian side Bangu at the Astrodome in Houston where Muhammad Ali had staged a couple of his World Championship fights. Later that evening Jim Scott and I were making our way back to the hotel after a couple of drinks when we ran into the big black full-back Cabrita and some of his team mates. Recognising us, we were immediately invited back to their room in the hotel for some more refreshments, and it was a fairly surreal atmosphere, none of us understanding a single word that the other was saying, communicating only by singing songs from our respective countries at the top of our voices.

Overall the trip had proved a relative success, winning four and drawing five of the 12 games played. The main problem had been the incredible amount of travelling, many of the games played in oppressive heat which certainly hadn't helped the European sides. We hadn't done a lot of training as the games were fairly close to each other and there had been plenty of time to take in the sightseeing trips that had been laid on for us, including a visit to, but not inside I hasten to add, San Quentin prison, although maybe some of us should have been inside, and also the famous Golden Gate Bridge. But in truth we were not really all that interested in sightseeing. We were mainly healthy young men away from home and all we really wanted to do was socialise in the local bars. During our first night in Toronto we decided to visit the residential Edinburgh Castle lounge that was situated in the basement of our hotel. As I approached the bar I was surprised to hear the bartender ask, 'What can I get you Eric?' It turned out that he was a Hibs supporter from Edinburgh and for the next few weeks he went out of his way to make our stay more comfortable.

With only a couple of games still to play, both against Irish opposition, we could well have qualified for the final, but in all reality few of us wanted to stay. Seven weeks had been far too long to be away from home for most of us, although some of the younger lads were keen to stay. We easily won our game against Shamrock Rovers-6-1, but by then we had set up a meeting with the manager regarding the situation. During the meeting I stood saying, 'Well, the rest of you can do what you like, but I am going,' and stormed from the room expecting to be followed by the majority of my team mates, only to find myself alone in the lobby. Our final game was against Glentoran in Toronto, but nobody celebrated the own goal that gave us the 1-1 draw. The result however meant that we could not now qualify for the final and it was only after we had been back in Edinburgh a few weeks that many of us realised just how daft we had been. It had been the holiday of a lifetime with very little training and plenty of free time. After the games we had been let off the leash and had been paid for it. Looking back it had been a truly fantastic experience, staying in the best of hotels and eating only the best of food. It had been one long holiday. We were all the best of pals, socialised together and it had been great bonding, particularly for the younger lads.

A few days before leaving, Bob Shankly had been approached by representatives from the local side Toronto City who wanted him to take over as manager. The offer while probably tempting, was eventually turned down by Shankly mainly because of his age, explaining that while the offer was a good one it was clearly a job for a much younger man.

In the final Eddie Turnbull's Aberdeen would eventually be defeated 6-5 by Wolverhampton Wanderers after extra time followed by a sudden death play-off.

Later Pat Stanton would be selected by the tournament organisers as the best right half in the entire tournament, a deserved honour for a player who had improved out of all recognition since his debut only a few years before.

CHAPTER NINE

See Naples and Die
and a Controversial Four Step Ruling
1967–68

THE PLAYERS THAT had taken part in the arduous transatlantic tour had been allowed a few extra days to recuperate before starting pre-season training, but both myself and John Murphy joined the boys on the traditional run around the Queens Park on the first day. My appearance was possibly something of a shock to the rest of the lads as it was well known that I wasn't all that keen on training. Another surprise visitor that day was Willie Hamilton who had been released by Aston Villa at the end of the season after failing to command a regular first team place. According to Willie himself he was only there to keep his fitness up, but it seemed fairly obvious to me that he was after a new contract. Although he had not yet turned 30, Willie's best days were already behind him, a situation that perhaps had not been helped by his undisciplined and often chaotic lifestyle. As it would turn out he would later sign for Hearts on a month to month basis, but would not remain at Tynecastle all that long, finally ending his career with the East of Scotland side Ferranti Thistle after short spells in South Africa, and later Ross County and Hamilton Accies.

By now Hibs had been notified that they had been accepted for that seasons Fairs Cup after all. This however meant that with second placed Rangers already accepted, the one city one team ruling meant exclusion for Clyde who had ended the previous campaign two places and four points above us in the league. Perhaps understandably the Shawfield side were far from happy regarding the situation and complained to the SFA who took their side, but as the Fairs Cup was still an invitation competition at the time there was nothing that the Scottish authorities could do. While we obviously had some sympathy for the Shawfield side, everyone at Easter Road was absolutely delighted to be in the first round draw.

Since his recent on-off transfer to Wolves, Jim Scott had become even more unsettled at Easter Road and had re-signed for the new season only on the understanding that the club would not stand in the way if any offers came in. The offers would not be long in coming and even before a ball had been kicked in anger Jim found himself on his way to Newcastle United for a fee in the region of £38,000 where he would meet up again with his former team mate John McNamee. One minute Jim was my best pal at Easter Road, the next minute he was gone, but as I have already mentioned, that is just the nature of the game. Jim would undoubtedly be a huge loss, but had probably only been allowed to leave because we then had several talented players about to break through at Easter Road, some of them highly promising forwards.

The new season didn't get off to the best of starts when we lost 6-2 to Blackpool in a friendly at Bloomfield Road, the entire game played in an absolute deluge of torrential rain. My immediate opponent that evening had been the legendary England international right-back Jimmy Armfield, who I found to be an absolute gentleman. Jimmy was a hard tackler, an extremely clever and tricky opponent, who like all the better defenders would jockey you into position instead of lunging in, but never for a minute did he resort to any underhand tactics. After the game I enjoyed a good chat with him in the bar and had nothing but respect for the man. Perhaps understandably though, a furious Bob Shankly was far from happy at the final result and we were all confined to barracks that evening. We were healthy young men however and most of us managed to sneak out later to sample the delights of the seaside holiday resort.

In a league cup section also comprising of Dundee, Motherwell and Clyde we could only manage to finish runners up in the group. The home game against Dundee which we lost 4-2 would turn out to be John Fraser's last ever appearance for the first team since signing from Edinburgh Thistle in 1954 as yet another potential understudy to the great Gordon Smith. John could play anywhere, on the wing, centre-forward, centre-half or full-back, you name it, and although he was never a superstar he was someone you would always want in your side. He was a great crosser of the ball and, although not as mobile as Neil Martin or Joe Baker, as a centre-forward he could certainly score goals. A very dependable player who never let the side down, John could tackle, was good in the air, could read the game, and to my mind would have made a great sweeper, a position that could well have extended his career for a couple of seasons. That afternoon he was replacing the injured John Madsen, but would soon join second division Stenhousemuir for a short spell as player-coach before later returning to Easter Road to train the youngsters in the evenings.

A few days later young John Murphy made a scoring debut at Fir Park with a brilliant 25 drive that flew past goalkeeper Peter McCloy to cancel out Motherwell's first half lead. That afternoon the fit again John Madsen was given an absolute roasting by his immediate opponent Dixie Deans, a player who would come back to haunt Hibs in the coming years. After Murphy's goal we came into the game and were the better side until a late winner by Lindsay denied us the opportunity to progress into the later stages of the competition. His impressive debut saw Murphy keep his place for the following few games including a great win at Tynecastle. We all had big hopes for John who looked every inch a real prospect and seemed certain to develop into a really outstanding player. He was brainy, had a great left foot and could hit a ball. Probably only because of his inexperience he would be left out of the side to face Porto in the forthcoming Fairs Cup tie, but for whatever reason he failed to re-establish himself in the first team. He always looked great in training, but possibly lacked a bit of confidence and didn't seem able to do it on a Saturday.

We made our way to Tynecastle for the first derby of the season in confident mood. By this time Willie Hamilton had returned to Hearts on a month to month contract and obviously would have been desperate to put one over on his former Easter Road team mates. That afternoon however Bob Shankly got his tactics spot on by designating Alan McGraw to man-mark Hammy, denying the Hearts player the opportunity to display his unquestionable skills. The extra space in midfield gave Pat Quinn the opportunity to take the game by the scruff of the neck. Pat, who had now settled his differences at Easter Road and withdrawn an earlier transfer request, was so effective that after not having scored a goal for well over a year and a half, that afternoon he took the opportunity to score hat trick. It was the first treble by a Hibs player since my three against Hamilton two years before, and the first against Hearts since Joe Baker's four in the famous Scottish Cup victory at Tynecastle in 1958. We had been the better side throughout, and the rumour that we about to sign the former Rangers player Alex Scott from Everton, if successful, would obviously be a great advantage if we wished to challenge the dominance of the 'Old Firm'.

By this time the ruling that substitutes could only be used in the case of injury had been relaxed, and in replacing Alan McGraw near the end of a 3-0 victory against Raith Rovers at Easter Road, Colin Grant became the first Hibs substitute to be used for purely tactical reasons in a competitive domestic fixture.

What became something of an on-off, on-off transfer saga regarding Alex Scott eventually proved successful and the former Rangers player made his debut against Oporto in the Fairs Cup at Easter Road a few days later. I was the only survivor from the last Hibs side to face a team from Portugal when we had defeated Belenenses in 1962, although Jimmy O'Rourke was still on the books, but then featuring mainly in the reserves.

Porto were far from the side they are today and were extremely fortunate to leave Easter Road only three goals in arrears. That evening we were absolutely magnificent, particularly in the first half when we could well have scored more had it not been for three goal line clearances and several brilliant saves by their international goalkeeper Americo. There were no failures in the Hibs team that evening and in the end our 3-0 win greatly flattered our opponents. Straight from the very start I found that I had the beating of full-back Valdemar who was booked after 25 minutes for only the latest of a series of cynical fouls on me, due no doubt to frustration as I had him going round in circles, Peter Cormack opening the scoring from the resultant free kick. Not long after, a brilliant defence splitting pass by debutant Scott allowed Cormack to win the race between himself and the goalkeeper before passing the ball into the empty net to double our lead. Just after half time the game was over as a contest after a Scott cross that had been headed on by Colin Stein allowed me to slip the ball past the advancing goalkeeper from close range. We were running riot now and our opponents had no answer. I myself had one of those games when it seemed as if I could do no wrong and Valdemar would have been mightily relieved to hear the final whistle. It had been a marvellous all round performance by the entire side, special mention must be made of Alex Scott whose inclusion had given our forward line another dimension. Obviously still lacking in match practice, Scott had managed just 60 minutes before being replaced by Colin Grant, but during this time he had shown just how good a player he was. At Ibrox he had been a permanent fixture in the side for several years, winning several Scotland caps and it was only the emergence of the outstanding Willie Henderson that Rangers felt that they were in a position to let the popular winger go. At Everton Scott had lined up alongside the former Hearts player Alex Young and both had been key members of the side that defeated Sheffield Wednesday in the 1966 FA Cup final at Wembley when the Merseysider's had famously come back from two behind to win 3-2.

For me European nights were always something special, playing under the lights and normally in front of big crowds. There was also the added interest of facing opponents that you hadn't met before, but it was the fans who really made these games memorable and there was always an atmosphere of expectancy inside the ground right from the start. In some games you often had to work at it, and it was only when you had created something that the crowd got right behind you. The European games however were different. You could sense the atmosphere even while you were still in the tunnel, and it obviously would have been the same for our opponents when we played abroad often in front of extremely hostile fans. I can't begin to tell you just what an incredible feeling it was running down the wing at Easter Road on those occasions, particularly on the stand side when the noise of the crowd was magnified by the huge seated structure in the background, and I can still hear Tom McNiven shouting encouragement from the bench, 'Go on Stevie, go on Stevie!' as I took off on a run.

On the Saturday at Easter Road I managed to score two goals in our 5-1 win against Partick Thistle a victory that would be an ideal boost to our confidence before the return game against Porto.

There was a slight hold up at Turnhouse Airport as we waited to board the flight to Portugal, when Alex Scott discovered that his passport had not arrived from his home in Liverpool in time. Fortunately, after a bit of haggling he was able to obtain a temporary visa. Meanwhile I had problems of my own. A slight injury picked up on the Saturday against Partick had threatened to prevent me from playing. Fortunately treatment right up to the kick-off from Tom McNiven who was using his 'secret weapon', a recently acquired bulky machine that was being used for the first time on the continent, eventually proved successful and I was able to take my place in the starting line-up at the Das Antas Stadium in Porto.

In the first game at Easter Road our defence had rarely been tested and if I am being honest we all probably thought that the tie was already as good as over. The return in Porto however would turn out to be something else. A goal from the penalty spot in the opening minutes after Stein had been fouled inside the box seemed more than enough to put the tie to bed. In a scene reminiscent of the Barcelona fracas at Easter Road a few years earlier, the game was held up for several minutes as the referee was surrounded by a pack of blue and white jerseys all protesting the decision while pushing and jostling the official. Order was eventually restored and the usually reliable Joe Davis gave us what was an unassailable 4-0 overall lead – or so we thought. Ten minutes before half time a tackle by Cormack wasn't particularly appreciated by his immediate opponent who promptly punched Peter in the face. Once again a melee involving several of the Oporto players led to the game being held up for several minutes before both players were eventually ordered off. We found our opponents to be a far different side to that seen at Easter Road as they really came at us, and after managing to hold out for just over an hour we conceded two goals in the space of two minutes. A few minutes later I was rugby tackled by the goalkeeper well outside the box, a challenge that probably should have led to a sending off, but unbelievably he escaped with just a warning. With 20 minutes remaining Valdir scored a third and it was backs to the wall as the home side went looking for more. At times I was so far back that I was playing more like a full-back than an outside-left and we spent the rest of the game kicking the ball anywhere in desperation during which time our opponents came within an ace of saving the tie as they pushed everyone forward, and we were all mightily relieved to hear the final whistle.

On the Saturday we again came up against a Celtic side at their very best. At that time we were still unbeaten in the league, but as often happens after an away midweek game in Europe, we really struggled and eventually went down to a heavy 4-0 defeat. The then European Cup holders had been knocked out of that year's competition in the first round by Dynamo Kiev in Russia a few days earlier, but they didn't seem to have shown any adverse reaction to their earlier midweek travels and were far too good for us from start to finish. At times we had managed to play some entertaining football, but lacked the punch of our opponents who looked as if they could score every time they went up the park and they were well worth the victory.

A few weeks later Colin Stein scored his first hat trick in senior football in a 5-0 home win against Airdrie, a result that saw us climb to second place behind league leaders Rangers. The Scotland boss Bobby Brown had watched from the stand and was believed to have been casting an eye over several Hibs players for possible inclusion in the Scotland side for the forthcoming game against Wales at Hampden. According to one newspaper:

> While the whole Hibs team play of a high class and slick order, no one will deny that Bobby Brown would have been particularly impressed by the displays put up by Colin Stein, who scored three beautiful goals in a row, Eric Stevenson, Pat Stanton and the very classy Peter Cormack.

So, once again the newspapers were suggesting that I was playing well enough to be considered for a Scotland call up, but as it would later turn out, none of the above would be selected for the game.

We now knew that our next Fairs Cup opponents would be the Italian side Napoli, the first game to take place in the beautiful city of Naples, which incidentally had been the most bombed city in Italy during the war. A few weeks before, during what had been an embarrassing 4-1 defeat at Annfield by bottom of the table Stirling Albion, I had felt a slight re-occurrence of my old groin trouble and had been replaced in the second half by Colin Grant. The injury would eventually mean me missing several games including the first leg against Napoli in Italy. For a while it seemed as though I could make it, but a late fitness test just before leaving Edinburgh had finally ruled me out. We were now really up against it. As well as myself, we would also be without the suspended Peter Cormack after his sending off against Oporto in the previous round. Alan McGraw had also been sent off at Dundee a couple of weeks previously, but luckily because the disciplinary committee had yet to meet, he was free to play in Naples. We were to suffer even more bad luck when Pat Stanton went down with flu shortly after arriving in Italy, but fortunately, although still not 100 per cent fit, he had recovered enough to take his place in a starting line-up that had inside-forward Colin Grant making his European debut.

At that time the Napoli fans had a reputation for being amongst the most volatile in Europe, and visiting teams playing at the Stadio San Paola had often likened it to looking into the very jaws of hell. In a recent game against Roma, the fans had still been fighting in the streets a full three hours after the game had ended, altercations that eventually resulted in over 40 supporters being taken to hospital. However, in front of a crowd of around 20,000 baying Napoli fans we gave every bit as good as we got, scorning several good chances in the first half before Napoli took the lead just before half time. The home side scored again soon after the break, but we were never out of it until the Brazilian Altafini, who was the game's best player by far, scored a third. Colin Stein gave us a lifeline ten minutes from time when he fired past goalkeeper Dino Zoff, only for Napoli to re-establish their three goal cushion five minutes from the end.

Back in Edinburgh nobody gave us much of a chance to reverse the score from the first leg, even our own fans, the lone dissenting voice that of manager Bob Shankly who publicly declared that we could still turn things around. According to Shankly-we would win at Easter Road, probably by the three goals needed, but I'm sure that if you had asked Bob in private he would have admitted that he was merely attempting to keep our spirits up. As far as most people were concerned the tie was already as good as over, particularly the Napoli background staff. The brilliant Altafini had been slightly injured on the Saturday before the return game in Edinburgh and although he could well have played, with such a commanding lead from the first leg it had been decided not to risk him at Easter Road. It was a decision that Napoli would come to regret.

I was still troubled by the injury and not really fully fit, but after the aid of an injection the manager decided to take a gamble and I took my usual place at outside-left in what would eventually turn out to be a quite incredible evening. We were all aware of just how difficult a task it would be to score even three goals against such formidable opponents while conceding none, but in front of over 21,000 fans, which I suppose was a more than reasonable turn out considering the score from the first leg, we scorned a great chance to take the lead inside the opening minute. The goal was only delayed however and right-back Bobby Duncan opened the floodgates a few minutes later with a fantastic strike from all of 25 yards that literally screamed past Zoff and into the top corner of the net. It was Bobby's first goal for the club and what a time to score it. Just over a minute later we were denied a stone wall penalty when Cormack was tripped inside the box only for the referee to award an indirect free kick, but already you could sense that the Italians were beginning to reel. We kept up the pressure for the remainder of the half during which time goalkeeper Wilson had not had a single save to make, and a few minutes before half time Pat Quinn took advantage of a rare slip by Dino Zoff to double our lead, a goal that seemed to completely knock the heart out of our opponents.

In an attempt to combat what had been our unrelenting attacks, at half time manager Pesalo replaced a forward with a defender, but the move made absolutely no difference. Napoli were clearly rattled now and the cracks were beginning to show as they resorted to defending at any cost while conceding numerous free kicks. With just 20 minutes left to play, brilliant headers, the first by Peter Cormack and then Pat Stanton gave us the overall lead when scoring twice within a minute resulting in Napoli going completely to pieces. I had been giving right-back Nardin and later the substitute Girado the run-around all evening. This eventually proved too much for Girado and midway through the half he lashed out, not only kicking me to the ground, but adding another kick as I lay there, and was promptly ordered off. With just five minutes remaining Colin Stein capped a memorable performance when he scored a fifth to complete not only Hibs biggest ever win in Europe, but one of the most astonishing comebacks ever by a Scottish team in a European tournament, the incredible result resounding throughout Europe the following morning. The watching Scotland manager Bobby Brown later congratulated us on our tremendous performance and he was not alone. After the game the Napoli president confessed that 'Hibs had been another team altogether from the one seen in Naples, their power, speed and force far too much for us.' The Hibs side that memorable evening:

WILSON, DUNCAN AND DAVIS, STANTON MADSEN AND MCGRAW, (A)
SCOTT QUINN STEIN CORMACK AND STEVENSON.

Once again our our inconsistency came to the surface and only a few days after one of the best performances ever by a Hibs side in Europe, we were beaten 1-0 by mid-table Morton at Easter Road. Although we had exerted tremendous pressure on the Cappielow defence after losing a soft goal, to their credit the visitors held firm and in the end were probably worth the victory. The win was thanks mainly to goalkeeper Russell who brought of several fine saves, and also to the sterling performance of the former Hibs player Morris Stevenson who as usual had been in tremendous form against his old side.

The next round of the Fairs Cup had handed us the daunting task of facing Leeds United the first game away from home, and a few days before Christmas we made our way to Elland Road to face arguably our biggest test of the season so far.

On a treacherous ice bound pitch that had only been passed playable a short time before, we appeared to handle the conditions better than the home team and produced a great fighting display against a team who were then rated one of the best in Europe. Leeds had lost to Dynamo Zagreb in the final of the previous seasons Fairs Cup, and at that time were not only still in the semi-finals of the league cup, but also in a challenging position for the league championship, and were clearly a side to be treated with respect. As early as the first minute Colin Stein had a great chance to open the scoring when he collected a beautiful through ball from Cormack, only to be cynically brought down on the edge of the box, the resulting free kick coming to nothing. This however was only the shape of things to come. As well as carving out a merited reputation for playing great football, Leeds were also a big powerful side who were more than capable of looking after themselves and we were kicked, pushed and shoved throughout the entire 90 minutes.

After only four minutes Eddie Gray capitalised on a poor kick out by Willie Wilson to give Leeds the lead, but for the remainder of the game the home side was often second best. They had set their stall out early however. Colin Stein had proved a particular menace to the Leeds defence in the early stages, constantly troubling the England centre-half Jack Charlton, and after just 30 minutes he was fouled twice in quick succession by Billy Bremner, the second a quite blatant and dangerous tackle that crudely bundled the Hibs forward onto the running track. Obviously in a fair bit of trouble, Colin was stretchered off in agony to be replaced by Jimmy O'Rourke, but to our utter disbelief and probably that of most of the huge crowd inside Elland Road, Bremner only received a mild ticking off from the Irish referee. Although he was a good lad off the field, on it Billy could be a dirty little demon and most of us felt that he should have been sent off. After the interval a brief spell of pressure from the home side created little danger and from then until the end of the game we were by far the more dangerous, creating several good chances although failing to take them.

Mick Jones, a recent £100,000 signing from Sheffield United had got absolutely no change out of John Madsen as our defence handled everything that was thrown at them quite comfortably, the only real threat when Wilson made up for his earlier mistake with a full length save from the future England international at point blank range in the final minute. Eddie Gray's early goal had been enough to win the match, but we certainly hadn't deserved to lose and had been much the better side for long periods of the game. I myself had been tightly man-marked throughout, first by Paul Reaney and then by his replacement Paul Madeley in the second half, both of whom had never left my side for a second, and consequently I had contributed little apart from one half chance in the first half when I shot narrowly past the post. The Leeds fans amongst the 32,000 crowd would possibly have been expecting a convincing victory against the upstarts from north of the border, but I don't think that the Leeds players would have been surprised at just how well we had played as the meticulous Don Revie, a manager famous for his thorough dossiers on the opposition would have seen to that, and it was all now to play for in Edinburgh.

In the New Year's Day derby against Hearts at Easter Road a Joe Davis penalty after I had been brought down in the box by full-back Davie Holt late in the game gave us our first home win against our great rivals in a Ne'erday match for several years. In what turned out to be an exciting encounter Hearts were the better side in the first half, troubling goalkeeper Wilson on numerous occasions. After the break attempts on goal were few and far between until we took the lead from the spot, after which Hearts staged an all out effort to secure at least the point that would have lifted them above us in the table, but we were able to hold out to the end.

Twenty-four hours after our victory over Hearts we faced Raith Rovers in Kirkcaldy. Alex Scott had picked up a slight injury the previous day and his place in the was side taken by the 17-year-old old Peter Marinello who was making his first team debut. At that time Raith were struggling near the foot of the table, but any thoughts that the game was going to be easy were quickly dispelled when the home side put up a tremendous display of attacking football to earn a well deserved draw. Rovers might well have scored twice in the opening minutes, but after Peter Cormack had given us the lead midway through the first half, the Hibs supporters in the crowd sat back waiting for a goal avalanche that never came. To be fair we had not played particularly well and according to the newspapers the following day the only visiting player to gain pass marks had been the young Marinello who had shown a confidence and ability far beyond his years. Peter could certainly play a bit, but his main weapon was his incredible pace that allowed him to skip past defenders with ease, and already, wrongly to my mind for a young player who was yet to be tested, he was being likened to the great Gordon Smith. Obviously because of his inexperience, at that time Peter was not particularly clever football wise, but it was amazing the number of times that his fantastic pace had allowed him to get on the end of through balls where he would often find himself face to face with the opposing goalkeeper.

The return game against Leeds in Edinburgh was eagerly anticipated and the kick off delayed to allow the huge crowd, estimated to be around the 40,000 mark, time to enter the stadium. Leeds had a reputation for being just as formidable a side away from home as at Elland Road and we were under no illusions that we were in for a very difficult evening. With young Marinello dropping out to make way for the more experienced Alex Scott, within a few minutes of the start Colin Stein had levelled the tie when he lobbed goalkeeper Sprake from a tight angle, the inrushing Jack Charlton only managing to help the ball into the net. As in the first game, I found myself closely marshalled by Paul Reaney, who never left my side for a second, and consequently I again saw very little of the ball. In those days wide players were expected to remain out on the wing and not go chasing the game, with the result was that once again I was reduced almost to the role of a spectator, creating little in way of danger inside the Leeds penalty area.

Although the game had been flat compared to the excitement of the match at Elland Road a couple of weeks earlier, there were several near things at either end. Egged on by a huge mainly partisan home crowd we managed to regain the upper hand and were well on top when with just 15 minutes remaining goalkeeper Willie Wilson was impeded by Peter Lorimer as he attempted to clear from his hands. Forced into taking one step too many Wilson was penalised by the controversial Welsh referee Clive Thomas, a man who was no stranger to contentious decisions. The four step rule had been introduced only at the beginning of the season and designed to prevent goalkeepers from wasting time, but the referee had allowed both goalkeepers to regularly flout the new regulation all evening and we were surprised to say the least at what appeared to be an over fussy decision. With extra time looming Jack Charlton headed Johnny Giles indirect free kick past Willie Wilson to effectively end any hopes of us winning the tie. To be fair to Leeds, at that time they had some great players, but we had got stronger the longer the game went on and I am still convinced that only the quite incredible decision by an over finicky official had prevented us from winning the tie, possibly in extra time.

Although all credit to Leeds. With players such as Johnny Giles, Eddie Gray Billy Bremner and Peter Lorimer in the side the entire team had great balance and it was no surprise to me when they went all the way to defeat the Hungarian side Ferencvaros in the two legged final.

We were still well in the running for the championship when we faced Celtic, this time in Edinburgh. The game started badly for Bobby Duncan when he put through his own net inside the opening few minutes, but unfortunately things would get much worse for the defender when he was carried from the field with a broken leg after a rash tackle by Celtic's John Hughes just before half time. Perhaps surprisingly Hughes was only spoken to by the referee as trouble broke out between rival fans in the covered area behind the goals. The Celtic goalkeeper Ronnie Simpson had been forced to flee his area after missiles were thrown onto the field, and the game held up for several minutes as the police attempted to regain order. The second-half was an anti-climax, no doubt due to the incident involving Duncan and Hughes and although we managed to exert some early pressure, the 2-0 final score in Celtics favour remained the same at the end. At that time the unlucky Bobby Duncan was playing the best football of his career by far and was on the verge of full international honours. The injury would keep him out of the game for almost a year and although Bobby may disagree I don't think that he was ever the same player again.

With Billy Simpson deputising for the unfortunate Bobby Duncan we overcame East Stirling much easier than the 5-3 score-line would suggest in the first round of that years Scottish Cup at Firs Park. The part timers had shocked us by taking the lead after just four minutes, but a hat trick by Colin Stein, another goal by Peter Cormack and the now almost mandatory penalty by Joe Davis gave us a 5-2 interval lead. The Shire scored again just five minutes after the restart, but there was never any danger of a giant killing act.

In the next round we had been drawn away to mid-table Airdrie at Broomfield. A goal two minutes from half time by wing half Derek Whiteford who had been released by Hibs only at the end of the previous season was enough to give the part timers a shock victory and end our Scottish Cup aspirations for at least another year. Whiteford had managed only one first team appearance during his time at Easter Road, but he was a good player although a bit cumbersome and with all due respect he had probably found his level with Airdrie. We came storming back and did everything but score against a resolute defence that was well marshalled by the future Hibs players Jim Black and goalkeeper Roddy McKenzie. We had played the football, but Airdrie had the strength and that was enough to allow the home side a meeting with St Johnstone in the third round. I was usually one of the first out of the bath after a game and instead of travelling back to Edinburgh on the team coach I was getting a lift back from a friend and was leaving the stadium at the same time as many of the Hibs fans who perhaps understandably started to give me absolute pelters. It was always a battle at Broomfield, but I knew that we had let them down and said nothing as I made my way to the car, their taunts still ringing in my ears. Broomfield was a very tight park which often made it difficult for the wide men, but if I am brutaly honest the main reason for our defeat was probably because we didn't have nearly enough battlers in the side.

We managed to gain a degree of revenge for the cup defeat a couple of weeks later, again at Broomfield, with a 2-1 victory in the league. Our winning goal however was a bizarre own goal by centre-half Jim Black whose pass back was allowed to trundle into the net by goalkeeper Roddy McKenzie who thought, wrongly as it turned out, that the whistle had already gone. The goal stood however, and with just over half dozen games left to play we were well placed to qualify for a European place, which as it would turn out was just as well. After a 2-0 home win against Dundee that saw John Blackley making his first team debut, we could only manage to take a solitary point from our following four games, including a 3-1 defeat by Rangers when I scored our goal with what was later described as a 'spectacular first time shot'. There was also a humiliating 5-0 defeat at Pittodrie. At that time Aberdeen had two really good defenders in Jim Whyte and Edinburgh born Jim Hermiston who both liked to play almost like wingers, particularly at home. Whyte was perhaps not the greatest of defenders, but at Pittodrie the Aberdeen system allowed him to play more like a forward and I often found myself marking him rather than the other way round. Fortunately Jim was far less adventurous at Easter Road where I usually got the better of him.

The Hibs team around that time was along the lines of:

WILSON, SIMPSON AND DAVIS,
STANTON, MADSEN AND MCGRAW,
A. SCOTT, QUINN, STEIN, CORMACK AND STEVENSON.
SUBS FROM: ALLAN, MARINELLO, BLACKLEY, COUSIN AND O'ROURKE.

After our premature exit from the cup, the club had arranged a friendly against Newcastle United at St James's Park and it gave us the chance to meet up again with our former team mates Jim Scott and John McNamee. In a 2-1 win for the home side, both players managed to score against their former club, but there were no hard feelings after the game when a few of us including Jim's brother Alex, caught up with the pair over a few beers.

A season that at one time had once again promised so much, finally came to an end a few weeks later with a 3-3 home draw against Kilmarnock, all our goals scored by Colin Stein, his third hat trick of the campaign. The game however turned out to be no typical dreary end of the season affair that the fans had become so accustomed to in recent years, and the crowd certainly got their money's worth as three times we managed to claw ourselves back from a goal behind to finally accomplish what was a more than credible draw.

In what was only his second season as a full time professional, Colin Stein had ended up as the club's top scorer in all games, closely followed by Peter Cormack and somewhat inevitably full-back Joe Davis who once again had kept up his incredible record of not having missed a single game during the entire campaign. I myself had scored a somewhat credible ten in all games including the goal against Porto in the Fairs Cup. Since making his debut against Morton just over two years before Colin Stein had become an almost automatic first choice and a gigantic favourite with the fans who always appreciated his determined all action style. In just over 70 games he had already scored 44 goals to become one of the hottest prospects in the country and an obvious target for predators.

Our third place finish had been the best by a Hibs team for 15 years. Not since 1953 and the days of the Famous Five had the feat been achieved at Easter Road. We had also managed to qualify for the following seasons Fairs Cup fairly comfortably, six points ahead of our nearest challengers Dunfermline, but a huge 18 points behind champions Celtic who were winning their third consecutive title, and 16 behind next best Rangers.

Just a few weeks earlier John Madsen had informed the club that he would be returning to Denmark at the end of the season to continue his career as an architect. John's wife had failed to settle in Scotland, but perhaps more importantly he wanted his children to be educated back in in Denmark which was quite understandable. With a year still to run on his contract Hibs were not particularly happy about the decision and it was explained that he would not be able to play for another side unless officially transferred. Nevertheless the Madsen family packed their bags and left for home, but it would not be the last we would hear of him at Easter Road. John was another good guy. With his shaven hairstyle he could look quite tough, but he was one of the few centre-half's that could play football. He was one of the lads and would often come out with us after a game, sometimes accompanied by his wife, and although he liked a drink I think he was amazed at how much alcohol some of us could consume and would often ask me, 'How do you do it, Eric?'

Probably due to the success of our previous visit to the country, we had once again been invited to tour America at the end of the season. Instead, the club had elected to explore new territory by accepting the offer of a five game tour of Nigeria and Ghana including matches against both national sides.

Meanwhile my former Edina Hearts team mate Chris Shevlane had been signed from Celtic just in time to accompany us on the trip. Chris had received a bad injury while playing with Hearts and had reluctantly been forced to retire. After a few months out of the game he seemed to have recovered sufficiently from the injury and after medical advice had been signed by Celtic. Unfortunately at Parkhead he had failed to hold down a first team place and after just four appearances for the first team, he had been handed a free transfer and was now ready to make up for lost time at Easter Road. With John Madsen now back in Denmark, Ian Wilkinson, a centre-half from Broxburn who had yet to play a game for the first team took Madsen's place in the Hibs party that made its way to Lagos for the opening game of the tour. Unfortunately, while in Africa the youngster injured his toe in training and failed to take part in any of the games. A tall likable guy, Ian would make several appearances for the first team the following season before joining Raith Rovers, later moving on to Hamilton Academicals.

In our first evening in Nigeria we were entertained to a lavish reception by many of the ex-pats in the local Caledonia Club, and I have to say that everywhere we went we were treated like royalty. Our hotel was different class, a far cry however from the shanty settlements not far outside town where some of the primitive living conditions and poverty was truly heartbreaking. Our first game against the Nigerian Olympic XI ended in a 1-1 draw. I had been limbering up before the game playing keepie-uppy, balancing the ball behind my head and all the other usual manoeuvres when I became aware that I was attracting considerable interest from the mainly black crowd who all seemed particularly appreciative of my skills. Encouraged by the other players I proceeded to really show off, and the more I performed the more the crowd went wild, jumping up and down and cheering madly, similar to what the Hearts fans did when I played at Tynecastle, only a bit friendlier.

Because of the high level of crime in the area, we had all been well warned not to venture too far from the hotel, but I had become friendly with one of the local journalists who told us the best places to go for a drink. My roommate Willie Wilson was not all that keen on the idea, but I had eventually convinced him that it would be alright, when there was a knock on our room door. Standing outside were Peter Marinello and

John Murphy who were both eager to join us, much against the advice of Wilson. On my first trip abroad with Hibs I had been well looked after by Willie Ormond, and now taking on the role of elder statesman I felt that it was my duty to look after the youngsters. The taxi driver took us to what appeared to be a respectable club that was mostly frequented by white ex-pats, many of whom worked in the local mines, and the drink flew freely all night everyone having a great time, the two youngsters perhaps having a better time than most. In the morning as I was going down for breakfast I knocked on the door of our previous evening's drinking buddies' room. For a long while there was no answer and just as I was about to leave, the door was opened slightly by a bleary eyed John Murphy. Looking into the room over John's shoulder I could see Peter Marinello sprawled on the bed, with sick everywhere. To this day I have never seen anyone as ill as this pair when they eventually made it down for breakfast, and I don't think they ever came out with us again, even back in Edinburgh.

We made our way to some of the games in an aircraft that looked as if it had been used during the First World War. At that time Nigeria was in the middle of a terrible civil conflict that would eventually cost over 75,000 lives. We only found out later that on arriving at the airport we had been mistaken for a group of mercenary paratroopers who had been airlifted in to fight on the side of the Federal troops. After a 1-0 win against Northern Lions and another solitary goal victory, this time against Western Rovers, we made our way to Ghana for the remaining two games of the tour. Our only defeat of the entire trip was against a South Ghana select who were made up of players eligible for the full international side and who would have been more than capable of giving any team in Scotland a game, before ending our visit with a convincing 2-0 victory against a North Ghana XI on an extremely waterlogged pitch.

The opposition during what had been yet another truly memorable trip, had all been amateurs. Some of them were good enough regarding ball control although they didn't have any savvy about going forward, but again this was well before Africa started to produce some really good players. The one down side of the trip had been the incredible heat that we all found a real problem, often as much as 100 per cent in the shade. Coming from Bonnyrigg I wasn't all that used to the sun, but apart from that it had been a truly incredible experience. One afternoon in Ghana we were taken by our hosts to a beautiful seaside lagoon to sunbathe. After a while we were approached by a group of Russian sailors who asked us if we fancied a game of football. They didn't have a clue who we were and it was only after scoring our seventh goal that we owned up that we were professional footballers and everyone had a good laugh.

Above: The arrival of Joe Davis and the departure of John Parke, November 1964.
Left to right: Parke Hamilton Quinn Davis and Baxter.

Right: Neil Martin, a prolific goal scorer and absolutely lethal in the air.

North American Tour 1965. Left to right: Baxter, Davis, (J) Stevenson, (B) Simpson and McNamee.

Hibernian 1965–66. Back row left to right: Blackley, Simpson, Stein, Duncan, Stevenson, Reilly, Allan, Watson, Whiteford, Falconer, Murphy, Martin, and Baxter. Centre row: Stanton, Fraser, Vincent, Cullerton, McNamee, Wilkinson, (C) Grant, McNeill, Gartshore, Hamilton. Front row: (R) Hogg, O'Rourke, Quinn, Cormack, Brown, Scott, (D) Hogg, Stevenson and Davis.

Peter Cormack (left) and 'penalty king' Joe Davis.

Always at my happiest wearing the
famous green and white jersey.

Above: Jim Scott in race to the ball with the Sunderland goalkeeper Jim Montgomery. Varsity Stadium, Toronto, 1967.

Fans' favourite John McNamee, whose very presence I am convinced scared some forwards to death.

Hibernian season 1967–68. Back Row left to right: (A) Scott, Simpson, Cousin, Wilkinson and (C) Grant. Middle row: Stanton, Blackley, Monaghan, Allan, Wilson, Murphy, Duncan and O'Rourke. Seated: (J) Hamilton, Shevlane, Quinn, Davis, Stein, Cormack, Pringle, Stevenson and McGraw. Front: Hastie, Brownlie, McEwan, Marinello and Jones.

A day that started badly for Bobby Duncan in a game against Celtic at Easter Road when he scored an own goal after just two minutes would get much worse when he was carried off with a broken leg after a challenge by John Hughes.

Above: Jimmy O'Rourke with the
Hibs supporters' player of the year
trophy. Left to right: Stanton, Hibs club
chairman, O'Rourke, Stevenson and
Tom McNiven.

Right: The much loved Tom
McNiven who on a couple of
occasions carefully nurtured me
back to full fitness.

Joe Baker's return to Easter Road January 1971. Back row left to right: Gillet, Blackley, (B) Duncan ,Black. Front row: (J) Hamilton, Graham, McEwan, Jones – Baker, Hunter, Stanton and Stevenson.

Eddie Turnbull returns to Easter Road, this time as manager, 1971. Back Row left to right: Shevlane, Stanton, Black, Baines, Blackley, Brownlie, McEwan and O'Rourke. Seated: Baker, Graham, McBride, (A) Duncan, Turnbull (manager), Hazel, Pringle, Davidson and Cropley. Front: McNiven (physio), Stevenson, Hamilton and Fraser (trainer).

Left: Eddie Turnbull, a great manager and a far better player than most folks believed. Photo taken during the filming of the Turnbull's Tornados video.

On the pitch at a recent event at Easter Road. From left to right: Daughter Sonia, grandson Aiden, wife Agnes, grandson Owen, son-in-law Alastair, granddaughter Lucy, Grandson Connor, daughter Lucy and myself.

CHAPTER TEN

A £100,000 Footballer
and League Cup Disappointment
1968–69

DURING THE PREVIOUS few years we had usually been well in the running until the final few weeks of the season when possibly a lack of mental and physical toughness and self-belief had come to the fore and we all knew that we would have to show far more consistency if we were ever going to challenge for major honours. Not that long before we had been described in one newspaper as possibly the most disappointing side in the country. According to them:

> Hibs were packed full of talent and one of the most entertaining sides in the country, but a good win would often be followed by an embarrassing defeat and they were far too good a side to consistently let their fans down.

It was clear that we faced another tough battle if we wished to dislodge a great Celtic side from the top of the table. Jock Stein had done a wonderful job at Parkhead since walking out of Easter Road so suddenly just over three years before. During this time Celtic had become not only the first British side to win the European Cup, but had also won the first three of what would eventually be a record nine consecutive titles, and were then recognised as one of the best club sides in Europe, if not the world – so no problem there then! The feat had been all the more remarkable for the fact that every player was home grown and all born within a 30 radius of Glasgow.

To make our prospects even more difficult, although they lagged behind their city rivals, Rangers were still a force to be reckoned with, and if we were to have any hope of competing for the honours that had so far eluded a side that on their day were capable of beating anybody, it was obvious that we would have to toughen up.

Bob Shankly reaffirmed the difficulty facing us in a newspaper article just before the start of the new season:

> A sustained challenge to the old firm is only possible when you have the financial resources to back you up, and to get the resources you must give the fans what they want most – trophies. Despite Hibs playing football of as high a quality as can be seen anywhere in the country, not one major trophy has been won.

The tour of Nigeria and Ghana had allowed the manager to experiment with team formations just as he had done during the trip to North America 12 months before. Those trips were also invaluable for building team spirit and camaraderie particularly amongst the younger lads, and John Blackley, Peter Marinello and John Murphy would all undoubtedly have benefited greatly from the experience. Although he had played in all our tour games, to all intents and purposes Chris Shevlane was a new signing as far as the Easter Road fans were concerned. He had done well in Africa and proved that he had lost none of the skill that had seen him earn two Scottish under-23 caps while with Hearts.

We were now back training at Seafield and Chris was joined on the first day by a handful of youngsters who had all stepped up from the juvenile ranks. Unfortunately, with the exception of Alex Cropley, John Brownlie and Willie McEwan who had all been signed from Edina Hibs during the summer, none of the others would make the breakthrough into the first team. Continuing in his role of club captain, Joe Davis was about to commence his fifth full season without missing a single game in any competition since December 1964, an incredible total of well over 200 consecutive appearances.

The new season opened with a home friendly against a Newcastle United side that would be competing in that seasons Fairs Cup. Not only would it be United's first ever experience of competitive European action, they would go all the way to the final and actually win the trophy, my good pal Jim Scott scoring one of the goals in the 6-2 aggregate victory over Hungarian side Újpest Dozsa in the two legged final. On the way to the final, Newcastle would knock out the Dutch side Feyenoord, Sporting Lisbon and our own Glasgow Rangers. The win against Rangers would be achieved, despite the Scottish fans invading the St James's pitch in an attempt to get the game abandoned when it became clear that their favourites would not win the game. Newcastle had finished tenth in the table the previous season and ironically had only qualified for the competition because of the obscure Fairs Cup ruling that only allowed one side from each city to take part, a ruling that meant exclusion for Everton, Arsenal and Spurs who had all finished higher up the table. As well as our former team mates Jim Scott and John McNamee, we would also be coming face to face with the ex-Hearts goalkeeper Gordon Marshall who had joined Newcastle in 1963. Ironically Gordon would end the current season as Hibs first choice goalkeeper after a short spell with Nottingham Forest.

In a match played in bright summer sunshine in front of a reasonable crowd for a pre-season friendly, the visitors earned a 2-1 victory in a game that might well have gone either way, the winning goal scored when a shot by the former Dunfermline player Jackie Sinclair was deflected past Thomson Allan by Chris Shevlane who was making his home debut. By now Alan Cousin had replaced the nomadic John Madsen and had done reasonably well against the dangerous Wyn Davies, but the undoubted star of the show was the former Hibs player John McNamee who was head and shoulders above everyone on the park. By a strange coincidence, in midweek we would come up against another future Hibs goalkeeper in the former Dunfermline and then current Scotland custodian Jim Herriot in a 2-0 victory against Birmingham City at St Andrews, a victory that set us up for the forthcoming league cup competition.

That year we had been drawn in a section that also comprised of St Johnstone, Raith Rovers and Falkirk, and with both Rangers and Celtic drawn in the same group as each other we were now 3-1 favourites with the bookies to at least reach the quarter-finals. This optimism however would be found to be sadly wanting when we crashed to 1-0 home defeat by St Johnstone, Joe Davis missing a penalty. It had been our first defeat on the opening day of the season for six years, but that didn't prevent the expectant Hibs fans from jeering us as we left the field at the end of the game, although I did have some sympathy for them after what had been an extremely poor display by us.

At Starks Park in midweek only a brilliant point blank save by Willie Wilson in the final minute allowed us to us to 'steal' both points after yet another mediocre display. The poor performances against both Raith and St Johnstone had forced Bob Shankly to make changes for the home game against section leaders Falkirk, and the inclusion of John Blackley as sweeper allowed us to utilise the skills of Pat Stanton in midfield where he could make more of an impact on the game. The move almost paid immediate dividends when Pat hit the post early on with a blistering drive from all of 25 yards, goalkeeper Devlin having to look lively to save the rebound. It took us almost an hour to break the deadlock until Jimmy

O'Rourke, who was making a rare first team appearance deputising for the injured Cormack, blasted home a twice taken free kick. Colin Stein settled things a few minutes from the end with his first goal of the season, the victory allowing us to top the section.

During a 2-2 draw against a pretty decent St Johnstone side at Muirton the following Saturday Pat Stanton was ordered off for the first time in his professional career when he retaliated after a hefty challenge by the rugged Bill McCarry. Pat would later recall that when my good pal 'Tiny' Wharton asked for his name he had replied, 'Pat, that's P-A-T,' at which point Wharton had apparently replied, 'Okay smart alec, can you spell ta-ta?'

A few days later, Pat Quinn became the second Hibs player to be ordered off in successive games when both he and Davie Sneddon of Raith Rovers were involved in a brawl that would not have disgraced a lightweight boxing contest. Sneddon had taken exception to being fouled by the Hibs player directly in front of the Easter Road tunnel and the subsequent 'bout' was level on points until the referee stepped in to end the contest by sending both players off. Pat Stanton who appeared to be relishing his new responsibility in midfield had given us a first half lead, a further two goals by Peter Marinello his first ever for the first team eventually giving us a convincing 3-0 victory. Once again the newspapers were comparing Marinello favourably with the great Gordon Smith as he 'glided past defences with ease while scoring goals as easy as Smith used to do,', but I didn't feel that they were doing the youngsters any favours at such an early stage in his career.

Peter however was only one of a handful of bright young prospects making the breakthrough into the game around that time. At Hibs we also had John Blackley who was then being described as one of the most promising talents in the game. Partick Thistle had Jimmy Bone who was featuring alongside another promising youngster in Arthur Duncan – I wonder whatever happened to him? – John Duncan at Dundee, Tommy Craig at Eddie Turnbull's Aberdeen, George Connolly at Celtic and Arthur Mann at Hearts, so at that time the future of the game north of the border looked assured.

In the first derby of the season a Pat Stanton strike gave us a first half lead at Easter Road, before three second half goals by a Willie Hamilton inspired Gorgie side gave Hearts what in the end was a thoroughly deserved, although possibly surprise, 3-1 victory. The *Pink News* that evening perhaps summed it up best when it described the Hibs forward line as a 'group of highly talented players who all perform as individuals, and that this had allowed the Hearts defence to mark them out of the game'.

Yet another defeat, this time at Starks Park meant that we were still sitting pointless at the wrong end of the table. Pat Stanton missed the game through suspension after his earlier sending off against St Johnstone, and midway through the first half Colin Stein who could be a fiery individual, became the third Hibs player to see red that season when he was overheard swearing by an over fussy referee. Interviewed after the game a still visibly upset Bob Shankly was stated that the dismissals were mainly because his players were the victims of persistent fouling, and probably because we were not playing well our frustrations had come to the surface. Whether indeed that was the case, the defeat in Kirkcaldy had hardly inspired confidence before our midweek trip to Yugoslavia to face Olympia of Ljubljana in the first round of the Fairs Cup.

Before the game could take place however, a surprise invasion of Czechoslovakia by Russian troops had destabilised the political climate in much of central Europe, and immediately put our game with Olympia in doubt. It had originally been decided that a completely new seeded draw should take place, but as neither Britain nor Yugoslavia were likely to be drawn into the conflict, both ourselves and our Scottish counterparts Rangers, who had been drawn against the Serbian side FK Vojvodina, were excluded from a partly revised draw and the games went ahead as planned. The only slight inconvenience as far as Hibs were concerned was the withdrawal of the Czechoslovakian referee who was replaced by an official from Austria. It would be the 100th appearance of a Scottish side in the Fairs Cup, and Hibs 20th in all European competitions.

The Bežigrad Stadium in Ljubljana was fairly unusual. Apart from a tiny structure on stilts at one end of the ground that housed the directors, press and the changing rooms, the entire stadium was completely bare of cover of any kind, the large running track around the perimeter of the pitch doing little to create an atmosphere favourable for good football.

With Stanton directing operations from midfield, it didn't take us long to find the measure of our opponents. According to one newspaper ,we proceeded to give 'a performance that the entire country could be proud of', our 3-0 victory Hibs' first away win in Europe since defeating Belenenses in 1962. Now, barring a complete shock at Easter Road, the first leg result surely meant that the tie was already as good as over. Midway through the first half I had blasted home a Pat Quinn free kick to open the scoring, Colin Stein adding another almost straight from the kick off. We heard later that our part time opponents were reputed to be on a bonus of £50 a man to win the tie, which would have been an incredible sum to them at the time, but a third goal by Peter Marinello late in the game from what appeared to be an almost impossible angle almost on the bye-line, surely meant all hopes of their bonus money going up in smoke before their very eyes.

At the airport waiting for our flight home, the *Evening News* reporter Stewart Brown, who as usual had accompanied the team, bumped into the Fiorentina manager Bruno Pesalo after their victory against Dynamo Zagreb the previous evening. Pesalo had been in charge of Napoli during our 5-0 victory the previous season. With his current side also looking likely to qualify for the next round, Brown had asked if he fancied meeting Hibs in the next round. At that Pesalo is alleged to have replied curtly – 'No thank you. Once was enough!'

In the return at Easter Road the last thing we expected from our opponents after their performance in Yugoslavia was a kicking match, but although it required two penalties by Joe Davis to secure our 2-1 victory we were never at any point in any real danger of going out of the competition. In front of a disappointingly poor crowd of well under 12,000, Olympia briefly shocked us when they took the lead in the fourth minute. Since the first game they had put together a decent run of results and we found them to be a far better side to the one we had faced at the Bežigrad stadium. For a while they were much the better team, but we gradually managed to claw ourselves back into the game and it was only then that we saw a different side to our opponents. With a rugged and at times ruthless, determination to hold on to their lead, they began to hack and kick at anything that moved, particularly myself, Peter Cormack and Peter Marinello, and in the end this probably cost them the game. Midway through the second half we were awarded a penalty after a defender had handled in the box, a decision that was hotly disputed by our opponents. Again the game was held up for several minutes before order was finally restored, Joe Davis eventually doing the needful from the spot. The goal would only be the catalyst for even more mayhem and once again the game was disrupted for several minutes as the Olympia players surrounded the referee, pushing and jostling the official before he again managed to bring the situation under control. Minutes later Jovanovic was sent off after just the latest of savage fouls on Peter Marinello. The culprit was not off the pitch seconds before I was upended inside the box by right-back Kokot who had been kicking me all game leaving the referee with no option, but to award us our second penalty of the evening. This time there were no protests as by then our opponents knew that the tie was already as good as over.

In the quarter-final's of the league cup a fairly comfortable 6-2 aggregate victory over East Fife set up a mouth-watering tie with Dundee in the semi-finals, the game to take place at Tynecastle, hardly a happy hunting ground for Hibs as far as league cup semi-final's were concerned. Dundee, probably with some justification protested at the choice of venue complaining that playing the game in Edinburgh would give Hibs an unfair advantage as it would be almost a home fixture for us. The protest however fell on deaf ears and Tynecastle it was. At that time Dundee were a fairly decent side with some very good players, particularly the outstanding Stevie Murray who would soon join Aberdeen before a later move to Celtic, Jocky Scott, the Edinburgh born George Stewart and the former Hibs centre-half Jim Easton. Like Hibs Dundee had often struggled to find consistency, but on their day they could be a match for anybody.

In 90 minutes of blood and thunder football that must have been exciting to watch, Dundee got off to a flying start when the former Rangers player George McLean opened the scoring after only six minutes to silence the Hibs fans in the huge crowd. However no sooner had the enthusiastic cheering of the Dundee fans died down when Colin Stein drew us level and it was now all to play for. In the second half there were several near things at both ends although it has to be said that Dundee were possibly the better side and looked the likelier to score what would in all probability have been the winner. Midway through the half Bob Shankly took a huge gamble. In an effort to beef up our attack he substituted Pat Quinn for Jimmy O'Rourke only for Alan McGraw to be carried off injured a few minutes later leaving us to play the final 15 minutes of the game with only ten men. With just five minutes remaining and extra time looming, to huge cheers from the Hibs fans Alan McGraw reappeared wearing a huge bandage on his injured left knee. Barely able to run Alan had obviously been reintroduced only as nuisance value hoping to tie up a defender. The atmosphere inside the stadium was now absolutely electric, and with just seconds remaining we won a corner on our left. Jimmy O'Rourke sent over a dangerous in swinging cross that was twice blocked on the line, but somehow McGraw, who looked incapable of movement, lunged forward to force the ball over the line with his injured knee. There was no time left for Dundee to come back and we had qualified for what would be only the clubs second league cup final, and its first for 18 years.

After the game Willie Wilson and myself walked from Tynecastle to the Grosvenor Hotel at Haymarket. We had all been on £50 a man to reach the final and we entered the bar to find only a handful of people inside. To the probable bemusement of the other customers, big-hearted Willie shouted in true western style – or as western as a guy from Wallyford could sound, 'The drinks are on me.' I'm not sure if he would have been as generous if the place had been packed, but it was still a great gesture. Willie was yet another great lad, but as the only son he was the most spoiled person I had ever known. I would often call for him at his house in Wallyford before going out on the town, to find his mother, two sisters and sometimes even his dad, running around after him as he was getting ready to go out. I used to say to his mother that she was spoiling him, but she just would reply: 'Och son, I bet you get spoiled like that at home!'

The win against Dundee had set up the daunting task of facing Celtic in the cup final. A week before the game was due to take place a Peter Cormack goal at Easter Road was enough to give us the points in a drab game against Kilmarnock in front of a very poor crowd of around 6,000 which for a side that had just reached a national cup final was extremely disappointing to say the least. We had now lost only once in our last nine games and it was felt that we were perhaps meeting Celtic at just the right time. A few days later, Colin Stein, who had won his first full Scotland cap against Denmark the previous midweek, learned that he had been suspended for ten days after his earlier indiscretion at Starks Park and would now miss the cup final. Hibs obviously, were far from happy at the timing of the ban. A similar situation had arisen the previous season when the authorities had allowed the suspended Jimmy Johnstone to play in Celtic's World Championship matches against Racing Club of Buenos Aires. I believe that Hibs did consider appealing the ban, but reluctantly decided to accept the verdict.

At that time Colin Stein was such a hugely influential figure for us that he would have been a massive loss in the cup final, but as it would turn out it we needn't have worried. A couple of days before the final, we were at our usual big match hideaway at Gullane when we were notified that there had been a serious fire in the main stand at Hampden that had destroyed both dressing rooms, offices, a restaurant and well over 2,000 seats, and in the circumstances it had been decided to cancel the game until a later date. Little did he know it then, but Colin had already played his last game for Hibs in the victory against Kilmarnock the previous Saturday, his last goal for the club, the equaliser in the victory against Dundee at Tynecastle a few weeks earlier. It was well known that Colin had been unsettled at Easter Road for some time. He was now involved in the international set up and mixing with some of the best players in the country, and as mentioned earlier it was a situation that often led to a player becoming unsettled after discovering just what could be earned elsewhere, particularly in England. At least two transfer requests had already been rejected out of hand by Bob Shankly, but on the very morning that it was announced that John Madsen would be returning to the club after his self-imposed exile, we were all disappointed to learn that Hibs had accepted a £90,000 offer from Everton for Stein. At that time it would have been the biggest transfer fee ever paid for a Scottish player, dwarfing the previous record £65,000 that Rangers had paid Dunfermline for Alex Ferguson just over a year before. It is now well known that Colin had asked for time to consider what was thought to be a more than generous offer. It was generally accepted that he would eventually sign for the English club, so it was a huge surprise to discover the following morning that he had decided to sign for Rangers who had now agreed to pay Hibs £100,000. As could well be expected Everton were absolutely furious, accusing Rangers of tapping the player overnight, but nothing could be done, and Stein himself would later confess that joining Rangers had been a boyhood dream come true. The deal would make him Scotland's first ever £100,000 player which was also a record transfer between Scottish clubs. Alex Ferguson had been offered to Hibs as part of the deal, but after he turned down the chance of a move to Easter Road the transaction went ahead on a cash only basis and against the wishes of a furious Bob Shankly, who had deliberately taken no part in the negotiations.

Shankly's views at losing his top players was well known. He had earlier walked out of Dens Park after several of his star men had been sold against his wishes, and it only became common knowledge some time later that he had actually resigned over the Stein deal, but had been persuaded to reconsider, a decision according to him that he would come to regret and I don't think that things were ever the same for him at Easter Road. Shankly was a member of the old school and known to value loyalty highly, but even so I was surprised to be called into to his office one day not long after to be handed a brown envelope containing a considerable amount of money. I was then the longest serving player at the club and apart from the temporary fit of pique after I had been dropped against Rangers, I had never asked for a transfer. It turned out that the payment was the managers way of rewarding this loyalty and I believe that several of the other long serving players also received the payment.

The following week Ian Wilkinson made his first team debut at right half in a 3-0 defeat at Love Street, one of only four appearances he would make during his time at Easter Road. Alan McGraw replaced Colin Stein in the middle of the forward line, but was not the answer as we surrendered meekly to a St Mirren side who at that time, perhaps surprisingly, were the only undefeated side in Britain.

Worse was to follow seven days later, when we travelled through to face Rangers and our former team mate Colin Stein at Ibrox. Colin had got his Rangers career off to a dream start the previous Saturday by scoring a hat trick on his debut at Arbroath and for him things were about get even better. After Stein's transfer our immediate priority had been the signing of another recognised goal scorer and Shankly had wasted no time in approaching Jock Stein at Celtic to secure the services of Joe McBride, and what a bargain he would turn out to be. Unfortunately that afternoon at Ibrox we came up against a Rangers side in a clinical goal hungry mood and were completely demoralised, Colin Stein scoring yet another hat trick in an emphatic 6-1 victory. Five behind at the time, our consolation goal was scored by Joe McBride on his Hibs debut when he beat goalkeeper Norrie Martin from close range. Not only was it Joe's first goal in Hibs colours, perhaps surprisingly it had also been his first ever against Rangers.

The much travelled McBride was then nearing the veteran stage of his career, but he had been a prolific finisher during his time with Kilmarnock, Luton, Partick Thistle, and Motherwell, with only a lean spell at Wolves, where he had failed to settle after his £12,500 move from Kilmarnock. At Fir Park he had been the top marksman in three consecutive seasons, form that had attracted the attention of a host of clubs including Celtic. Consequently in 1965 he became manager Jock Stein's first signing–for a fee of £22,000, ending his first season at Parkhead as joint top goal scorer in the country, level with Alex Ferguson of Rangers. During Celtic's historic European Cup winning season McBride had scored a remarkable 35 goals in all games before Christmas including the four against Hibs in their 5-3 victory at Easter Road. Another four against Clyde had brought his tally to 15 in ten league cup games as Celtic progressed all the way to the final, where they would eventually defeat Rangers, their first success in the competition for nine years. Unfortunately a bad knee injury picked up against Aberdeen had forced him to miss the rest of the season including Celtic's historic win in Lisbon. Now fully fit again he had struggled to re-establish himself in the first team at Parkhead and jumped at the chance to resurrect his career at Easter Road.

Joe was probably past his sell by date when he arrived at Easter Road, but he was still some player. At five foot eight he was not all that tall for a striker, but was very good in the air. He could also hold the ball, but knew his limitations. Don't ask him to run about daft, but he was lethal in the penalty area as he would soon prove with ten goals in his first six games for Hibs including four in our 5-0 home win against Morton, and I don't think I have ever seen anyone strike a dead ball with such power. A very clever player, unlike many strikers, Joe would always give you the ball if you were in a much better position, and I found him to be an absolute delight to play alongside. Capped twice at full level for Scotland with another four appearances for the Inter League side, he was perhaps a better goal scorer than Colin Stein although not nearly as mobile. Joe hadn't been at Easter Road very long when he gave me a huge compliment when telling me that he hadn't realised just how good I really was until playing alongside me.

McBride soon proved that his goal at Ibrox was no fluke by scoring all three in our 3-1 home victory against Locomotiv Leipzig in the Fairs Cup a few days later. It was the first ever hat trick by a Hibs player in a competitive European game and made him an instant favourite with the fans. All our goals had been scored in the first half playing towards the 'Dunbar' end of the ground. Now kicking down the famous slope in the second half against a side that hadn't really given us any problems and also with the advantage of a strong wind behind us, the fans sat back expecting a second half goal rush only to be disappointed. Centre-forward Naumann gave the visitors a glimmer of hope for the second leg when he pulled one back 20 minutes from the end. Not long after, Alex Scott, who had been on the receiving end of some harsh treatment from full-back Geissner all evening was sent off after striking out after he had been fouled one time too often. Many of Geissner's fouls had gone unpunished by a weak referee, sadly a common occurrence in European games, but even with the ten men we managed to hold on to our lead quite comfortably until the final whistle.

Joe McBride went one better on the Saturday when he scored four in a totally one sided 5-0 victory against Morton, Pat Quinn getting the other. In the Morton side that day was a 21-year-old Joe Harper who had just returned from a fairly unproductive spell with second division Huddersfield and George McNeil who had recently joined the Cappielow side on a free transfer from Hibs.

Heartened by our impressive win on the Saturday we made our way to Turnhouse Airport for the return leg against Locomotiv Leipzig in good spirits, unaware that the trip would turn out to be an absolute nightmare. At that time the chartering of a private plane was not yet common practice for football clubs in Scotland and our journey to Leipzig would eventually entail three separate flights and a long bus journey, something that would be considered laughable nowadays. The trip to London proved uneventful enough as did the connection to Amsterdam, but while in Holland the weather closed in, and after an eight hour delay at the airport it was decided that we should remain overnight in the Dutch capital. Some of the players did manage a trip to the nearby famous red light district, but only as sightseers I hasten to add. In the morning we managed to catch an early flight to Berlin where it was decided to continue the rest of the journey to Leipzig by coach. At that time the Berlin Wall was still in place and as we passed through Checkpoint Charlie, police armed with machine pistols boarded the coach to check our passports, a situation that many of us found quite threatening. East Germany was like being in another world, a completely different way of life, and certainly unlike anything we had been used to back home. Everywhere we went there were long lines of people. At first we thought they were queuing up for some event or other, until it dawned on us that with the huge food shortages in the eastern sector, they were waiting patiently in line to be served in the poorly stocked shops and it made you appreciate life back in Scotland all the more. However after a long and exhausting 125 mile coach journey, we eventually arrived at our destination a full 24 hours after leaving Edinburgh.

If they were to have any hopes of winning the tie Locomotiv would need an early goal, but luckily for us when the goal did arrive it was scored by Colin Grant. Only-three minutes had been played when I sent over a cross from the left. The ball was fumbled by goalkeeper Friese, but fortunately dropped straight at the feet of Grant who wasted no time in prodding it into the empty net from close range and already we were as good as in the next round. The early goal completely knocked the heart out of our opponents, destroying any faint hopes they might have harboured of a comeback. Using the ruse Hibs had employed against Roma several years before, Colin Grant had switched jerseys with danger man Joe McBride in an attempt to confuse our opponents. The deception was so successful that we really should have scored several more goals, but the solitary strike was enough to see us safely through to the next round. It would be Joe McBride's first game since joining the club that he had failed to figure on the score sheet. Some praise however has to be given to a Locomotiv side who never totally gave up and did their best to pierce a confident Hibs rearguard, but their efforts came to nothing against a defence that was once again magnificently marshalled by the brilliant Pat Stanton.

The journey back to Scotland was no better than the incoming trip. After a 5 am rise we made the long trek by coach back to Berlin and Checkpoint Charlie where we were eventually able to catch a flight to London. Incredibly in London we were to face even more delays including a change of aircraft due to engine trouble, finally arriving back in Edinburgh just before midnight.

It was around this time that Willie Hunter, another player who was to become a great pal, was signed from the American side Detroit Cougars. Born only a few hundred yards from Easter Road and a keen Hibs supporter as a boy, Willie had been an integral part of the great Motherwell 'Ancell Babes' side of the late '50s and early '60s when lining up alongside the likes of Pat Quinn, Bert McCann and Ian St John, while winning several Scotland caps at full and league level. Although he was not yet 30 his career had been hampered by an arm injury that had kept him out of the game for some time and he was possibly already past his best. A tricky and versatile individual who could play equally well at inside-forward or on either wing, at Motherwell Willie had never stopped running, covering every blade of grass while spraying his intelligent passes all over the field. To my mind however, at Easter Road Willie didn't attempt to change his style of play which had relied on his earlier pace and I always felt that he could well have extended his career by playing further back, where he could have used his considerable football brain and experience to far greater effect. As it would turn out he would not play many games for Hibs during his three seasons with the club before ending his career with the South African side Cape Town City after a short spell with Hellenic. Willie was a forthright character who could also be very opinionated at times, but nevertheless we became great pals and remain so to this very day. Later he would be appointed assistant to his former team mate Ian St John at Portsmouth, before entering management himself with Queen of the South and latterly with the Highland League side Inverness Caley.

At Easter Road a few weeks later Joe McBride would come up against his former colleagues for the first time since leaving Parkhead, but it would turn out to be an afternoon that Joe and the rest of us would want to forget. Tommy Gemmell had opened the scoring for the visitors from the penalty spot early in the game, only for goal scorer supreme McBride to equalise with a header midway through the half. In what turned out to be another hotly contested affair we were giving Celtic as good as we got and that remained the score at the interval. In a real blood and thunder encounter all the real drama was reserved for the final few minutes of the game. With just 15 minutes remaining Joe Davis gave us what many thought was a deserved lead from the penalty spot before the roof caved in. Up until then we had been more than holding our own, but all that changed when master tactician Jock Stein switched the rugged John Hughes from the wing into the middle. Alan Cousin, who was perhaps too much of a football player, found big 'Yogi' too hot to handle and Hughes scored four times inside the final ten minutes to give the visitors what was a highly embarrassing although to my mind a somewhat flattering 5-2 victory.

A few days later we managed to shrug of the frustration of the Celtic defeat with a brilliant performance at Pittodrie that completely floored Aberdeen. Once again there were goals galore, but this time most of them were scored by Hibs. With John Madsen now reinstated at the heart of the defence, his first game back after his self-imposed exile during the summer, an Aberdeen side that had blossomed under the guidance of manager Eddie Turnbull during the past few years, reaching the final of the Scottish Cup the previous season only to lose to Celtic, found us far too hot to handle. Man-of-the-match Peter Cormack scored his first hat trick for the club since his three against Airdrie four years earlier and was a particular thorn in Aberdeen's side throughout.

5-1 ahead at the interval, the result had never been in any doubt and not only the final 6-2 score, but the all-round sterling performance had given us confidence for the forthcoming Fairs Cup tie against the German side Hamburg.

At that time Hamburg, who were then the oldest club in the country, lay second in the German league. They could boast of no fewer than six full internationals including centre-forward Uve Seeler who had played in the 1966 World Cup Final against England at Wembley and centre-half Willie Shultz, and were unbeaten at home in Europe. Shultz however was still on international duty in South America and would miss the game, but even without his presence in midfield we knew that we were in for a tough time.

A heavy fall of snow in Hamburg the previous day had for a time threatened the cancellation of the match. On the day of the game there was still a slight covering of snow on the ground, but this particular threat had receded to be replaced by an equally serious concern because of a thick blanket of fog that had hung over the city all day. Fortunately, although visibility still remained at a premium, by late afternoon the fog had lifted sufficiently to allow the game to go ahead.

Both sides were led on to the pitch by a piper from the Royal Scots who were stationed nearby, the players appearing as ghostly silhouettes in the mist as they took to a heavily frost bound pitch. Once the game started Hamburg took the lead after only five minutes when Honig blasted past Thomson Allan from just inside the penalty area and things were already beginning to look ominous. Slowly, but surely however, superbly marshalled by both Pat Stanton and Alan Cousin at the back, we started to reassert ourselves and eventually managed to hold a very good Hamburg side to that single goal.

At times it had been backs to the wall, our chances few and far between, although Peter Cormack had missed a great opportunity from close range late in the game. In the very last minute Joe McBride seemed certain to score, but slipped just as he was about to strike and the danger was cleared. With the return game at Easter Road still to come the narrow defeat had given us a great chance to proceed into the next round. The super confident Bob Shankly had been so sure that in his post-match interview he had boldly stated that, 'Hibs will win in Edinburgh.'

On New Year's Day Chris Shevlane made his first return to Tynecastle since leaving almost two years before. In a completely one sided first half we totally dominated proceedings and only some incredible misses by Joe McBride had prevented us from taking a commanding lead. After the break however it was a different story as Hearts stepped up a gear to take command of the game. The future Hibs player Alan Gordon had proved a handful for John Madsen throughout, but only Alan could explain just how he managed to miss an open goal from three yards in the closing minutes when it seemed far easier to score. The chance was probably much easier than several that had uncharacteristically been passed up earlier by Joe McBride and the no score draw was probably a fair result although Hearts would have been disappointed in failing to win a New Year's Day game at Tynecastle for the first time since 1955.

The narrow defeat in Hamburg had created a great interest in the return leg in Edinburgh and there were almost 30,000 inside Easter Road when the sides took the field. Encouraged by an expectant and extremely vocal home support, we were by far the better side in the first half and had two seemingly good goals chalked off by the Swedish referee, who I have to say had an absolute shocker. Hamburg had set their stall out early determined to hold on to their slender lead from the first leg, and all our forwards, particularly Peter Cormack who had obviously been singled out as the main danger man, were subjected to 90 minutes of close attention that often bordered on sheer brutality. Hamburg's cause had been helped by an extremely lax referee who, as well as failing to notice that the German goalkeeper was wearing a green jersey that clashed with the green of Hibs, had regularly failed to punish the offenders. With just a few minutes of the first half remaining Cormack was scythed down inside the box. This time there could be no option, but to award a penalty only for the normally reliable Joe Davis to shoot past the post with the goalkeeper stranded.

Midway inside the second half we eventually managed to score the goal that our play had deserved when who else, but Joe McBride placed a shot past goalkeeper Ozcan after a melee in the goalmouth, and it was now game on. With just ten minutes remaining we were going all out for the winner when centre-forward Seeler intercepted a misplaced cross field pass from Bobby Duncan to shoot past Thomson Allan from 15 yards to give Hamburg the overall lead only for Joe McBride to score his second of the evening in the final minute to level the aggregate scores. Because of the new away goals ruling almost everyone in the crowd was aware that the game was already over, except it seemed the inept official who was preparing to play another 30 minutes' extra time until informed otherwise by one of his linesman. Hamburg were through to the next round only on the recent ruling that goals would count double in the event of a draw and the visitors left the field to a background of jeers from a Hibs crowd that had been less than enamoured by their constant fouling, time wasting and at times brutal play. Peter Cormack in particular had done well to withstand the 90 minutes of ferocious tackling. After the game he was almost unable to walk, his legs a mass of black and blue, and later had to be driven home by Tom McNiven.

A 3-0 defeat at Broomfield on the Saturday, a game we had dominated until gradually slipping into what one newspaper described as a performance of mediocrity, was followed by an early Scottish Cup exit after a dismal display at Ibrox when a Colin Stein goal midway through the second half was enough to put paid to our Scottish Cup aspirations for yet another year. The return of John Madsen however had provided a strength and resilience at the back that had been lacking for some time. At Ibrox Madsen had been head and shoulders above his green shirted colleagues and at times only he had stood between us and a rampant Rangers scoring more than the solitary goal. In the final minutes of the game we were perhaps fortunate to escape conceding a penalty when the ball ran up the entire length of Madsen's arm, but to the disbelief of almost everyone in the 50,000 crowd, referee Bobby Davidson waved away Rangers appeals for a spot kick, an extremely rare occurrence at Ibrox.

In midweek I went down with a virus missing the home game against St Mirren on the Saturday, my place in the side taken by the 19-year-old Alex Cropley who was making his first team debut. John Blackley was making a return to action after a five month absence since breaking a toe in a game against Airdrie, his return once again allowing us to move the influential Pat Stanton into a more productive midfield role. Midway through the first half young Cropley almost made it a dream start to his professional career when he rounded the goalkeeper only to hit the post with his shot.

You could see immediately that Alex was going to be a player, but it was obvious to me that he was never going make a wide man. While he could certainly beat a man, to my mind he was not direct enough to be an out and out winger. It had been always been drummed into me that once you had beaten your man you were to get to the corner flag as quickly as you possibly could, and I would like to think that I was as fast with the ball at my feet as I was without it. However Alex was like Superman coming out of the phone box. Similar to myself he was very quiet in the dressing room, almost painfully shy, but once on the field he was like a man possessed. A very brainy player and a great passer of the ball, for his size he was also incredibly tenacious in the tackle. Five foot nothing and weighing around eight stone soaking wet, he tackled like a heavyweight. Even at that early age he had very few weaknesses and you could see immediately that he was destined for much bigger things. He had a terrific shot, mostly with his left foot – you always had a chance if you were left sided – and for a man his size he was extremely good in the air. When we lined up together he would always give me plenty of the ball, and I only wish that we could have played together longer. I had recovered from the virus the following week and it was back to the reserves for Alex, but you could tell even this early that he could not be held back for long.

At Cappielow the following week a second half hat trick by a player the press were already describing a 'pocket dynamo' had cancelled out our 2-1 interval lead. The diminutive Joe Harper had made his debut for Morton as a 16-year-old a few years earlier scoring 29 goals from just 30 appearances during the 1966–67 campaign before a move to English Second Division side Huddersfield the following season. For some reason his time at Leeds Road had not been particularly successful and he soon returned to Morton where he immediately started banging in the goals again. Lining up in direct opposition to the in form John Madsen that afternoon he had given the experienced former Morton defender the run around, Harper's goals earning his side a deserved 4-3 victory, their first league win for almost two months. He would soon be on the move again, first to Aberdeen then Everton, and it is now history that he would later sign for Eddie Turnbull at Hibs.

Although Turnbull would never admit it, to my mind the signing of Harper would be one of the very few serious mistakes he would make during his tenure at Easter Road. According to Eddie, Harper had usually been the top goal scorer wherever he had played and he had been brought to Easter Road with the intention of playing him up front alongside Jimmy O'Rourke and Alan Gordon, but it had never quite worked out. The popular pairing of O'Rourke and Gordon had formed a particularly prolific goalscoring partnership, but both would soon be on their way out of Easter Road to make way for Harper, and for the love of me I could never quite work out why Turnbull had broken up such a successful side so early.

Meanwhile the defeat at Cappielow would be just the start of a ten game run without a win of any kind that saw us drop from eighth place to 12th, our worst league position since the near relegation in 1963. We now trailed champions elect Celtic by an enormous 23 points and were seemingly well out of the running for qualification for the Fairs Cup, and the frustrated Hibs fans were beginning to call for Bob Shankly's head. A 3-0 defeat at Tannadice just days before meeting an in form Celtic in the postponed League Cup final, did nothing for our confidence as we slumped to what was possibly our worst performance of the season. Even worse, two of the goals that day had been scored by my good pal and former Hibs player Davie Hogg. His first a tremendous 30 yard drive after a pass from the former Hearts player Alan Gordon who had been signed only that morning, the other in the very last minute of the game. Kenny Cameron made amends for an earlier miss from the penalty spot, when scoring United's other goal, and in truth it could well have been more as we slumped to 13th in the table or sixth bottom.

A League Cup rehearsal at Parkhead a couple of weeks before the rearranged final had seen us achieve what in the circumstances had been a commendable 1-1 draw. Moreover, it was a game we could well have won. In the first half, Celtic had been well on top, but after the interval it was a vastly different story as we took a grip in midfield. With only 20 minutes remaining Joe McBride equalised an earlier goal by Willie Wallace and from then until the end it was all Hibs. During this time Celtic had been extremely fortunate to survive, as twice shots had been cleared off the line and our performance had clearly shaken the home side. Since his signing Joe McBride had been such a big player for us, but unfortunately as he had already played in the competition with Celtic earlier in the season, he was cup tied and would miss the cup final. He would prove to be an enormous loss.

For some reason, instead of spending the few days leading up to the final at our usual big game hideaway at Gullane which had been Hibs base for many years, we spent the days leading up to the game at Turnberry on the Ayrshire coast. Although we had drawn the league game at Parkhead a few weeks earlier, the bookies had made Celtic red hot favourites to lift the cup, and with just two points from our previous half dozen games we were not nearly as optimistic as we had been at the time of the original fixture when we had been playing well.

On a bright sunny afternoon the teams took the field at the national stadium to the rousing cheers from over 75,000 exuberant fans, a great number of them having made their way through from Edinburgh. Inside the opening few minutes I passed up an easy chance to give us the lead when I attempted to smash the ball into the net from close range with power instead of placing the shot and the opportunity was missed when the ball flew harmlessly past the post.

From then until half time we gave a fairly good account of ourselves while managing to create another couple of decent chances, but we had been guilty of conceding goals far too easily and Celtic's 3-0 interval lead had already given us a mountain to climb. At that time Celtic were a very talented, powerful and confident side and once they managed to get on top we just couldn't get near them. Jimmy Johnstone in particular was in irresistible form that afternoon, and at times we were left chasing shadows.

After the interval we again conceded goals far too easily and with just minutes remaining we trailed 6-0, although to be fair I felt that the score-line flattered Celtic somewhat. We finally managed to give the final result a slight semblance of respectability when we scored twice in the closing minutes, the first when Jimmy O'Rourke scored from close range, the other when I headed past the Celtic goalkeeper John Fallon from well inside the six yard box. It may sound ludicrous considering what was a more than convincing final result, but I felt that we could take some credit from the game. We had put up a fighting performance, but in truth Celtic had just been far too good for us. The final result admittedly had been a major embarrassment, and we aware that we had let down not only ourselves, but the huge number of Hibs fans who had made their way to Hampden for the game. We were a team packed full of talent, however it is one thing playing pretty football and turning on the style, but the game is all about scoring goals and you have to take your chances when they come. As we left the field after collecting our losers medals, I just wanted to hide and as you would expect the mood in the dressing room was sombre, like a morgue, each one of us sitting in embarrassed silence. I can't remember now if the club had anything laid on for us back in Edinburgh, but I just couldn't face going back on the team coach. I caught a lift back in a friend's car and spent a pretty miserable evening back in the city. I have to confess though that later that night I ended up with some friends in a well-known hostelry in the West End, something I wouldn't recommended today after a particularly embarrassing defeat in a cup final, although I do believe that it happened fairly recently after a game against Hearts, many of the dejected supporters later complaining to the club.

It would turn out to be my only cup final in top class football. Perhaps the last word should be left to a despondent and bitterly despondent Bob Shankly in his post-match interview:

> I thought that the team had done quite well, creating far more chances that they had managed in the last six games, but the truth is that there were some good players out there who didn't give as much as expected of them.

The papers quite rightly gave us pelters, most of them of the opinion that it was time for Hibs to get tough, and how could anyone argue with that.

HIBS: ALLAN, SHEVLANE AND DAVIS, STANTON MADSEN AND BLACKLEY,
MARINELLO, QUINN, CORMACK, O'ROURKE AND STEVENSON.
SUB: HUNTER.
SCORERS: O'ROURKE AND STEVENSON.

CELTIC: FALLON, CRAIG AND GEMMELL, MURDOCH, MCNEILL AND
BROGAN, JOHNSTONE, WALLACE, CHALMERS, AULD AND LENNOX.
SUB: CLARK.
SCORERS: LENNOX (3) WALLACE AULD-CRAIG.

REFEREE: W SYME (GLASGOW)

We had spent the past few weeks languishing in the bottom half of the table and after the humiliation at Hampden we badly needed a victory against Dundee the following week. However after yet another home defeat the fans were not slow in showing their displeasure towards the manager and the cries of 'Shankly must go' were clearly audible around the ground.

What had been yet another dreadfully disappointing season finally limped out with a 4-1 win against St Johnstone at Easter Road watched by a very poor crowd. The Leicester City manager, Matt Gillies, was in the directors' box believed to have been watching Peter Cormack who scored twice, but the win couldn't prevent us from ending the season in 12th place, our lowest finish since the near relegation in 1963.

Willie Wilson and Thomson Allan had been sharing the goalkeeping duties throughout most of the campaign. Neither had been exuding confidence although it couldn't have been all that easy playing behind an often porous defence, and only weeks before the end of the season the former Hearts goalkeeper Gordon Marshall had been signed from Nottingham Forest. Gordon had made his first team debut for Hearts at the tender age of 17, and had been part of the great Hearts side of the late 1950s and early 1960s, but with the emergence of the promising Jim Cruickshank in 1963 he had been allowed to join the English second division side Newcastle United. Transferred to Nottingham Forest earlier in the season for a fee around £18,000, he had played only a handful of games at the City Ground before jumping at the chance to return to Edinburgh with Hibs. I had played against Gordon several times over the years while he was at Hearts and had actually played on the same side as him in the full scale practice match at Saughton Enclosure when I was training with the Gorgie side as a youngster. Born in Surrey, he had been recommended for the Scotland under-23 side while at Hearts until it was pointed out that he had actually been born south of the border, and had since made several appearances for the England under-23s along with Hibs Joe Baker. Now at almost 30 he was still a very good goalkeeper although-possibly a bit slower than at his peak, but he was still big and brave as most goalkeepers are. A good all round pro, the vastly experienced Marshall was also very good in dealing with the youngsters.

Our position in the lower half of the table, a massive 23 points behind champions Celtic and five behind eighth placed Hearts, was not nearly good enough for such a talented side and a far cry from third place the previous season. Although we had reached a national cup final, several indifferent performances had been our undoing and had cost us a place in the following seasons Fairs Cup.

Perhaps unsurprisingly Joe McBride had ended the season as top marksman with 24 goals in all games, 19 in the league, and six more than Colin Stein had managed to score for Rangers since his £100,000 move to Ibrox.

CHAPTER ELEVEN

Willie MacFarlane
and a Scottish League Cap
1969–70

DURING THE SUMMER Jim Black had been signed from Airdrie and was joined on the first day of the new season by John Brownlie and Willie McEwan. Both the latter had had been training with Hibs in the evenings and farmed out to Pumpherston Juniors on a Saturday, but had now joined the full time ranks at Easter Road.

In yet another change of venue we were now training at the Civil Service playing fields at Silverknowes which was a world away from the public park at Seafield. Although much further from Easter Road, Silverknowes was quiet, had very good facilities and a couple of full size pitches well away from the gaze of the general public although we continued to change back at Easter Road. At that time Willie Hunter had a tape player in his car which was a fairly modern innovation at that time and myself, Willie Wilson and Hunter would make our way to Silverknowes each day singing all the current hits of the day at the top of our voices. It was not the only change at the club around that time. Previously, all the players had received a chitty for lunch at the Osborne Hotel at the West End, but the club had now decided to employ its own cook and we would have all our meals at the ground.

The cook Mrs McDougal also came from Bonnyrigg and she always made sure that not only did I have plenty on my plate, but also that I had second helpings, particularly my favourite, Steak Casserole, the crawler in me replying in my best patronising voice: 'That's lovely Mrs Mac'. The joker Johnny Hamilton used to wind her up by constantly complaining 'Oh no, not Beef Casserole again'. But Mrs Mac, who didn't suffer fools gladly, would simply reply unsmilingly – 'Take it or leave it.'

At that time Easter Road was a happy camp. We had nicknames for everyone. Jimmy O'Rourke had christened trainer Jimmy Stevenson

Doberman after the character from the Sergeant Bilko series on TV that was very popular at the time while Bobby Duncan thought that Jimmy himself looked like a Chinaman. One day on our way to a game, Bobby spotted a Chinaman walking down Easter Road and quipped, 'Look, there Jimmy', accompanied by roars of laughter from the rest of us, Jimmy taking it in good heart and joining in. They were great days that I thought would go on for ever.

Jimmy O'Rourke was a very humorous guy. The serious injury received earlier in his career had greatly disrupted his progress at Easter Road and after a bright start he would be in and out the first team for several years, usually only covering in case of injury and never quite managing to hold down a regular place. He now seemed to have forced himself back into the picture and although he was perhaps not the greatest of footballers, and I'm sure that Jimmy himself would be the first to admit it, his never say die attitude and hundred per cent commitment, allied to the fact that he was a self-confessed Hibs fanatic, made him a huge favourite with the fans.

A pre-season friendly against the newly promoted Coventry City at Highfield Road had been arranged after heavy snow had forced the cancellation of an earlier game between the sides the previous season, and it allowed us to catch up with our former team mates Gerry Baker and Neil Martin who had recently joined the 'Sky Blues' from Sunderland. By this time Pat Stanton had taken over the role of club captain from Joe Davis, and with new signing Jim Black performing well on his debut, a fairly drab encounter that looked certain to end goalless, spluttered into life with just a few minutes remaining. After beating three men on a solo run I had managed to slip the ball past the advancing Coventry goalkeeper Bill Glazier from close range and this looked like being the winner until Neil Martin equalised with a trademark header in the very last seconds of the game. It turned out to be another of those games when everything I tried seemed to come off and I had had the beating of the highly rated Coventry defender Mick Coop all afternoon. Over the piece I thought the whole team had played well and interviewed after game Neil Martin was of the opinion that, 'Hibs would have opened a lot of eyes down here. They were the better side in the second half and I thought that Eric Stevenson who took his goal well, was their best forward.' A compliment that was really appreciated.

Later Willie Wilson and I spent the night with Neil and his wife, missing the team coach for the journey back to Edinburgh that had left immediately after the game, and if I remember rightly we were later fined by Bob Shankly. That evening Neil had told me that he was always on at the Coventry manager Noel Cantwell to sign me, only to be told that he

193

had already had me watched and that I was no better than what he already had at his disposal. Evidently after the game Neil didn't miss Cantwell, reminding the manager that I had 'just taken one of his favourite players to the cleaners.' Although Neil's compliment had been welcome I was extremely happy at Easter Road and had absolutely no desire to move, either to England or anywhere else.

Willie Wilson and I had made it back from Coventry in plenty of time to face Newcastle in yet another friendly at Easter Road on the Saturday. Newcastle had the former Aberdeen player Jimmy Smith in their line-up while we would be without the suspended trio of Peter Marinello, John Blackley and Peter Cormack who would all miss the start of the new campaign after their indiscretions the previous season. Midway through the first half of what would turn out to be a rather uninspired no-score draw, we were to suffer another huge blow when Joe McBride was stretchered off after a clumsy challenge. Although the former Hibs player John McNamee was on the bench, this time there would be no place for my pal Jim Scott and he would soon be on his way to Crystal Palace.

Both Jim Black and 19-year-old Johnny Hamilton made their competitive debuts in our opening league cup game against Clyde that was won easily enough, even without four of our regular first team players, both the newcomers acquitting themselves well. Hamilton had been signed from Cumbernauld Juniors a couple of seasons before, after impressing manager Bob Shankly, who had actually gone to watch another player, and already big things were expected of him. A member of the Glasgow contingent that motored through from the west each day, you could normally hear 'Hammy' well before you saw him. Highly regarded as a youngster, after breaking through into the first team he would usually line up in midfield alongside Pat Stanton and myself and the boy could certainly play a bit. Sadly Johnny would be yet another who passed away during the writing of this book.

Since taking over at Pittodrie a few years earlier, Eddie Turnbull had put together an extremely talented squad of players and they had been tipped as our main challengers for qualification to the later stages of the league cup. Runners up to Celtic in the final of the Scottish Cup two years before, at the end of the coming season they would go all the way and win the trophy and were a side not to be taken lightly. Even without Jimmy Smith after his recent move to Newcastle, the teenage prodigy Tommy Craig who had become the first £100,000 teenager when he joined Sheffield Wednesday not long before and the hugely influential Martin Buchan who had recently been injured in a car crash they would still prove extremely difficult to overcome. One big plus point as far as I was concerned was that this time I wouldn't have to face right-back Jim Whyte who was out of favour and would soon be on his way to Kilmarnock. As I have already mentioned I had always found 'Chalkie' to be a particularly difficult opponent, particularly at Pittodrie where Eddie Turnbull would have him playing almost as an out and out winger on the overlap. This meant I had to do far more back tracking than I was normally used to and I was pleased to see his name missing from the team lines. We started the game well, but the dropped point in a 2-2 draw despite twice coming back from behind, now meant that if we were to have any chance of progressing into the latter stages of the completion it was imperative that we overcome Aberdeen by at least two clear goals in Edinburgh in midweek. Unfortunately, at Easter Road we would come up against an extremely confident and well organised Aberdeen defence, who dealt comfortably with all that we threw at them and in the end they deserved the no score draw that allowed them to progress into the later stages of the competition. Encouraged by a huge home support, we had tried hard enough, but even with the fit again Joe McBride we lacked penetration, leaving the Hibs fans to lament the disappearance of the high scoring side of previous seasons.

However things were about to get much worse. As Turnbull's Aberdeen were coasting to an easy 6-0 home win against over Clyde in the opening game of the new league season, we were crashing to a humiliating 3-0 defeat at Somerset Park against the newly promoted Ayr United. Worse still, our opponents had been forced to play almost an hour with ten men after the future Rangers player Quintin Young had been sent off after aiming a kick at Colin Grant. Our supporters had paid good money in making their way to Ayr, and it must have been excruciating having to witness a display that for some reason had been completely lacking in spirit, dedication and determination. According to one newspaper the following day:

> The Easter Road side have skill aplenty, but players like Marinello, Cormack and Stevenson must give more than pretty football. If it was a court of law Hibs would have been found guilty of desertion while under fire.

Shankly himself would later claim that it had been the worst performance by far of any Hibs side during his time at the club. Exaggerated or not, our performance, or lack of it, had been a huge embarrassment to the players and we were all determined to make amends against St Mirren at Easter Road on the Wednesday.

Just before the St Mirren game we learned that left-back Joe Davis had been dropped, bringing to an end his incredible run of 273 consecutive games in all competitions. Although he had been unsettled at Easter Road for some time and had already asked for a move the news still came as something of a shock. He was replaced in the side by Mervyn Jones who was making his debut. Before the kick off there had been some talk that manager Bob Shankly would be resigning after the game which we all took to be just paper talk, but immediately after the final whistle the rumours were confirmed with the announcement that the manager would be standing down with immediate effect, a move that apparently also took the board of directors completely by surprise.

The two goals by Peter Cormack that had given us a 2-0 victory that in a small way had made up for the previous Saturday's embarrassment were almost forgotten in the furore that followed Shankly's shock announcement. When asked, the manager had refused to give a reason for his resignation, but it was well known in some quarters that he had been unhappy at Easter Road for some time. Only now did it become common knowledge that he had offered his resignation immediately after the transfer of Colin Stein, but had been persuaded to stay, a decision that he now admitted to be a mistake.

Shankly was a man of principle who had already walked out on Falkirk and Dundee over their policy of selling their best players, and during his time at Easter Road the club had already sold Willie Hamilton, John McNamee, Neil Martin, Jim Scott and Colin Stein, all against the managers wishes, and at that time Peter Cormack was being closely watched by a host of top English clubs. Possibly feeling that it would be hopeless in trying to keep the unsettled Cormack who had made it abundantly clear that he wanted a move, this had probably played no small part in his decision to resign. Apparently there had been no pressure put on him to go. It had been his decision and his decision alone, but the manager would later admit that all the fun had gone out of the game. An idealist, who believed in pure football, he had no time for what he called the cloggers, and believed that attractive football with entertainment was as important, perhaps more so, than results and was what the public wanted.

As usual the newspapers were full of potential candidates for the Easter Road hot seat, the front runners former players Eddie Turnbull at Aberdeen and Willie Ormond who was then manager of St Johnstone. Meanwhile, with the help of some of the senior players Tom McNiven would pick the team. John Blackley had earlier stated a preference to play in midfield instead of his usual position as sweeper and was given the opportunity in our next game, a 5-1 victory over Partick Thistle. However it only took John about 20 minutes or so to realise that midfield was not for him and he soon reverted back to what was undoubtedly his best position in the middle of the back four.

During the few weeks without a manager we were undefeated with wins against Partick Thistle and Raith Rovers and gained a slight degree of satisfaction after the embarrassing defeat in the League Cup Final when we defeated Celtic 2-1 in Glasgow. The home side had taken the lead midway through the first half after Jimmy Johnstone had intercepted a poor pass from Jones to score, and at that stage Celtic were well on top scorning a couple of good chances to increase their lead. We just kept plugging away however and could well have equalised just before half time when after a mazy run by Marinello that had left several defenders floundering in his wake, his inch perfect cross was met by the inrushing Cormack who headed past goalkeeper John Fallon only to see the ball to come crashing back off the crossbar before being cleared to safety. In the second half Celtic still had the majority of the play, but we were dangerous on the break and it was no surprise when Hamilton finished the best move of the game when he shot past Fallon from close range. With just seven minutes remaining a magnificent 25 yard drive by Pat Stanton gave us the points and an extremely satisfying victory.

One morning not that long after Shankly's resignation, Willie Hunter and I were having a coffee in town before training, when who should walk past, but Willie MacFarlane, who was then the manager of Stirling Albion. Willie knew MacFarlane slightly and joked that maybe he would get the Easter Road job. We both just laughed, but on arriving at Easter Road we were astonished to see MacFarlane's car in the car park. It later turned out that he was being interviewed for the job and would soon be unveiled as Hibs sixth manager since the war. His appointment had come as a huge surprise to everyone, including apparently the man himself, who had felt that either Willie Ormond or Eddie Turnbull had been the front runners for the job. A former miner, MacFarlane had signed for Hibs from Tranent Juniors in 1949 and had played in the home leg against the German side Rot Weiss of Essen in 1955 when Hibs had become the first ever British side to take part in the inaugural European Cup competition. That season the rugged defender had been something of a first team regular, but had never quite managed to hold down a first team place, and after almost ten years at Easter Road he joined Raith Rovers in 1958. After his playing days were over he had managed the East of Scotland sides Gala Fairydean, Eyemouth and Hawick Royal Albert before taking over as boss of second division Stirling Albion in 1967.

MacFarlane's Hibs career second time round got off to a flying start with satisfying victory over Hearts at Tynecastle in his first game, a result that saw us topping the table level on points with Dunfermline. At that particular time I was playing some of the best football of my career from midfield. The manager however wanted me to revert back to the left wing until Joe McBride stepped in to suggest that I was playing out of my skin, so maybe it would be better if we leave things as they were in the meantime. I remained in midfield against the Hearts and the decision was justified. Even though I say it myself, I had one of my best ever games as we cruised to a comfortable 2-0 win against our city rivals. I had one of those games when it seemed as if I could do no wrong, beating men with ease to set up several gilt edged chances. Peter Cormack opened the scoring in the first half when he headed home a McBride cross. McBride himself scored our second on the hour mark with a goal that appeared to everyone inside the ground to be well offside, including the player himself, who hesitated briefly waiting for a whistle that didn't come, before crashing the ball past Cruickshank in the Hearts goal. It was a satisfying and well deserved victory and one that was particularly enjoyed by the supporters, but typical of MacFarlane, if there was any glory to be had he wanted it all to himself and took the full brunt of the praise for the win in the following days newspapers.

The new manager had organised an after match party back at Easter Road with all the staff ordered to attend. I had a previous engagement that had been arranged some time before, but was told that if I didn't turn up I would be fined a week's wages. I was usually first out of the bath after games and duly arrived at the ground early to find that apart from the barman only MacFarlane and myself were in the place, the atmosphere rather surreal as we both sat there in total silence. Soon the rest of the guys began to arrive and after a few drinks I was about to leave, when MacFarlane demanded to know where I was going. I replied frostily that 'I had been ordered to turn up and I had. Now I was going'. Even this early I already had the distinct impression that for some reason or other I wasn't going to be one of the managers' favourites. Perhaps he felt that I got too much attention from the fans, but from that moment on there was never any danger that were going to get along. It wasn't just me. Later that evening Peter Marinello who had been booked that afternoon, our first yellow card of the season, was taken aside to be told that he was being fined for his earlier indiscretion and this obviously this didn't go down too well with Peter. As far as I was concerned MacFarlane was too brash, often well over the top, and everything was always about him and what he was going to do.

To give the manager his due at that time we were playing well and a

Pat Stanton goal against Morton at Easter Road was our sixth straight victory in a row, the first time the feat had been achieved by a Hibs side since season 1954–55 and things were about to get even better.

It was also around this time that an article appeared in the *Pink News* suggesting that I was 'the best uncapped winger in Scotland and that I had all the potential in the world', comments that were obviously very welcome. The article went as far as to suggest that on recent form, 'Hibs had found a new Eric Stevenson who was ready to fight for the international honours that have so far eluded him.'

The following week at Ibrox, all the forwards decided to swop jerseys to confuse the Rangers defence and it worked a treat. I immediately grabbed the number nine shirt in tribute to my great idol Lawrie Reilly and lined up at centre-forward. The Rangers manager Davie White had taken the opportunity to give young Brian Heron his debut at full-back after just two games for the reserves, but unfortunately it would prove to be a baptism of fire for the youngster who had no answer to the pace of Peter Marinello who scored twice, and in all honesty could well have scored five or six. It was all too easy for me to put the ball through for Peter to run on to, and poor Brian just didn't know which way to turn. Joe McBride scored our other goal, but it was Peter's game. That afternoon he was in absolutely unbeatable form as he repeatedly tore the Rangers defence to ribbons and I'm positive that it was this game that eventually got him his move to Arsenal. At times I almost felt sorry for Herron who didn't quite know what had hit him as Peter gave him the run-around for the entire 90 minutes. I don't know if it had anything to do with it, but Brian would soon be on his way to Motherwell. At the final whistle Rangers, who had fielded a strong side with the likes of Baxter, Greig, Johansen, Wilson and Stein, were booed from the field by the few supporters that had bothered to stay until the end, but I don't think that they had fully appreciated just what their favourites had been up against that afternoon. The Hibs side at Ibrox was:

MARSHALL, SHEVLANE AND JONES, BLACKLEY BLACK AND STANTON,
MARINELLO HAMILTON MCBRIDE CORMACK AND STEVENSON. SUB:
MADSEN.

Trainer Jimmy Stevenson had joined the club along with Jock Stein in 1964, but had now decided to return to Dunfermline leaving the way clear for former player John Fraser to step up as first team coach. Not long before leaving to join Stenhousemuir as player-coach a couple of seasons before, John had had been promised by Bob Shankly, that if ever the situation arose he would bring him back to Easter Road and for the past few months he had been training the youngsters in the evenings. He would prove a valuable and popular addition to the first team back room staff.

We had now gone seven games without defeat, were sitting top of the table and even this early in the season were being tipped as potential champions. A friendly had been arranged against Aston Villa and we were brim full of confidence before facing the then second division side at Easter Road. Unfortunately, with a young Alex Cropley making one of his few first team starts at outside-left we were murdered 4-1.

It had been obvious for some time that MacFarlane had been keen to ring the changes, but with things going so well he had naturally decided against it. Now the heavy defeat by Villa had given him the perfect opportunity. Out went the settled side that had done so well in previous weeks, with O'Rourke, Grant, Hunter, Graham and McEwan all among the many positional changes made.

We were still sitting on top of the table a few weeks later when we made our way to-Muirton to face a St Johnstone side that had lost only narrowly to Celtic in the League Cup final the previous Saturday. A goal by the talented John Connolly in the second half gave the home side both points and Willie MacFarlane his first defeat as Hibs manager. The absence of the injured Cormack and Marinello had been a serious handicap, but could not in any way be used as an excuse against a spirited and confident Saints side that included my immediate opponent John Lambie. John was a rugged competitor who had recently joined the Perth club after almost ten seasons with Falkirk and would later join Hibs as a coach under Eddie Turnbull. In a late dramatic fight back we twice had shots cleared off the line by left-back Coburn as we tried desperately to take something from the game although to no avail and the loss of the points was enough to knock us from the top of the table.

With Joe Davis now at Carlisle, Mervyn Jones and Willie McEwan had both been sharing the left-back position, but in midweek Willie MacFarlane returned to his former club Stirling Albion to sign Erich Schaedler. A couple of previous bids for the player had been rejected by Albion who were keen to hold on to the defender, but an increased offer of just under £7,000 for a player who would go on to become a legendary figure at Easter Road eventually proved successful. Erich was another really nice lad, but at that time he was still very raw, although you could see immediately that he had something. Very pacy, he was good on the recovery and extremely strong in the tackle although at that time he was prone to commit himself by diving in. He was also not the greatest of passers although he did get better, particularly under Eddie Turnbull, who got the best out of him. Erich was mad, but in a nice way. Unbelievably brave, he tackled with his entire body and would go right through you. I remember Jim Black saying to me one day at training that if you were ever in a fight with Erich, the boy would die before you beat him and you would probably have to kill him. The son of a captured German prisoner of war who later settled in Peebles, Erich was a bit of a loner with not a lot of humour and after a game he would usually go his own way rarely mixing socially with the rest of us. He made his debut for the first team when he replaced Willie McEwan at half time in a friendly against the Polish side Gornik at Easter Road just before Christmas. It didn't take him long to demonstrate what would soon become his legendary ferocious tackling skills when Peter Cormack was carried off injured after both men had gone for the same ball. Considering that Gornik were wearing white jerseys that evening and Hibs their distinctive green, the incident perhaps demonstrated Erich's determination to succeed.

The manager was far from finished in the transfer market and a few days later, Johnny Graham was bought from Second Division Falkirk for a fee of around £28,000. Johnny was another who was to become a great friend. More reserved than most of the other Glasgow lads he was fairly quiet, although at times he could be a bit cocky, but was a gem of a bloke and I would occasionally stay at his home, even after I stopped playing. He was a good player who could be quite tricky and usually played off the front men. Although he was not the greatest of workers, he could beat a man and could certainly score goals as he proved on his debut against Airdrie just hours after signing for the club. That evening he was the star of the show and an immediate hit with the supporters when he scored twice in our 3-1 home victory, our other goal scored by Peter Cormack.

Our good run continued by taking 11 points from the following six games, the only drawback a 1-1 draw with Motherwell at Easter Road. The game was played on a light covering of snow which may well have been responsible for goalkeeper Peter McCloy allowing a weak header from Johnny Graham to slither through his legs before trundling over the line. To give Motherwell their due, justice was done when left half Oglethorpe scored with a magnificent drive seven minutes from time to earn his side a share of the points

We were now well out in front of the table, four points ahead of our nearest challengers Rangers although Celtic still had two games in hand, and were now being strongly tipped in many quarters to win the league. Under the new manager we had won seven of the ten games played with two drawn, results that were enough for Willie MacFarlane to be voted manager of the month. Ludicrously, but perhaps predictably knowing the Scottish authorities, MacFarlane had been allowed to receive the trophy, but somewhat absurdly the league rules at that time prevented him from collecting the £50 prize money that went with the award.

I myself, I was about to receive what was without doubt the greatest honour of my career when I was selected along with my Easter Road team mates Pat Stanton and Peter Cormack for the Scottish League side to play the Irish League at Ibrox. I can't remember now if I was notified by letter or by the club, but for days it had been in all the papers that I could be in the running for possible selection, and I was absolutely delighted when the rumours were finally confirmed. My uncle Tam ran me through to Glasgow and at the pre-match reception captain John Greig rose to officially welcome me into the side by introducing me to the other players as 'someone that they all knew well, and that the honour had been long overdue,' a gesture that was well appreciated. I can't remember too much about the game itself except that I was played wide on the left and consequently didn't see that much of the ball. After the game, a 5-2 win for Scotland, there was no reception or anything like that and in the dressing room I was simply handed a plaque to commemorate the occasion before we made our separate way home. Later I would receive a medal in the post. The framed jersey still has pride of place in my home hanging on the wall alongside the one from my earlier appearance for the Scottish Juvenile Select. My grandson Owen now has the inter-league medal and my other grandson, Aidan, who lives in Australia, has my league cup runners-up medal.

At one time, particularly during the immediate post-war years the inter-league matches had been well capable of attracting big crowds, mainly games against the Football League, but after several one sided contests against both the Irish League and the League of Ireland, the fans interest had waned somewhat and that evening at Ibrox there were only around 4,000 inside the huge stadium.

The first ever Scottish inter-league game had taken place against England at Bolton as far back as 1892, the game ending in a 2-2 draw. Scotland's first game against the Irish League took place in Dublin the following year, a 3-2 victory for the home side, one of only five victories managed by Ireland in the 87-year history of the fixture. Unlike full internationals that in Scotland were normally all played at the national stadium, the inter league games were usually spread throughout various venues around the country. The Scottish team that evening at Ibrox was:

DONALDSON (DUNDEE) CLUNIE (HEARTS) AND GREIG (RANGERS),
THOMSON (HEARTS) SWEENEY (MORTON) AND STANTON (HIBS),
CORMACK (HIBS) HARPER (ABERDEEN) INGRAM (AYR UNITED) ROBB

(ABERDEEN) AND STEVENSON (HIBS).
SUBSTITUTE: W JOHNSTON (RANGERS).
GOAL SCORERS: HARPER (2) CORMACK, ROBB AND JOHNSTON.

Willie MacFarlane's manager off the month award was to prove the kiss of death for us and we could only manage to pick up three points from the following half dozen games. The results had also been more than a bit embarrassing after the bold MacFarlane had publicly stated a short while before that the title was now in our own hands and only seven wins away. A 1-0 defeat at Dens Park had been followed by a no score draw against Hearts in the New Year derby at Easter Road. In a nasty bruising and ill-tempered match that was marred throughout by crowd trouble, Peter Cormack was sent off after kicking full-back Oliver as he lay on the ground. At first Peter refused to go until escorted from the field by trainer John Fraser as fighting broke out between rival fans in the covered enclosure behind the goals, the off field incidents probably influenced by the events taking place on the pitch. For most of the game Hearts had been by far the better side, hitting the post twice with another effort cleared from the line, and we were fortunate to escape with a share of the points. Peter Marinello watched from the stand as rumours spread throughout the ground that he was about to sign for Arsenal.

Later that evening the rumours were confirmed when we learned that Peter had indeed agreed to join the Highbury club for a fee believed to be around £90,000, which I suppose was a fantastic bit of business for a player who had only been at the club a little over three seasons and had cost them nothing. Peter could certainly play a bit. He was good with the ball at his feet, but his main weapon was his electric pace. Relatively inexperienced, and at that time with limited football intelligence, I always felt that the move to Highbury probably came a bit too soon for him. He was a wee gem of a lad though who mixed well and was popular with everyone. He was fairly quiet, but could also be quite funny, sometimes unconsciously. On the Monday morning after training I was in the dressing room when Peter came downstairs after meeting the representatives from Arsenal. I got on well with the lad and he told me that they wanted to sign him, but that he didn't have a clue regarding terms. I made a few suggestions and I believe that he later got what he asked for.

Willie MacFarlane wasted no time in securing a replacement for Peter, when he travelled through to Glasgow to sign Arthur Duncan from Partick Thistle for a club record fee of around £35,000. I had played against Arthur a few times, and while he was a very good player, like Marinello, his main asset was his incredible pace. At that time he was being closely watched by Manchester City who were believed to be about to make an offer for him, but City's loss was Hibs gain and he would eventually go on to make a record number of appearances for the club and earn himself a testimonial game against Newcastle United. Very direct and with a fantastic never say die attitude, Arthur himself would admit that he was never the best football player, but he could beat a man, had an eye for a goal and was well capable of scoring from 30 yards. With his seemingly unlimited energy he would chase back when dispossessed, never gave up, and became an instant hit with the fans who thought he could do no wrong. He couldn't really beat a man with football, but unlike myself who was comfortable with the ball at my feet, Arthur's main strength was his amazing pace in his forays down the wing. It didn't take him long to become one of the boys and he would join us for a drink after the game, although he wouldn't stay long, leaving the rest of us to face the long night that lay ahead. He was comfortable either at centre or on either wing, but with Joe McBride playing well in the middle of the attack it was obvious to me that he had been signed to play on the left wing in direct competition to myself for a regular first team place.

At training in midweek rumours were going around that Arthur would be taking my place on the left wing for the game against Celtic on the Saturday, and in a full scale practice match when the first team took on the reserves, the whispers seemed to be confirmed when I was selected for the reserves. Needless to say, I was far from happy and was in a bit of a huff until I was approached by Joe McBride who told me not to worry saying, 'Look who you are up against,' – a reference to Erich Schaedler who would be in direct opposition – 'go and show MacFarlane just how good you are.' As I have already mentioned, at that time Erich was still very raw and had not yet really acclimatised himself to the pace of the game at the higher level, and I have to admit that I tore him up, taking him on both inside and out, and I am sorry to say that I took a little bit of the mickey out of him, a performance that must have impressed the watching manager.

On the Saturday I was surprised, but obviously delighted to be selected in my usual place at outside-left against Celtic with Arthur making his debut on the right. As usual the manager took all the credit, telling anyone who would listen that he had only played me against Erich in the practice game in midweek because he knew that the former Stirling Albion player would be up against the elusive Jimmy Johnstone on the Saturday and had only wanted him to experience difficulties similar to what he was likely to face then.

Such was the demand to see the game against league leaders Celtic that the kick off had to be delayed several minutes to allow the huge crowd, estimated to be well over 45,000, time to enter the ground. Arthur got his Easter Road career off to a great start by scoring on his debut when he shot past goalkeeper Evan Williams through a ruck of players midway through the second half. It would be only one of many he would score for the club and equalised an earlier strike by Billy McNeil header from a free kick. There were several near things at either end until John Hughes secured the points for the visitors a few minutes before the end to hand us our first league defeat of the season.

For a second successive season we would make a first round exit from the Scottish Cup at Ibrox. Joe McBride was on the bench after picking up a slight injury against Celtic the previous week, but even with Joe in the side that afternoon Rangers would still have been far too good for us and we were second best throughout the entire 90 minutes. Hibs were still a big draw, particularly in Glasgow, and once again the kick off had to be delayed with well over 60,000 inside the stadium. Rangers had opened the scoring not long after the start, but the familiar 'easy-easy' chants from the huge home support were silenced a few minutes later when a fumble by goalkeeper Neef allowed Johnny Graham to put us level from a free kick. However an absolutely stunning strike by Andy Penman from all of 35 yards and another goal by Alex McDonald, his second of the game a few minutes after half time, put the tie well beyond us. I was replaced late on by substitute McBride. Once again I was far from happy and handed in a transfer request immediately after the game.

I was very content at Easter Road. Life was good, I was playing well and with a great group of lads, but my demand for a move was purely because of my strained relationship with a manager who was probably the worst that I had ever played under. As far as I personally was concerned Willie MacFarlane was totally lacking tactically and was not a great motivator. Maybe he impressed some of the younger lads, but he certainly didn't fool me or the more experienced players. Although I knew that our dislike was mutual, my decision to ask for a transfer was more than just a clash of personalities. It was about football, and for me he hadn't a clue. He was always wanting to change things, even when it was going well, and I sometimes found it difficult to hold my tongue.

When news of my transfer request reached the newspapers, I was contacted by several of the sports reporters including Alex Cameron of the *Daily Record*. I explained that in my opinion the manager hadn't a clue and that I had had enough. The next day at training a furious MacFarlane pulled me aside demanding to know why I had spoken to the newspapers. I replied that I hadn't said anything that I hadn't said to his face. At that I thought he was going to explode as he screamed, 'You will never f***ing play for Hibs again.'

Since taking over from Bob Shankly four months before, MacFarlane had known nothing but relative success, but by now our great start had begun to falter. Although we were lying third in the table we were a huge nine points behind leaders Celtic and to all intents and purposes already out of the championship race.

After the fall out with the manager, I sat out the following half dozen games, not even featuring for the reserves and also missed out on possible selection for the Scottish League side that had faced the Football League in Coventry. During my enforced absence the first team had managed only the one win although three games had ended level including a 3-3 draw with St Mirren that saw Cormack sent off for the second time in three games after lashing out in frustration at the future Hibs player Ian Munro after a rash tackle. Peter had been extremely unhappy at Easter Road for some time, posting several transfer requests that had all been turned down as the club tried desperately to keep one of its best players. In recent years he had watched as a succession of players made the move to England and the much better money on offer south of the border, and had become even more unsettled since the transfer of Peter Marinello to Arsenal. Now despite all their efforts it was evident that it would prove very difficult if not impossible for the club to keep hold of him.

One Saturday morning a few weeks later, I was sitting in the house when I received a telegram ordering me to report to Waverley Station immediately for Hibs' trip to Aberdeen and I was on the left wing as we harried and harassed the cup semi-finalists to their first defeat in almost two months – so much for being told that I would never play for the club again! It was backs to the wall as we had to survive a brisk opening spell of pressure when the home side were well on top, but all this changed when Joe McBride opened the scoring from the penalty spot after I had been sent sprawling in the box. The foul had brought to an abrupt end a mazy run when I had taken on and beaten several men. As if to prove a point to the manager it had been another of those games when I simply could do no wrong and from then on we were simply far too good for the Dons, a second goal scored by the unsettled Peter Cormack who had been made captain for the day making sure of the points.

Back in our hotel after the game, several of the players including Joe McBride, Willie Hunter, Johnny Graham and myself were enjoying a few drinks in our room, when who should walk in but the bold MacFarlane who complimented us on our great victory. Spotting the beer on the table he was about to take a bottle when I piped up: 'Leave them alone. You're not welcome here.' Joe McBride tried to calm me down, but I insisted. 'No. He is not getting one.' At that, the red-faced MacFarlane stormed from the room, but I think I had made my point.

At the end of the month Peter Cormack was sold to Nottingham Forest clearly against the wishes of the manager who to give him his due, had done everything in his power to keep the player at Easter Road. Peter had been desperate to leave Easter Road for some time and was always going to go. A clearly disappointed MacFarlane refused to even discuss the situation after the deal was completed and Cormack became the twelfth Hibs player to be transferred for a big fee since I had joined the club at the beginning of the decade. Ironically, Bob Shankly who had resigned at Easter Road on a point of principle after the sale of Colin Stein, was then the Scottish scout for Forest and no doubt would have had some input in the transfer going ahead.

Just a few days later both Alex Cropley and myself formed a left wing partnership for the very first time in a competitive fixture against Kilmarnock at Easter Road, Alex scoring one of the goals in our 2-1 victory. It had been clear from the very start that Cropley was going to be some player and he showed it that evening with an overall display of fast, confident and aggressive ball control, the newspapers the following morning suggesting that he would soon make the fans forget all about Peter Cormack.

Games against the Hearts were always keenly contested affairs, but that year's East of Scotland Final at Easter Road would later be described by the experienced Joe McBride as possibly the dirtiest game that he had taken part in, and that included several encounters between Celtic and Rangers. According to Joe this was the toughest ever. 'I have been with seven clubs and have never even attempted to kick a player deliberately, but I came close it last night against Hearts. These games are becoming so bitter that it's scarcely believable.'

The behaviour, by the players, of both sides it has to be said, later cast doubt on future of the fixture. In an ugly bad tempered game McBride scored from the penalty spot after Alex Cropley had been brought down inside the box in the later stages of the game, but by that time Hearts were already two goals ahead. Such was the intensity of the occasion however that it was a surprise that only three players had been yellow carded, none sent off, only one penalty awarded and just the one player needing to leave the field for treatment. I myself had been on the receiving end of several what were described as merciless tackles, but later earned the appreciation of the crowd by appealing against a booking for Alan Sneddon after he had committed what I felt to be a comparatively innocuous foul.

A few weeks later I was part of a Hibs side that had taken part in the relative calm of the Uniroyal Five-Side tournament, an indoor competition organised by the Leith Round Table. After defeating Stirling Albion 5-1 and Hearts 9-1 in the opening rounds, a strong Hibs side of Thomson Allan, Alex Cropley, Mervyn Jones, Willie Hunter, young Brian Ness and myself easily defeated Dunfermline 5-0 in the final. These competitions were always fun to play in, were enjoyed by the fans, and could often be a welcome distraction from the pressures of the competitive season.

Some time before, Peter Marinello and myself had been invited to represent Hibs in a national head-tennis tournament in Manchester. On the train down we bumped in to Willie Johnston and my old pal Willie Henderson who would be representing Rangers and were invited to join them in the buffet car for a few refreshments. There was money at stake for the winners of a competition that I felt we were more than capable of winning, so being the consummate professional I refused their generous offer, although I have to admit that I found it very tempting. The first thing Peter wanted to do on arriving at our hotel was find a bookie, but I insisted that we take the whole thing seriously and rest. The rules of the competition allowed only two touches of the ball, but in our first game against Manchester City, Peter being Peter couldn't resist demonstrating his intricate ball skills and took more touches than was allowed despite several reminders from myself. The upshot was that we lost both our games 15-1, as I believe did the pair from Rangers. The competition however gave me the opportunity to meet up again with Joe Baker who was representing Nottingham Forest and we had a few drinks in the bar afterwards, deeply regretting that I hadn't taken advantage of Willie Henderson's invitation on the journey down.

In the penultimate game of the season at Easter Road we came up against an Aberdeen side that had defeated Celtic 3-1 in the Scottish Cup final only a few days before at Hampden. Before the kick off we lined up as a guard of honour to welcome the cup winning 'Dons' on to the park and I was particularly pleased for my former colleague Eddie Turnbull, who had finally led Aberdeen to success after losing in the final three years before. Aberdeen went ahead against the run of play, but their lead lasted just five minutes when I smashed an unsavable drive past Bobby Clark to level things. We were in rampant mood in the second half and a lesser team would have buckled, but with just 15 minutes remaining the former Rangers player Jim Forrest ran through to slam a Robb pass past Thomson Allan to deny Hibs a winning end to our home league programme.

A season that had again promised so much only to deliver nothing but disappointment, particularly for the loyal Hibs fans who had been entitled to expect so much better, finally came to an end at East End Park. In the absence of the injured Pat Stanton, MacFarlane gave a first start to the 17-year-old John Brownlie who lined up alongside Jim Black in the middle of a back four. The 2-1 victory allowed us to finish the season in third place, a massive 13 points behind champions Celtic who were winning the title for the fifth consecutive season, but six ahead of our nearest rivals Hearts, to again qualify for the Fairs Cup.

For some time now the supporters had been accusing the Easter Road board of lacking ambition, merely content just to amble along, but the manager had missed the Dunfermline game on a so called spying mission in an attempt to bring in another big money signing. During the season just ended several promising youngsters in Cropley, McEwan, Schaedler, Hamilton and now Brownlie, who would all stand the club in good stead in the near future, had either made their debut or consolidated their challenge for a first team place. Gordon Marshall and centre-half Jim Black had each missed only one game all season because of injury, while I myself had missed nine, mainly because of the recent bust up with the manager. The long serving Joe Davis who had joined English Second Division side Carlisle earlier in the season had made seven appearances in all games. It was no surprise however that goal scorer supreme Joe McBride had once again ended the campaign as our top marksman with 23 goals in all games, 11 ahead of the next best Cormack and far more than my disappointing tally of only one in the league, a 2-1 defeat by Aberdeen, and another in the pre-season friendly against Coventry.

At the end of the season captain Pat Stanton would be voted the Scottish Football Writers Player of the Year, well ahead of second placed Bertie Auld of Celtic. Pat had been the recipient of the inaugural Hibs Supporters Player of the Year award a couple of seasons before and the tribute by the football writers was merely a recognition of his remarkable consistency since making his debut just over six years before. It was fairly rare for the award to go to a non Old Firm player, but was hugely deserved. The popular Stanton had been a regular member of the Scotland set up for several years now, but would undoubtedly have won far more caps during this time had he played for either of the two big Glasgow clubs, and I was just one of several of his team mates that made their way to Glasgow to watch him collect the prestigious award.

CHAPTER TWELVE

The Ibrox Disaster, a Liverpool Fiasco and Dave Ewing

1970–71

ALTHOUGH I WAS still only 28, I had been at Easter Road for almost ten years and was then the longest serving player at the club. It was an age when my best years should still have been ahead of me, but although I couldn't know it at the time, it would turn out to be my last full season as a Hibs player.

The club had accepted an invitation to take part in a three game pre-season tour of Germany and Holland before the start of the 1970–71 campaign and we were joined on the trip by the former St Mirren centre-forward Jim Blair, who had been the target of the managers mystery trip at the end of the previous season. Jim was a nice big lad, but as far as I was concerned he fell far short of being Hibs class. A prolific scorer with St Mirren, I had played against him several times and always thought he looked decent, but with all due respect, although he should have benefited by full time training for the first time in his career, he didn't do much during his short time at Easter Road. He would soon return to Love Street where he would again start to score goals, so perhaps it was the system at Easter Road that didn't suit him.

With draws against a very good German side Schalke, the Dutch side Nijmegen and a comprehensive 3-0 defeat of Maastricht, I suppose the tour could be considered to have been a reasonable success. After each match there had been the usual post-match banquet which gave us the opportunity to mingle with the opposing players when we would discuss the various merits of the game. I must say though that I really had my eyes opened at the Dutch style of football, which was just beginning to make a real impact in Europe around that time, particularly with the rise to prominence of sides like Ajax, PSV Eindhoven and Feyenoord. The thing that impressed me most however was the amount of time their players spent on the ball. My game was to 'knock it past the defender and run, get to the byline and cross the ball', but in direct contrast the Dutch played a pass-and-go system that made it extremely difficult to get the ball from them.

These trips were always a great experience particularly for some of the younger lads who perhaps had not been abroad before. It was just like being on holiday, but being paid for it, and with plenty of free time on our hands we were allowed to roam freely

The one downside of the trip was the flight back to London which eventually turned into a nightmare and almost put me off flying for life. Unknown to everyone on board a tyre had burst on take-off. Some of us, including the pilot, had heard a dull thump, but didn't think too much about it. Obviously taking every precaution, the plane had been ordered to circle the observation tower at the airport to allow them to check for any potential damage, and at one point a small aircraft had even flown underneath us trying to get a better look. By this time we realised that something was wrong and we were all ordered to assume the emergency position. It was then that I noticed that even the stewardesses were crying which unnerved me even more. The entire procedure took almost an hour while the plane circled the airport burning up fuel before we were finally allowed to land well away from the terminal where the plane was immediately surrounded by fire appliances and ambulances. I was a terrible flyer who normally spent the entire journey with my eyes tightly shut, and I have been told that I could be heard shouting at the top of my voice: 'That's it – the next time I'm taking the bus.' We eventually managed to catch another flight to London, but believe me it was an experience that none of us would wish to go through again.

At that particular time Jimmy O'Rourke was still finding difficulty in establishing himself as a first team regular and had refused to re-sign for the new season, a decision that ultimately had cost him a place in the squad that had made its way to the continent. Jimmy had initially been offered to St Mirren as part of the Jim Blair deal, but he had not fancied the idea of part time football and turned the move down, although still retaining his desire for a move. Jimmy had always been a popular figure with the fans because of his wholehearted approach to the game, and a couple of years before had been voted the Hibs Supporters Association's Player of the Year, even although he had not been a regular in the side. At that time he was normally called upon only in the case of injury and had made just seven appearances the previous season. Highly rated as a youngster with a great future ahead of him, several serious injuries had severely hampered his progress at the club. He was also unlucky in that even when he did finally achieve full fitness there were so many really good forwards on the books at that time that it was difficult for him to force his way back into the first team. However, the situation was about to change in a way that he could never have imagined.

Once again, several newspapers were tipping us for big things in the season ahead and we were all raring to go. By now we were back training much nearer to home at Meadowbank stadium. Meadowbank had been completed in time for the 1970 Commonwealth games that had been held in Edinburgh. With the competition now over Hibs had been offered the use of the then brand new state of the art facilities that included a Tartan track and all weather pitch, and obviously jumped at the opportunity. The stadium's location also made it convenient for the traditional pre-season trek to the top of Arthur's Seat which had been endured by generations of Hibs players before us. Apart from Jim Blair, the only other newcomers at the club were several provisional signings from the minor ranks, but unfortunately none would make the breakthrough at Easter Road, although one, 16-year-old Willie Pettigrew would later make a name for himself with Motherwell, Dundee United, Hearts, Morton, Hamilton and Scotland.

In a change to our normal routine, there were no pre-season friendlies arranged for Easter Road. Near the end of the previous season Willie MacFarlane had visited London to watch Peter Marinello in action for Arsenal, and had returned claiming that he had arranged reciprocal home and away friendlies against the English First Division club. Perhaps unsurprisingly these games had failed to materialise and we kicked off the new season with an away game against St Johnstone in the league cup.

In a group that also consisted of Airdrie and for a second consecutive season, Eddie Turnbull's Aberdeen, the competition got off to a flyer with a 3-1 victory over Willie Ormond's Saints in Perth. A long delay caused by heavy build-up of traffic meant us arriving at the ground only 20 minutes before the kick-off, but fortunately the delay didn't appear to have had any adverse effect and Johnny Graham gave us the lead after only nine minutes. Our other goals were scored by Arthur Duncan and Joe McBride, and although Aitken pulled one back for the home side we managed to hold out quite comfortably till the end. In the second half, substitute John Brownlie took over from the injured Chris Shevlane and gave a display that suggested that Hibs had unearthed yet another diamond. Playing out wide, I was accustomed to receiving the ball first time from the full-back, be it Shevlane, Joe Davis or Bobby Duncan, but this young lad just kept flying past me up the wing, and indeed could well have been playing in my position as he overlapped the St Johnstone defence with ease to set up two of our goals. To say he had been immense would be an understatement, and I can remember telling Chris after the game, only half in jest, that he had better start looking for a long nail to hang his jersey on or find another club. You could see immediately that Brownlie was going to be something very special. Tall and gangly, he was a supremely confident lad and went past players for fun. Never the greatest of tacklers, he made up for it by his reading of the game and was very difficult to get past. I don't think that any of us had realised in training just how good John was, but we soon had our eyes opened.

Both ourselves and Aberdeen had been made equal favourites with the bookies to top the section and a 1-1 draw at Pittodrie meant that once again it would all come down to the final game at Easter Road, a win for either side guaranteeing automatic qualification for the later stages of the competition. I was now featuring mainly on the right wing with Arthur on the left, and I found out later that Eddie Turnbull had instructed the 'Dons' left-back George Murray that he was not to leave my side for a minute. Man marking was not Aberdeen's usual style, and apparently Murray had told Turnbull not to worry as he could handle me no bother while still playing his normal game. To cut a long story short we murdered them. 4-0 ahead at half time, qualification was already assured. In one of the best 45 minutes of my entire career I took poor George to the cleaners and although I say it myself, I was unstoppable that evening. Murray had just tried to carry on as normal which left me acres of space and I murdered him. Turnbull would tell me later that he gave the player a withering glare as he left the field at half time as if to say – I thought you could handle him. It had been our best display for some time and although the second half was a bit of an anti-climax, I could hardly breathe after the energy I had expended during the opening period. Although there had not been a failure in the side, I think it would only be fair to mention both Jim Black and Pat Stanton who had been particularly outstanding at the back in repulsing everything that Aberdeen could throw at us.

The following week I would score what would turn out to be the first of only two competitive goals I would score that season in a 1-0 victory at Dens Park, before facing our great rivals Hearts at Easter Road. Unfortunately it would turn out to be another typical derby, one of several drab goalless games between the sides around that time. Although both sides had applied effort in abundance, good football was at a premium and a share of the spoils was perhaps the right result. There were just seconds of the game remaining when I pulled up suddenly with a recurrence of my old groin trouble. It didn't seem all that serious at the time, but unfortunately once again it was to keep me out of the side for several months, missing amongst others the Fairs Cup games against both Malmo and Guimaraes.

With Alex Cropley making his European debut, our Fairs Cup campaign got off to a great start with an easy 6-0 victory over Malmo at Easter Road, Joe McBride scoring his second European hat trick in a Hibs jersey. Our other goals that evening were scored by Arthur Duncan who got two and Jim Blair, the final result ensuring that even with the second leg in Sweden still to come, that qualification for the next round was already a mere formality.

A couple of days later I picked up a newspaper to learn that chairman William Harrower who had only rarely been seen at the home games recently, had sold his shares to the 48 year-old self-made millionaire businessman and lifelong Hibs supporter Tom Hart. The former Hibs and Scotland goalkeeper Tommy Younger was already at the club as PR man, and he was immediately co-opted on to a new Hibs orientated board of directors along with another former goalkeeper Jimmy Kerr. They were joined on the committee by the eminent surgeon Sir John Bruce who assumed the role of chairman with Harrower remaining on the board as President. I had always got on well with Tom Hart who was great Hibby and had been a regular visitor to the Easter Road boardroom. Never a man to mince his words you always knew exactly where you stood with the forthright Hart. Tommy Younger I knew quite well from his days as owner of the Peacock Hotel in Newhaven. A player during the Famous Five era before his move to Liverpool in 1956 he was still a bit of a hero to the older fans. A big jovial character, he could be quite loud and gregarious, but was also very generous. In contrast I rarely had much to do with Jimmy Kerr who usually preferred to stay very much in the background. A very quiet and unassuming man, our contact was usually limited to just a polite hello in the passing.

I had been visiting the ground every day for treatment from Tom McNiven in the hope of making the return game against Malmo and was included in the party that made its way to Sweden. Unfortunately despite receiving treatment right up to the kick off the injury failed to respond in time, and I watched from the side-lines as the 18-year-old Kenny Davidson made not only his European debut for the club, but his first ever start for the first team. Davidson had been signed from Loanhead Mayflower only a few weeks before, making an immediate impact by scoring a hat trick against Cowdenbeath reserves in his very first game. Although he was just a slip of a lad he was an extremely tricky ball player with a great turn of speed. He could beat men for fun, and it seemed certain that a brilliant future lay ahead of him. Showing very little sign of nerves in his first European game Davidson had looked a real prospect and his wonderful ball control and acceleration that took him past defenders as if they were standing still seemed to confirm that Hibs had signed another star in the making. We all thought that Kenny was going to be something very special, but unfortunately a couple of serious injuries would severely hamper his progress at Easter Road. The long soul destroying recovery periods would eventually take a heavy toll, and failing to re-establish himself in the first team he would soon be on his way to Dunfermline where he would link up again with his former Easter Road colleague Joe McBride.

Another surprise inclusion in the Hibs side in Sweden had been full-back Bobby Duncan, who was making his first appearance of the season and only his second start since breaking his leg against Celtic just over two years before. It was probably even more of a surprise when Bobby opened the scoring just after the interval, his first goal since the famous wonder strike against Napoli a couple of years before, but nowhere nearly as spectacular. We managed to recover from a poor start to win 3-2 and it was only fitting that captain Pat Stanton, the best player on the park by a mile, should score the winner with just ten minutes of the game remaining. Willie McEwan got our other goal, his first ever for the first team.

Between both Malmo games Joe McBride had scored twice in an impressive 2-0 victory against his former side Celtic at Easter Road. Watched by the club's new owner Tom Hart, Joe's second from around 20 yards when he struck the ball first time on the turn was a real beauty that brought the house down.

At that time we were playing well and were desperately disappointed to exit the league cup, after losing 3-1 in the second leg of the quarter-final tie at Ibrox after a similar score-line in Edinburgh. At a wind lashed Easter Road Rangers had opened the scoring in the very first minute of the game and proved far too good for us on the night. In the return at Ibrox a couple of weeks later the home side again took advantage of an early goal and the game was as good as over although McBride missed a penalty that could have levelled the scores on the night, and who knows just what might have happened then.

By now Willie MacFarlane and I were barely managing to tolerate each other, but after lengthy discussions with the manager I was persuaded to withdraw my earlier transfer request and agreed to sign a new two year contract with a two year option. The deal would keep me at Hibs until I was 32 and suited me down to the ground, as apart from my feelings toward McFarlane I was extremely settled at Easter Road.

After an absence of several weeks I appeared to have recovered from the groin complaint and was champing at the bit to get back playing again. I had expected to make my return in the home game against Guimaraes in the Fairs Cup, but unfortunately broke down again in a reserve game against Motherwell a few days before. Although the groin injury itself had seemed to have cleared up, I had now pulled a muscle and once again it was back to the treatment table under the caring hands of Tom McNiven.

Against Guimaraes I was a frustrated spectator as I sat through an unimpressive 90 minutes at Easter Road during which time we failed to penetrate the visitors defensive blanket until two goals in injury time gave us a great chance of proceeding into the next round. It had probably been one of Hibs worst ever displays in Europe and the jeers of the Hibs fans at the end let the players know that they hadn't been all that impressed either. The 90 minutes had elapsed goalless, and with the referee looking at his watch in injury time, Arthur Duncan opened the scoring. Incredibly the game had barely restarted when Pat Stanton doubled our lead with what was literally the last kick of the ball. Probably the only positive that could be taken from the game apart from the final result was the performance of young Kenny Davidson who had shown once again that Hibs had uncovered another cracker.

In the return game in Portugal we recovered from a disastrous first half during which time we conceded two goals that cancelled out our lead from the first leg, and were now in very real danger of a European exit. In sweltering sunshine, conditions that were far from conducive for fast attacking football, the oppressive heat initially seemed to affect our early play until Johnny Graham scored the best goal of the game from a Joe McBride free kick in the second half that was enough to earn us a passage into the next round. After Graham's goal our superior fitness told with Jim Black who had recently withdrawn a transfer request, head and shoulders above every player on the park, as Hibs totally outclassed Guimaraes in the closing stages of the game. A special mention must also be made of goalkeeper Roy Baines who had since taken over from Gordon Marshall and was playing in his first ever European tie. Roy also had a great game that evening and kept us in it in the early stages with a couple of fine saves. Perhaps surprisingly after 14 years as a full time professional the vastly experienced Willie Hunter would also be making his European debut, but he had almost missed the game. It was only after arriving at the airport in Edinburgh that he discovered that his passport had expired, and a quick dash by taxi to the passport office in Glasgow was required, only just managing to catch the next plane to Portugal. He finally arrived at our hotel several hours after the rest of his team mates.

Since defeating Celtic a couple of months before we had taken only five points from a possible 14, but a superb 3-2 victory against Rangers at Easter Road had stopped the rot. By now we knew that our next Fairs Cup opponents would be an extremely good Liverpool side who were then managed by the legendary Bill Shankly.

The Liverpool manager had watched the Rangers game from the stand and interviewed after the game had confessed that he had found what had been a fiercely competitive affair 'very brutal but interesting', although he could not have failed to have been impressed with Hibs resistance to the usual powerhouse tactics of our opponents. Late in the game Willie Johnstone of Rangers was sent off after an altercation with Jim Blair as we prepared to defend a free kick, Blair booked for his part in the incident. It had taken Jim some time to settle at Easter Road, but his two goals that evening took his total to four in three games and he was now starting to live up to his early promise.

It was around this time that the former Manchester City player Dave Ewing was-appointed assistant first team trainer to Tom McNiven, a move I'm sure that would have been against the wishes of Willie MacFarlane, and had in all probability come as an even bigger surprise to the manager as it had the rest of us. It had been fairly obvious for some time now that MacFalane and Tom Hart didn't always see eye to eye. This had become even more apparent a few weeks previously when a game against Morton at Cappielow had been abandoned after only half an hour when play had proved impossible on a waterlogged pitch due the incessant rain that had been falling all day. In his post-match interview MacFarlane had been highly critical of referee Callaghan's decision to even start the game, but there soon followed an obvious rebuke in an official release from Easter Road distancing themselves from the manager's comments, stating that Hibs wished to abide by all referee's decisions-regardless of circumstances.

For me personally the past few months had been a nightmare. My groin injury had failed to respond to treatment and it was only after a few days in the Western General Hospital for tests that the cause of the mystery ailment had been detected and finally treated. I had been out of the game for over three months, but eventually managed to come through a couple of reserve games unscathed, and was earmarked to make my return on the Wednesday against a Liverpool side who at that time were considered to be one of the best teams in Europe.

We were at our usual pre-match hideaway at Bissett's Hotel in Gullane the day before the game when Willie MacFarlane was summoned back to Easter Road. The manager arrived at the ground to be told in no uncertain terms by Tom Hart that neither Joe McBride nor Johnny Graham were to be included in the Hibs line-up for the following day's game. Back at

Gullane later that evening Macfarlane informed both players that they would not be playing the following day until Joe McBride piped up. By then we all knew that MacFarlane and Tom Hart did not get on and Joe said, 'Boss, they are going to sack you anyway. If you want to come out of this looking like a man, tell him that as manager of this club nobody can tell you who or who not to select, and you will come out of all this with your head held high.' After relaying the news to Tom Hart in the morning that both players would be playing later that evening, MacFarlane was asked to resign. Refusing point blank to do so, he was promptly sacked on the spot. I still have no idea to this day why Tom Hart wanted McBride and Graham left out of the side. Maybe it was because they both came from Glasgow or possibly that he just didn't like them. One thing was for certain, although I personally always got on well with Hart, he was that type of guy. It was his club, and if he thought that your time was up, your time was up. He could, and would do what he liked as he demonstrated some time later over the signing of George Best. Eddie Turnbull didn't want George Best, but what Tom Hart wanted Tom Hart got, the only surprise for me was that Eddie put up with it. Hart was his own man while Willie MacFarlane always wanted to be top dog and something just had to give. The owner was also a working class man who didn't suffer fools gladly and for me it had only been a matter of time until they clashed.

As expected the decision to sack Willie MacFarlane in the circumstances provoked outrage and outright condemnation, not only in Edinburgh, but throughout the entire country. According to one newspaper: 'The club had become so much smaller because of this decision.' And another: 'On the eve of one of the most important matches in the history of the club, Hibs have managed to behave as if they were intent on some sort of soccer suicide.' As had been correctly forecast by Joe McBride, Willie MacFarlane left Easter Road with his head held high and his dignity intact. The manager himself was quoted as saying: 'A board of directors have the prerogative of choosing a manager and of sacking him if he is a failure, but while he is still in charge he must be allowed to exercise his judgement.'

The following morning after only a few weeks at the club Dave Ewing was duly installed as manager. Maybe it was always going to happen, but probably not as soon. I always found Dave to be a nice big lad and a decent enough coach. Although he had been born in Perth he had spent most of his football career down south and spoke with a fairly refined English accent. A team mate of the legendary former Hibs player Bobby Johnstone at Manchester City, he had played in the consecutive FA Cup finals in 1955 and '56 when City had lost to Newcastle and then defeated

Birmingham City the following year in what famously became known as 'the Bert Trautmann final. He obviously must have known 'the game, but at Easter Road under Willie MacFarlane, Dave hadn't shown a lot tactically and Tom McNiven would take the warm up as usual, with Dave on the periphery as the manager himself took the actual training.

After an absence of over three months I finally made my return to first team action against Liverpool. There would be no place for Johnny Graham, but perhaps surprisingly Joe McBride was on the substitutes bench.

It was vital that we put the recent off-field events to the back of our minds, and we started the game well. Only five minutes had been played when we were denied a stonewall penalty after Larry Lloyd had blatantly pulled back Kenny Davidson well inside the box, but incredibly the referee waved aside our furious appeals. As we expected Liverpool proved to be tough opponents, well organised and dangerous on the break. We were also capable of creating several dangerous chances ourselves, but unfortunately they all came to nothing. With the usually inspirational Pat Stanton less commanding in midfield than normal, it took a rare Jim Black blunder, his only mistake of the evening, to allow John Toshack in to score the only goal of the game. Throughout the entire 90 minutes, the home crowd had been very vocal regarding the events of the past few days with constant demands for the introduction of McBride. They eventually got their wish and with only half an hour remaining the former Celtic player replaced Kenny Davidson. He was only on the field five minutes when he was involved in the main talking point of the evening. I had sent over a long cross field pass from the left which was perfectly met by Arthur Duncan who bulleted a header past Clemence. The referee however disallowed the goal, claiming that McBride had fouled the goalkeeper as he went for the ball, a claim that was vociferously denied by the player in the dressing room after the game. The referee's decision stood however and after nine years of competitive European football it would be Hibs first ever defeat at home. Even more concerning was the fact that it had been our third consecutive game without even scoring a goal

After a dour no-score draw against Clyde at Shawfield on the Saturday, we made our way to Liverpool for the return leg in less than confident mood. With Joe McBride reinstated in the side we put up a much better all-round performance at Anfield than we had in the first game at Easter Road, playing some of our best football for some time, but again defensive mistakes were to cost us dear. One particular memory I have of the game is receiving a generous round of applause from an always appreciative Liverpool crowd after I had brought a high ball under instant control.

As for the game itself we created several good openings that may well have led to goals, but unfortunately came up against a future England goalkeeper in Ray Clemence who was in international form. For Hibs, John Brownlie, Jim Black and John Blackley had been immense at the back, although I felt that goalkeeper Roy Baines could possibly have done much better at both goals in our 2-0 defeat, particularly the second when he allowed a speculative and harmless looking lob to completely deceive him before dropping into the net.

As I have already mentioned, during my time at Hibs, Easter Road was always a happy camp although like every other club we did have our fair share of training ground bust ups. One particular occasion that comes to mind is the day we were having a full scale practice match on the Easter Road pitch. I always wanted desperately to win every game and after Roy Baines had conceded what I considered to be a soft goal I started to remonstrate with him. One things led to another with heated words being exchanged. Roy who is a big lad was obviously not too pleased with my comments and punched me full in the face, an altercation that resulted in a visit to the doctors for stitches to my eye. Afterwards Roy was very apologetic, but the incident was soon forgotten by both of us. Years later, I was on a licensed trade day out at Newcastle Races sponsored by Booker's Cash and Carry, when who should get on the same coach, but Roy Baines? We hadn't seen each other for many years and I was apprehensive as to how Roy would react, but I shouldn't have worried and we got on like a house on fire. On another occasion my good pal Jim Scott and I were playing snooker at the ground after training, when an argument started over the score. Once again voices were raised with one thing leading to another ending in all seriousness by Jim threatening to hit me with the cue. Things were quickly sorted out however and a short while later we were in the pub together having a few pints.

The return at Anfield would be Joe McBride's last game in a Hibs jersey. It later turned out that Hibs had already rejected an earlier offer for the player, but incredibly, with the club struggling to score goals with just two in the past six games, one of the best goal scorers in the entire country was allowed to join Dunfermline for what must surely have been the bargain of the season at just £4,000. Joe would later tell me that he had wanted to stay, but it was clear, particularly after the fiasco before the first Liverpool game that he was not wanted at Easter Road and that there was no point in hanging around. No disrespect to Dunfermline, but Hibs were a far bigger club. In just over two years at Easter Road Joe McBride had scored 62 goals in 96 appearances in all games and for me it had been a huge mistake to let him go.

As McBride was making a scoring debut for his new side in a one sided 5-0 victory at Ayr, at Easter Road young John Hazel was making his first team debut as we slumped to a 1-0 defeat at the hands of Dundee United. Both Johnny Graham and Hazel himself had struck the post with shots, Jim Blair missing an absolute sitter in the second half, but regardless of the booing of the Hibs fans we had been by far the better side. Only a string of outstanding saves by goalkeeper Hamish McCalpine had kept United in the game, leaving Jackie Copland a recent signing from Stranraer to score the winner just two minutes from time.

The New Year's derby at Tynecastle was the second holiday fixture in consecutive years to end goalless and only the latest in a series of drab encounters between the sides. The referee had added an extra three minutes at the end of the game, but in truth both sides could have played all night and still not have scored. For Hibs it was just a continuation of our lean spell. With the exception of a 2-2 home draw with Dunfermline it had now been eight games since we had last found the net and had dropped into mid-table. I had not been selected for the Hearts game and was an interested spectator as we scorned at least three gilt edged chances to secure the points, a couple of decent chances falling to the inexperienced John Hazel. John was a promising youngster who had been signed from Dunipace Juniors and was yet another player at Easter Road at that time with real potential, but I often felt that his attitude left a lot be desired. I could be wrong, but to John a defeat was just a defeat, unlike some of the other players, including myself, who just hated losing.

The following day 2 January 1971 I was in the reserve side that travelled to face Cowdenbeath at Station Park. As the first team were scraping a 2-2 draw against the Fife side at Easter Road, a tragedy then unparalleled in the history of the British game was taking place just minutes before the end of a Rangers-Celtic game at Ibrox. That afternoon football results paled into insignificance with the breaking news that 66 fans had lost their lives after a barrier at stairway 13 had collapsed resulting in a major crush. It is now thought that the horrific accident was caused when a youngster being carried on the shoulders of an adult had fallen, causing literally hundreds of supporters to collapse on top of each other. We were out later that evening when we first became aware of the tragedy and were immediately concerned as my wife's sister had been at the game. There were no mobile phones in those days and understandably we were all extremely anxious until she finally managed to phone home to tell us she was safe. The following Saturday both Celtic and Hibs took the field at Parkhead wearing black armbands, the minutes silence before the start meticulously observed in eerie silence by both sets of fans, as it had been at grounds throughout the country. Given the circumstances ,the game was played out in an almost surreal atmosphere, Celtic coasting to an easy win against a Hibs side that had offered no real threat. Pat Stanton scored for us a few minutes before the end of a 2-1 defeat, but the result meant little after the harrowing events at Ibrox only a few days before.

A disaster fund had been quickly set up and a considerable sum was eventually raised for the dependants of those who had lost their lives. Later a Scotland XI featuring George Best, Bobby Charlton and Chelsea's Peter Bonnetti would play a Rangers/Celtic select at Hampden, all the proceeds from the game going to the fund.

We had now gone ten games without a win and clearly something had to be done. The answer was to re-sign cult hero Joe Baker from Sunderland. Joe had become a great pal and whenever he was back in Edinburgh we would always meet up. He was some man, a larger than life character who was great to have around the dressing room. One day before a friendly against Queen of the South in Dumfries, the pair of us were passing the time in a local café when Joe asked me if I wanted a coffee. I wasn't all that keen on coffee and politely declined. Not to be outdone however the bold Joe returned from the counter with two coffee's. Reluctantly I took a sip out of mine only to find out that it had been laced with Brandy. 'I didn't get it for you' snapped Baker who promptly downed both himself. As I say with Joe around there was never a dull moment.

His first game back was against Eddie Turnbull's high flying Aberdeen who at that time were sitting comfortably at the top of the table four points clear of the rest. They had gone 15 games without dropping a single point and had not even conceded a goal for 1,093 minutes, which was a Scottish record. I watched from the side-lines as captain for the day Baker led the team out wearing distinctive white boots which were a rare innovation in those days. His electric pace had gone, but his brain was as sharp as ever and he would still get stuck in like the Baker of old. He celebrated his return by scoring our second goal a few minutes after Pat Stanton had smashed Bobby Clark's unbeaten record, our 2-1 victory severely denting Aberdeen's title aspirations.

By now I was 100 per cent fit again, but finding it very difficult to force myself back into the picture except for a brief recall in Hibs convincing 8-1 Scottish Cup victory against Forfar during which I had managed to score one of the goals. Unfortunately I was to spend a couple of soul searching months in the reserves champing at the bit and missed not only the great victory against Aberdeen, but also a very satisfying Scottish Cup victory over Hearts when goals by John Hazel and Arthur Duncan had given us a

2-1 win at Tynecastle. I would also miss the cup game against Dundee in the next round when a Jimmy O'Rourke penalty would be enough to see us through to the next round. After a 4-2 home defeat by Morton I was eventually recalled to the side to face Dundee in a league game at Dens Park, but unfortunately it was not to be a happy return when Dundee gained revenge for the earlier cup defeat by winning 1-0.

By now Jim Blair had returned to his old club St Mirren. For some reason it hadn't worked out for Jim in Edinburgh. During the previous six months he had often struggled to secure a regular first team place and had managed only six goals from 21 starts in all games which unfortunately was poor return for the amount of money Hibs had invested in bringing him to Easter Road. He had certainly tried hard enough, but unfortunately things hadn't come off for him. On his return to Love Street he would start to score goals again and I was delighted for him when he later got a decent move to Norwich City.

We had been drawn against Rangers in the semi-final of the Scottish Cup, but in the weeks leading up to the game a weakened Hibs side went down 2-1 to St Johnstone. Worse was to follow with a heavy defeat at Kilmarnock the following week. It was during this game that I was sent off for the first and only time in my professional career, indeed in almost ten years of first class football I had not even been booked before. I was having personal off-field problems at the time and perhaps my head wasn't as it should have been. Tommy McLean who was soon to sign for Rangers, was a niggly irritating type of player and I remember him chipping away at my heels as I moved upfield with the ball. It was a situation that I had experienced countless of times before, but for some reason this time I turned and lashed out at him. Retaliation wasn't remotely my style. During my entire career, even as a juvenile, I had had to endure more than my fair share of heavy, often unfair and at times brutal tackling, but never before had I lost my cool. Normally I would just have got up and walked away, but for some reason this time I lost it. Regardless, referee Wilson of Glasgow had no hesitation, and probably no option, but to send me packing and I was a despondent figure in the dressing room, only too aware that not only had I let myself down, but also my team mates. The afternoon had started badly for us when we lost a goal inside the first minute and we were three behind after just half an hour when I saw red, literally and metaphorically. John Blackley eventually managed to pull a goal back, but the heavy 4-1 defeat was hardly an ideal preparation for the semi-final in midweek.

Against Rangers at Hampden we were much the better side in a game that at times threatened to turn into a hacking match, although by that time we were well capable of taking care of ourselves on that score. We perhaps surprised our opponents by matching their customary physical style of play and for a while Rangers were teetering on the brink of defeat. For long periods of the game we had them on the back foot, but once again our failure in front of goal was evident. The nearest we came to scoring was when John Greig cleared a shot of the line in the very last minute of the game and it was on to a replay the following midweek. In was in the dressing room after the game that manager Dave Ewing uttered his now infamous comment, 'Rangers are rubbish.' Unfortunately this ill-advised comment, whether true or not, was overheard by a newspaper reporter while the dressing room door was open and the next morning the headlines were emblazoned across the back pages of the newspapers. Rangers not unnaturally were absolutely furious.

We had now gone six games without a victory and yet another embarrassing home defeat against Falkirk did little to boost our confidence as we made our way to Hampden for the cup replay. With the same players again taking the field, perhaps understandably Ewing's comments had done little to defuse the tense atmosphere. Playing wide on the right once again I was giving my immediate opponent Billy Mathieson a hard time and we were by far the better side for long spells of the game, but unfortunately Rangers scored the goals that mattered. Jimmy O'Rourke had levelled an earlier goal from Alfie Conn when he scored from close range after an Alex Cropley cut back from near the byline and with the scores still level Johnny Graham somehow contrived to miss the best chance of the game when he shot weakly past the post with only goalkeeper Peter McCloy to beat. In the closing stages we had another couple of good chances that unfortunately came to nothing before Willie Henderson scored the goal that was enough to send Rangers into the final where they would eventually lose to Celtic after a replay.

HIBS: MARSHALL BROWNLIE AND JONES, BLACKLEY STANTON AND PRINGLE, GRAHAM O'ROURKE BAKER CROPLEY AND STEVENSON. SUB: BLACK.

RANGERS: MCCLOY JARDINE AND MATHIESON, GREIG MCKINNON AND JACKSON, HENDERSON CONN STEIN MCDONALD AND JOHNSTONE. SUB: PENMAN.

REFEREE: BILL MULLEN (DALKEITH)

Out of the cup and stranded in the lower reaches of the table there was now nothing left to play for, but pride, and a 5-1 home win against Clyde in our final league game that was played in front of our smallest crowd of the season, estimated to have been well under 4,000, turned out to be our biggest win of the entire campaign.

The curtain finally came down on the season with a home friendly against the Dutch side Maastricht. The visitors took the field with the unusual sight of goalkeeper Korver wearing glasses which he wore all through the game. I was in the stand as Hibs gave the 17-year-old schoolboy Bobby Mathieson a debut at left-back in a 3-0 victory. Once again the game was watched by an extremely disappointingly crowd of under 4,000, most of them no doubt looking forward to their summer holidays and just pleased that a season that had again promised so much and delivered so little was finally at an end.

Yet again we had failed to live up to expectations. With only 47 goals scored, the same as in our near relegation season of 1962–63, and 53 conceded, the statistics perhaps tells its own story. Of the 36 league games played only ten had ended in victory with another ten drawn. Perhaps surprising Joe Baker who had played in only around a third of the games, had finished the season as our top league goal scorer, although this time with a derisory eight goals, a far cry from his club record of 42 in season 1959-60, and two ahead of the next best Jimmy O'Rourke.

It was difficult to put a finger on just what had gone wrong with a club that had been capable of doing so much better. A change of manager during the season had certainly not helped, but that surely couldn't have been the only reason for the slump. We had beaten the top sides in the league in Celtic, Aberdeen and Rangers, but had still dropped to 12th place in the table, nine places below that of the previous season. Perhaps at times our attitude had been wrong, guilty of approaching games against lower league sides with the mentality that the points were already in the bag.

A proposed end of season tour of America, Canada and Bermuda had been cancelled almost at the last minute and instead, after a whistle stop tour of central England with games against Wigan and Oldham, we made our way to Majorca for a 14 day stay. Surprisingly, but perhaps ominously giving forthcoming events that were shortly to enfold, Dave Ewing did not accompany us on the trip, leaving John Fraser and Jimmy McColl to take charge of the group. Just a few days before Bertie Auld had been signed from Celtic, Dave Ewing's last signing for the club, but too late to be included in the party that made its way to the holiday town of Arenal, although coincidentally Auld and his wife had already booked a holiday at the same resort for later in the month. Bertie was some man. Later, during pre-season training under Dave Ewing, Joe, Bertie, myself and some of the other lads would often pop into the Learig pub in Restalrig Road for a few refreshment before returning to the ground for the afternoon sessions. In those days the bars closed in the afternoons and one day the barman refused to serve us any more drink as it was after time. At that I can still see Bertie leaning over the bar and grabbing the barman by the throat threatening to punch him, and it eventually took four or five of us to calm him down. Later back at the ground Joe, Bertie and I would go through the motions of sprinting, but we certainly wouldn't have fooled Eddie Turnbull, whose arrival was imminent, although obviously we weren't aware of it at that at the time.

After losing his place in the first team to Pat Stanton in the latter part of the season, Jim Black had asked to be placed on the transfer list and remained back in Scotland as the rest of us made our way to the Majorca. Once again the trip was a great experience with plenty laughs along the way. It was mainly a holiday with little in the way of training and only the one game against the islands top side Real Majorca which we eventually lost 2-1, Joe Baker scoring a fantastic long range shot for our goal. In the evening's we would all gather at the local bar and soon we would be half pissed and singing the popular pop song of the day: 'Chirpy-Chirpy-Cheep-Cheep' by the Scottish band Middle of the Road at the top of our voices.

One morning we were all sitting around the pool when Tom Hart suddenly appeared. I can't remember now how it came about, but Hart turned to the rest of the younger lads pointing in the direction of Joe Baker and myself, and urged them to take a lesson on how to look after themselves properly from two dedicated professionals, the chairman completely oblivious to the fact that we were both absolutely pissed at the time.

Although I was not to know it the time, after ten years as a Hibs player this would turn out to be my last trip abroad with the club.

CHAPTER THIRTEEN

Almost the End
1971–72

PRE-SEASON TRAINING HAD already started when Dave Ewing suddenly announced his resignation, stating a desire to return to coaching in England. The news had come completely out of the blue to everyone, as it was believed that all the backroom staff had just signed new five year contracts. One of the departing manager's last acts had been to pay a £50 fine after he had mistakenly entered Kenny Davidson's name on the team sheets for the Scottish Cup semi-final against Rangers a couple of months before instead of my own. As usual there was a long list of candidates as to who would replace Ewing, including perhaps predictably the former Hibs players Willie Ormond, George Farm who was then manager at Raith Rovers, and even Bertie Auld. Other possible contenders included the then Dunfermline manager Willie Cunningham and the Aberdeen assistant manager Jimmy Bonthrone. Eddie Turnbull's name had also been mentioned, but it was thought highly unlikely that he would leave an Aberdeen side that he had built into potential league champions having missed out on the title by only two points at the end of the previous season.

I can't remember now how I first heard that Turnbull would be returning to Easter Road, but I can remember being over the moon at the news. Before his arrival, Easter Road had become something of a holiday camp with the players more or less allowed to do just as they pleased, but all that changed instantly under Turnbull. Dave Ewing's normal pre-season routine had consisted of morning and afternoon sessions at Easter Road, and as I have already mentioned, a group of us including Joe Baker and Bertie Auld would often wander along to the Learig pub in Restalrig Road for a few pints before returning to the ground for the afternoon session. The new manager however knew exactly what was going on and soon sorted that out. Turnbull was not a big man, but he had a presence and believe me he could be a very frightening figure if the occasion warranted it. In the past some of us had been able to get away with skiving during training, but all that stopped immediately. Under Turnbull the training was hard, usually always involving the ball, but enjoyable, even for a notoriously poor trainer like myself. Tactically brilliant and with meticulous eye for detail, for the first few weeks Eddie would take the back four back for extra sessions in the afternoons until they were able to perform as a complete unit, a move that would soon pay dividends for the club.

As far as football was concerned he was on a different planet. I knew that he respected me, a feeling that was more than mutual. I knew the game, was not afraid to speak my mind and although I was a bit intimidated at the beginning I felt that we were both on the same wavelength. It was only now that I found out that on a couple of occasions he had tried to sign me for Aberdeen, once when I wasn't in the first team, but for some reason although I wasn't then in the set up his advances had been rebuffed. One day after training he took me aside to say that he was relying on me. I nodded, but deep down I knew that I could no longer do it. At the time my personal problems had worsened. My head was all over the place, I couldn't concentrate and hadn't been training properly. The last thing I wanted was to let him down, but I knew even then that I wasn't capable of living up to what was expected from me.

Eddie had been some player, far better than I ever thought when watching him from the terracing as a youngster, and it was only when I later played alongside both him and Willie Ormond at training that I really appreciated just how good they both really were. A leader with a great football brain, Turnbull had been regarded by many to have been mainly the engine room of the great Hibs side of the late '40s and early '50s, but all I can say is that if Gordon Smith, Bobby Johnstone and Lawrie Reilly were better than Eddie Turnbull and Willie Ormond then they must have been some players. I am occasionaly asked who was the better manager, Jock Stein or Eddie Turnbull, but I really couldn't say. Both were tactically brilliant and well ahead of their time, but undoubtedly Stein was a better man-manager who would give the players more credit, something that Eddie seemed to find difficult. Stein would treat everybody differently depending on their own individual personality, while Eddie would treat everybody the same which didn't always work for some players. For instance I don't think that he would have tolerated Willie Hamilton's wayward habits or sit down and talk with him as Jock had done, and consequently would not have got the best out of him. Although in saying that he managed to take the wee man from Dunfermline in hand. Both were great managers in their own right, but perhaps Celtic's nine titles in a row plus a European Cup speaks for itself.

Turnbull's first game in charge was a friendly against the English Second Division side Middlesbrough at Easter Road with new signing Bertie Auld making his debut for Hibs. Bertie was a smashing bloke. I already knew him from playing against him several times over the years. He was a leader, but unfortunately by the time he arrived at Easter Road he was well past his best. A very clever player who could read the game, he could also make a pass as well as score goals. He was also as hard as nails and one of the dirtiest players I had ever come across when the occasion warranted it. During the Middlesbrough game, a 2-0 victory for the visitors, Bertie was quite clearly 'done' by the former Manchester United and England player Nobby Stiles who himself had a bit of a reputation for mixing it. It was obvious that Bertie was badly hurt, but he refused to go off, pleading with trainer Tom McNiven just to give him five more minutes. You just knew what was coming next, and within minutes Stiles was writhing in agony on the ground after Bertie had gone 'over the top' before making his way to the touchline for treatment. It later turned out that Auld had broken his collarbone, but had been determined not to go off until he had extracted his revenge. That was Bertie. He could be loud and opinionated and was certainly someone you wouldn't get the better of easily.

Both Gordon Marshall and Thomson Allan had been freed at the end of the previous season, leaving Roy Baines as our number one goalkeeper. Unfortunately Roy had been injured in training and we were forced to call upon the former junior internationalist Eddie Pryce who had only joined the club a few weeks before from Shettleston Juniors. Eddie had played well enough in games against Middlesbrough, both at Easter Road and in the return at Ayrsome Park and also in the home friendly against the German side Shalke a few days later. Before the Shalke game, the long serving Jimmy McColl was presented with a watch by his favourite all time player Gordon Smith in front of the assembled for the evening Famous Five to commemorate his 50 years service with the club.

For me though Pryce was a bit on the small side for a goalkeeper, his lack of inches a definite handicap. Although he had acquitted himself reasonably well it was probably unfair to pitch the inexperienced player into the deep end, and possibly with this in mind Turnbull had wasted no time in signing the former Dunfermline, Birmingham and Scotland goalkeeper Jim Herriot from the South African side Durban City. Herriot's registration papers had been delayed, but the bold Turnbull took a chance and played him anyway in our final pre-season game against York City at Bootham Crescent under the name of Pryce and incredibly although Herriot was a former Scottish international no one appeared to notice. I had played against Jim several times when he was with Dunfermline and found him to be a terrific and an extremely reliable goalkeeper and would be an asset to the side.

The new season opened with a win against Motherwell in in the league cup. I had managed to lay on the second goal for Johnny Hamilton in our 3-0 victory, but in truth my mind was not really on the job in hand. By now my off-field personal problems had worsened. My head was somewhere else and I was finding it extremely difficult to concentrate. I was not putting 100 per cent into training, lacked motivation, could not get interested in anything, even the game, and had already made up my mind at that point that a move would probably be for the best. I had several meetings with the boss who felt that I could work my way through it, but I wasn't doing it on the park. To be fair to Eddie he listened, was understanding, but typical of the man there was never even any hint of sympathy.

We managed to get through a league cup section comprising Dundee United, Motherwell and Kilmarnock to qualify for the quarter-finals with two games to spare. In the home game against United I had hit the post with a header and had another cleared off the line, but although we managed to win 2-0 I clearly hadn't been at my best. In the return at Tannadice the following week, a 4-1 victory, the United defender Jim Cameron was sent off after blatantly attempting to kick John Brownlie out wide on the far touchline. From the resultant free kick, my 35 yard cross completely deceived everyone in the box including goalkeeper Hamish McCalpine to land in the back off the net. It would turn out to be my last ever goal for Hibs.

Our league campaign opened against local rivals Hearts at Tynecastle. We eventually managed to come out in top of what was considered to be one of the drabbest derbies in many years thanks to two late goals from Alex Cropley and Johnny Hamilton, both scored in the final few minutes of the game. In just a few weeks Turnbull had instilled a new sense of purpose and self-belief into the side and the satisfying result now meant that we hadn't lost a league game at Tynecastle for eight years, our opponents failing to even score a goal in the last six. Sadly, that afternoon I myself had what can only be described as the proverbial nightmare. I was not fit, could not concentrate on the game, and was substituted after an hour. With all due respect to the Hearts full-back's Alan Sneddon and Roy Kay, normally I would have had no problem against them, but that afternoon nothing was coming off for me. Regardless of how hard I tried I just couldn't get past them and perhaps I was starting to feel a bit sorry for myself. It would turn out to be my last ever first team start after 11 years at Easter Road, and it is perhaps ironic that it all ended where it had started all those years before, at Tynecastle.

It was not quite the end however. I was listed as a substitute for the next few games although not used, and my very last action for the first team came when I replaced Johnny Hamilton for the last 30 minutes in a 4-1 victory against Dundee United at Tannadice on Saturday 18 September 1971. The Hibs team was:

HERRIOT BROWNLIE AND SCHAEDLER, STANTON BLACK AND BLACKLEY, HAMILTON HAZEL O'ROURKE AULD AND CROPLEY. SUB: STEVENSON.

By this time Johnny Graham had joined Ayr United, a move ironically that would prove to be the catalyst for my own move to the coastal holiday town a short time later. After a bright start at Easter Road Johnny had found it difficult to hold down a permanent place in the first team, particularly after the Liverpool fiasco. During his time at Easter Road he had been capped for the Scottish League against the League of Ireland and had also made a substitute appearance in a game against the Football League, but so far that season he had failed to feature at all in the first team. It was obvious that Turnbull either didn't like him or rate him as a player, and with all due respect, although he was a big pal of mine, I didn't think that Johnny good enough for Hibs.

I would make several more appearances for the second team before even they eventually dried up, one of them perhaps ironically, a 7-2 defeat by Ayr reserves at Somerset Park. My last ever appearance wearing the famous green and white jersey that I had dreamed of wearing since I was a boy, was a 1-1 draw against Motherwell reserves at Easter Road on 2 October 1971. The Hibs team that day was:

BAINES, MCEWAN AND SHEVLANE, MATHIESON, GRANT AND PRINGLE, STEVENSON, SPALDING, GORDON, SMITH AND DAVIDSON.

After several Saturdays idly spent twiddling my thumbs, it was now more evident than ever that I just had to get away from Easter Road. During my absence from the first team I had been approached by several other clubs about a possible transfer, but I was at a crossroads of my life and lacking direction. Meanwhile Johnny Graham had been doing well at Ayr, scoring five goals in the previous two games. Unknown to me he had also been putting in a good word for me with manager Ally MacLeod, although I don't think that that would have been necessary as the manager knew all about me from our time playing together several years before. It was around that time that the rules regarding eligibility to play for either of the home international countries were relaxed and the Aldershot-born Alex Cropley won his first Scotland cap when lining up alongside his Hibs team mate Pat Stanton for the game against Portugal at Hampden. After the game Ally MacLeod had bumped into Eddie Turnbull either by accident or design, and they had ended up discussing my situation at Easter Road. It was Johnny Graham who got in touch to tell me about the meeting and once again I went to see Eddie Turnbull to discuss things. As usual Eddie showed not a flicker of sympathy. If I had been fully fit there is absolutely no doubt in my mind that he would have wanted me to stay, but fully aware of what was going on in my head, his advice was that possibly a move would be in the best interests of all parties. Consequently, after a meeting with Ally MacLeod a few days later I eventually agreed to sign for Ayr United for a fee that I believe was in the region of £10,000.

I left Easter Road with the parting shot in one newspaper: 'Eric Stevenson has only the one representative honour to his name which is scant reward for such a skilful player.' The compliment however came far too late for me, but it was welcome all the same. So, after over ten years, more than 400 first team appearances in all games and 77 goals, plus another 66 appearances for the reserves, something that I thought would go on for ever, had finally come to an end.

To give Eddie Turnbull his due, he had wasted no time in weeding out the slackers at Easter Road including I'm sorry to say both myself and Joe Baker, until he finally got what he wanted. I always felt however that one of Eddie's big problems was that he always had to be the main man. It's well known that both he and Pat Stanton did not get on and I think the main reason was that the manager was jealous of Pat's popularity with the fans. Even the praise he rightly received for the great Turnbull's Tornados side of the early '70s was never enough, he had to be the main man. However he wasted no time in signing my replacement, and who is to say that he made the wrong decision when he travelled the short distance to Fife to sign Alex Edwards from Dunfermline.

As for myself I knew almost immediately that I had made the wrong decision in agreeing to sign for Ayr, even before I had played a game. Part time football and the long trips to Ayrshire twice a week for training was far removed from the world that I had grown accustomed to. I was far from fit, but knew that although they had some good players including the future Scottish international goalkeeper Jim Stewart, Quintin Young who would soon sign for Rangers after a short spell with Coventry and Johnny Doyle who was to lose his life so tragically in a domestic accident while playing for Celtic, I felt that they were mostly inferior to me, and even under the charismatic leadership of manager Ally MacLeod, we would end the season in the bottom half of the table.

As Hibs were going down 2-1 at Pittodrie on the Saturday I was making my way to Ayr for the game against Clyde where I met up again with my old friend Joe McBride who scored twice in Clyde's emphatic 5-0 victory. I personally had a very poor first outing and I have to admit that in my almost 30 appearances for Ayr I don't think that I ever played well, and was fully aware that I had let Ally MacLeod down. I was unfit, was not playing well and had fallen out of love with the game, sometimes not even bothering to turn up. What made things worse was that Ally was such a good pal that he never once castigated me, although I knew that he must have been bitterly disappointed. He knew the kind of guy I was and never once complained. Although he was that bit older, Ally and I had always got on well when he was at Hibs. A big jovial lad, he could be a bit loud, could talk for Scotland and often interrupted when someone was talking, and although the most of the players liked him well enough he was a bit too brash for some.

A few weeks later I came up against my former team mates for the first and only time. It turned out to be an almost surreal and ultimately disappointing occasion for me personally when we went down to a 2-1 defeat at Somerset Park. Playing on the left wing that day I came up against John Brownlie and for the entire 90 minutes I found myself marking John instead of the other way round as he consistently tore me up. He also scored one of the Hibs goals after goalkeeper Stewart somehow managed to punch his speculative lob from 40 yards into his own net. There is no doubt that I had been a poor second best that afternoon, but I consoled myself with the thought that with all due respect to John it would have been an interesting contest if I had been at my peak.

After only a few games at the start of the following season, I gradually fell out of the picture altogether at Ayr not even featuring in the second team, but I was still expected to turn up for games. Often I wouldn't even make the training when I would be easily distracted by a visit to Bertie Auld's pub on the way through to Ayrshire. It was around that time that Hibs reached the final of the League Cup. I went to see Eddie Turnbull about tickets for the game and was at Hampden early to see my former team mates warming up, several of them spotting me in the crowd and giving me a wave. Hibs won the cup that afternoon, Pat Stanton giving as good a performance as he had ever done in a 2-1 win against Celtic, a victory that was far more decisive than the final score-line would suggest. After the game there was no invite to the official function at the North

British Hotel in Princes Street, not that I expected one, and it was back to Bonnyrigg to celebrate with my pals.

Jock Stein must have mentioned to Ally MacLeod that he had seen me at Hampden and when I reported for training on the Tuesday evening Ally took me aside to ask where I had been on the Saturday afternoon. He obviously knew, so there was no point in lying and I told him that I had been at Hampden watching my team beating Celtic. Ally then informed me more in resignation than anger that he would have to fine me two weeks wages, but as far as I was concerned it was well worth it to see Hibs winning the cup.

As luck would have it Hibs very next game was against Ayr in a league game at Easter Road. I watched from the stand with mixed emotions as Hibs put on what many thought to be their finest performance of the season in destroying poor Ayr 8-1, their first goal scored by Alex Cropley after only eight seconds. One half of me was relieved that I was not playing that afternoon, the other half wishing that I had been wearing the green and white jersey.

It was to get even better for the Hibs fans a few weeks later, when a side that was already being hailed as Turnbull's Tornados travelled the short distance to Tynecastle on New Year's Day to record a famous 7-0 victory over their greatest rivals. I had managed to get a couple of tickets for the game, and a Hibs fan in the crowd that I knew offered me a drink of whisky from his hip flask when Jimmy O'Rourke opened the scoring. We both took another drink each time Hibs scored and by the final whistle we were both almost reeling.

At the end of the season Ally MacLeod took me aside to tell me that reluctantly he would have to let me go, which I totally understood. I had enquiries from a couple of clubs including Queen of the South, but on hearing my terms, nothing ever came of it. There had even been an offer from my old Hibs team mate John Young to play in Canada and another from a South African side, but by that time I had opened a newsagents/licensed grocers shop in the Bonnyrigg area that was beginning to thrive, but apart from that I wanted to remain in Scotland.

Things might well have turned out differently had I been fit, but apart from being an unenthusiastic trainer, my off-field lifestyle had taken its toll. It had been a great life, visiting countries that I would never have visited had it not been for football and being well paid well for it. I had thought that it would go on for ever, but now at just over 30 years of age, a time when as a footballer I should just have been reaching my prime it was over.

Near the end of my time with Hibs, I had met my future wife Agnes at a nightspot in town. Meeting Agnes who lived at nearby Restalrig, only a couple of hundred yards from Easter Road was to change my life and was the best thing that has ever happened to me. We were married a few months later in a quiet ceremony at Montrose Terrace Register Office in Edinburgh with my former Easter Road team mate Davie Hogg as my best man.

I had now decided to retire completely from the game to concentrate on our business interests, which at that time were doing really well. I had always fancied going into the pub game and when the Waverley Hotel in Bonnyrigg came up for lease I applied for it and was successful. Although the venture was lucrative enough it didn't take me long to realise that the pub game was not for me. A guy who would later become a director of the club ran a bus for all the Hibs games both home and away leaving from the pub before picking up more people from Dalkeith on the way, and occasionally a Celtic bus would leave for some of the bigger games. We also had our own football team who played in the Sunday morning pub league and I would usually go along and watch them, I helped them to buy strips and had given them the run of the hotel until one day they decided that they could get a better deal elsewhere. I have to say that I felt very let down by their actions and myself and a few of the other regulars decided to form our own side. It later gave me great satisfaction when we defeated the previous team three times in the same season and although it was not really in my nature, I found great difficulty in stopping myself from telling them that I thought we now got to keep them. The hotel had several rooms above that I let out and although we kept the place for several years I eventually got fed up with the seven days a week commitment as well as running the shop and decided not to renew the lease.

Looking back, do I have any regrets? Certainly, particularly when I saw the great side that Turnbull was putting together at Easter Road, one that I could well have been part off. A couple of years ago I bumped into John Brownlie and John Blackley who are still great friends at the airport. During our chat they were kind enough to say that if I had remained at Easter Road and regained my fitness then to their mind Hibs would undoubtedly have won the League. Exaggerated or not the compliment meant a lot to me.

It took me a long time, perhaps several years to get over not playing on a Saturday. I missed the whole thing, the environment, the camaraderie and the dressing room crack. I had played all over Europe, North America and South Africa, making many great friends along the way and had been paid for doing it, and now, almost in an instant it was over.

For several years both my wife Agnes and I attended all the home games at Easter Road until we got fed up with what we were watching. I couldn't believe the quality of some of Eddie's later teams, very few of the players Hibs class. A few years later I was at a game against Aberdeen at Easter Road that had ended in Hibs being relegated. After the final whistle we went across for a drink at the Fifty Club that was situated just across from the stadium and were surprised to find the place almost empty. I asked where everyone was and was stunned when the barman replied that they would still be in the stadium applauding the team. To say I was dumfounded would be an understatement. Christ, the team had just been relegated and the supporters were giving the players a round of applause !

Like every fan a great thrill for me was meeting some of the players from the old days that I used to watch from the terracing when I was a boy. In later years I would occasionally spend some time with John Paterson, father of Craig, who had been centre-half or left-back during the halcyon days of the Famous Five who would talk fondly of the time, me an enthralled listener. I also managed to meet Bobby Johnstone briefly at a function. I had only missed playing alongside Bobby at Easter Road by a few weeks, but unfortunately that evening I was unable to spend much time with him. On another occasion I was having a few drinks in a bar in Rose Street in Edinburgh when I was introduced to Jock Govan who had been right-back in the great Hibs side of the late '40s and early '50s. It turned out that he was a big admirer and we spent a couple of hours discussing the game and the personalities from the old days. Then there was my hero, the great Lawrie Reilly whom I used to idolise from the terracing, later spending hours kicking a ball about in the street imagining myself to be him, and I am glad to say that he and I later became great friends.

A few years ago I was asked to join the Hibs Former Players association and started attending games again. For me the modern game can be boring with too much emphasis on winning and not enough on entertaining although and have to say that I enjoyed the Tony Mowbray era and enjoyed Alan Stubbs early days at Easter Road.

I have now been married for 44 years during which time my wife Agnes has presented me with two wonderful daughters. Sonya the oldest, is married to Alistair whose father Robert was a Hibs director for a while. They both work in insurance and have two children, Owen who plays for the Bonnyrigg Rose under-10 side and Lucy who plays for the under-9's. The youngest daughter Nadia is a nurse in Australia and is married to Scott who is a tiler. They too have two children Aidan and Connor who also play football, but their real passion is street dancing. At the time of writing Nadia and Scott are expecting a third child and we will be going out to Australia for the birth. I also have three children from my first marriage Eric, Gary and Elaine. Eric and his wife Donita have given me two granddaughters Lisa and Stacey and a great granddaughter Ella-May

In 2012 I received the great honour of being inducted into the Hibernian Hall of Fame and was almost overcome with emotion when I was presented with my plaque by my hero Lawrie Reilly.

Looking back, I wish now that I had behaved better, trained harder and with less partying. Plenty of football players like to socialise, but most could train hard to get it out of their system. I believe that if I had handled things differently then I could well have played on, certainly into my mid-30s, and could possibly have ended my career as manager at Easter Road.

However there is no use looking back as things can't be changed, but I will always have the satisfaction of having achieved my boyhood ambition of playing for the Hibs.

CHAPTER FOURTEEN

My Dream Team

I HAVE OFTEN been asked who the best players were that I played both with and against. During almost 11 years as a professional footballer, I encountered so many truly wonderful individuals that it would be an extremely difficult decision for me to choose the best. However at the risk of disappointing some of my best friends in the game, after much soul searching and changes of mind I have finally decided. Any team of mine would line up in a 4-2-4 formation entirely geared to attack. I admit that it might sometimes be over run in midfield, but it would certainly be capable of scoring goals and if the opposition were to score four then this side would be more than capable of scoring five.

The first position is relatively easy. I would have absolutely no hesitation in selecting Ronnie Simpson as the best goalkeeper that I have played alongside, with Willie Wilson a close contender. Ronnie though was far and away the best. Extremely agile with wonderful reflexes, he had great anticipation, was brilliant with crosses and when he punched the ball it would travel 30 or 40 yards and well away from the danger area. For a keeper he was also fantastic on the ground and I have lost count of the number of times he would save with his feet, far too often for it to have been accidental. Yet another great lad, joining Hibs was thought to be his swan song, but history would write a different script. Willie Wilson was not all that far behind Ronnie, and who knows just how good he might have been had it not been for the serious back injury he received early in his career. Some say Hibs rushed him back too quickly with the result that the injury would trouble him for the rest of his days.

Three players are in contention for the right-back position. John Grant, Bobby Duncan and John Brownlie. The Scottish international John Grant was probably the best defensive full-back of the three, but in choosing an attacking team, I am going to go for Bobby Duncan on the right, with perhaps surprisingly John Brownlie on the left. Bobby was a very confident lad who would run up and down the pitch all day.

Perhaps not the greatest defensively, but he more than made up for it with his reading of the game and his flair for going forward. He was on the verge of full international honours when he received the horrific injury against Celtic, and although Bobby might not agree I don't think that he was ever the same player afterwards. Brownlie had originally joined the club as a midfielder. He would make a name for himself as a right-back, but John was so good that he could have played anywhere. Although he could tackle, perhaps he wasn't the greatest of defenders, but played more like a forward, his frequent incursions up the wing constantly creating menace in the opposition penalty area. A determined character with a bit of fire about him and you could see immediately that he was going to be something special. His first game when he looked as though he had been in the side for years told you all you needed to know about him. Like Bobby Duncan had also to battle back from a horrific leg break against East Fife, but he too recovered well enough to earn more Scotland caps and a later move to Newcastle United.

In the middle of the back four I would look no further than the pairing of Pat Stanton and John Blackley. What is there to say about Pat that hasn't already been said? As influential at the back as he was in midfield he would be my sweeper, although he would be asked to break from defence carrying the ball just like Franz Beckenbauer, something he did to great effect at Easter Road, although as far as I was concerned he never did it often enough. Pat led by example and who will ever forget his magnificent performance in the 1972 League Cup Final when he led the side to victory against what was then one of the best sides in Europe. For me it was his best ever game in a green and white jersey, but Pat's problem was possibly that he never fully realised just how good a player he was. John Blackley, or 'Sloop' to his team mates, could read the game and was good in the air for a man his size. He had the confidence to play football in a crowded penalty area while the rest of us were fainting all around him, and was also an exceptional tackler, although don't ask him to make 30 yard passes after he had won the ball. Although Pat could play anywhere, John was at his most effective sweeping up in the middle of a back four and was good enough to earn several Scotland caps.

In midfield I would have the pairing of Davie Gibson and Alex Cropley. Although they were both left sided players, Davie was more than capable of playing on the right. Unfortunately I didn't play long with either of them, mainly in the reserves, but always felt comfortable in their company. The wee man could tackle, while Davie relied more on his positional play although both were extremely clever players who could read the game and had a great touch. With just the two of them in midfield we might occasionally be overrun, but they would be great to watch as they powered forward to set up chances for the forwards while chipping in with a few themselves.

Considering the number of great forwards at Easter Road during my time with the club, selecting the front four was never going to be easy, however after much deliberating I have managed to come up with the following. During my time at Easter Road Hibs had been blessed with the talents of Colin Stein, Joe McBride, Peter Cormack, Johnny McCloud and Gerry Baker to name, but a few, but I am going to go for the following front four. At outside-right I would choose my great pal Jim Scott, but not only because of sentiment. Jim's best time for the club would be after he had been moved into the middle of the forward line by Jock Stein, but for me he was also a quite exceptional wide man and I can still picture watching him from the terracing in a game against Rangers before I joined the club, waltzing past a string of defenders before casually placing the ball beyond the goalkeeper. An extremely tricky player Jim sometimes looked as if he was dreaming, but the next minute he would be ghosting past players as if they weren't there. Some say that he could be a bit timid, but believe me you wouldn't last long at the top level if you were timid, and would certainly not have become a Fairs Cup winner.

There are two contenders for the left wing position. Because its my team I would select myself for the first half and Willie Ormond for the second. Willie was perhaps the ideal winger. He was strong, worked hard, was clever on the ball with his magical left foot and could score goals. His record for both the Famous Five and Scotland, both as a player and a manager speaks for itself, and as a boy I can still remember watching him from the terracing charging down the left wing leaving a string of defenders floundering in his wake. Willie was another great lad and liked a laugh. I had always been a great admirer and later considered it to be a great privilege to have been considered a friend.

In the centre there would have to be a place for both Joe Baker and Neil Martin. (sorry Lawrie!) Joe was a very clever player with quite fantastic pace and all round ability, while Neilly, who also had a great football brain worked like a Trojan and was prepared to go in where it hurt. Both were great competitors who could score goals that the other could only dream about. Unfortunately I only managed to play a few times with Joe before his move to Italy and again after his return, while I often lined up on the left with Neilly. Whenever I found myself in trouble out on the wing I would just send the ball over and Neil would always be lurking somewhere in the box, and I have lost count of the number of phenomenal goals he scored with his head, both inside and outside the area. With their different strengths they would be an explosive combination together.

As manager of the side I couldn't select Eddie Turnbull as there is no way that he would let the side play an all-out attacking formation without attempting to defend. He would also have wanted it all his own way, and besides probably wouldn't have picked Pat. (I hope Eddie's not up there somewhere watching) Instead I am going to go for Bob Shankly. Bob was always a great believer in entertaining the public and would just have let the players get on with it.

4-2-4 FORMATION

RONNIE SIMPSON

BOBBY DUNCAN, PAT STANTON, JOHN BLACKLEY, JOHN BROWNLIE

DAVIE GIBSON, ALEX CROPLEY

JIM SCOTT, JOE BAKER, NEIL MARTIN, WILLIE ORMOND (ERIC STEVENSON)

MANAGER: BOB SHANKLY

I have also selected a team from among the best players that I was lucky enough to play against during my ten years at Easter Road. For the reasons previously mentioned Ronnie Simpson would be in goal. Then considered to be well past his best he had been allowed to join Celtic mainly as a backup to goalkeeper John Fallon, but it would turn out to be only the beginning of a fairytale for the veteran. The oldest player ever to make his full debut for Scotland in the famous 3-2 victory over England at Wembley in 1967, just weeks after a historic European Cup win in Lisbon, Simpson's name will go down in Celtic folklore.

My full-backs would be the Rangers pair Billy 'Sandy' Jardine and Eric Caldow. I always found playing against either of them extremely difficult. Neither would lunge into the tackle, but instead would jockey you into position until a colleague came to their aid and only rarely did I manage to go past them. Both were pacey and brave, but were mainly defensively-minded full-backs, who didn't venture forward nearly as much as Danny McGrain and Tommy Gemmell of Celtic who were much more adventurous.

There is only one candidate for the centre-half position and that is Billy McNeill of Celtic and Scotland. Almost unbeatable in the air, Billy could also play a bit on the ground and was an inspirational figure who was never beaten. A leader during his medal laden time with Celtic and a regular for Scotland for many years his career speaks for itself. My choice of sweeper may surprise some, but I am going to go for Eddie Thomson of Hearts and later Aberdeen although there is a bit of sentiment attached to his selection. Eddie hails from Rosewell which is not all that far from Bonnyrigg and when he was a youngster I would often give him tickets for the Hibs games at Easter Road. Eddie could play a bit. He was good reader of the game, could pass the ball and was a dogged competitor. He was really a centre-half, but I always thought that he would have made a great sweeper.

The midfield trio of Bobby Murdoch, John Greig and Jim Baxter would almost be unbeatable. Murdoch on the right hand side was a fantastic passer of the ball who, although he lacked a bit of pace, would be up and down the park making those accurate 40 or 50 yard passes while scoring the occasional goal himself. Jim Baxter was more of an inside-forward than a wing half, but when he decided to play he was absolutely brilliant, unstoppable, gliding past players like a fairy. Unfortunately, like myself he wasn't the greatest of trainers and would retire from the game almost obscenely prematurely at just over 30 years of age, a time when he should have been at his peak which was almost criminal for someone with his sublime talents. John Greig in the centre of midfield was a far better football player than many gave him credit for although not quite in the same class as Murdoch and Baxter. A pacey rugged competitor who never knew when he was beaten, he was a leader and often carried the side on his shoulders. He would later be voted Rangers best ever player, which considering the many great players that the Ibrox side have had at their disposal throughout the years speaks for itself.

There would have to be a place for both Jimmy Johnstone and Willie Henderson in my side so I would play Johnstone wide on the right and Henderson on the left. Jimmy was an out and out outside-right, but Willie was well capable of playing on the other wing. Jimmy could beat three men then go back and beat them again, while Willie was far more direct and both Jimmy Miller and Ralph Brand would often be fighting each other to get on the end of his accurate crosses from the byline. All the players I have selected so far played the majority of their football in Scotland, but I am going to cheat a bit by selecting Dragoslav Šekularac of Red Star Belgrade in the centre-forward position, although he usually played a bit further back breaking through into the attack. Quite simply, he was the best player by far that I played against which is saying something. He was out of this world, a genius and it was almost impossible to-take the ball from him. He was a confident lad and had once been asked to name the best three players in the world. His reply? Di Stefano, myself and Pele. Unfortunately not long after arriving back from the 1962 World Cup finals in Chile when he had apparently been voted the best player in the tournament, he would be suspended for almost 18 months for assaulting a referee during a game. He would return to the game however, finally retiring in 1975 at the age of 38.

4-3-3 FORMATION

RONNIE SIMPSON
SANDY JARDINE, BILLY MCNEILL, EDDIE THOMSON AND ERIC CALDOW
BOBBY MURDOCH, JOHN GREIG AND JIM BAXTER
JIMMY JOHNSTONE, DRAGOSLAV ŠEKULARIC AND WILLIE HENDERSON

CHAPTER FIFTEEN
And Finally

JUST AS THIS book was about to go to press Hibs defeated Rangers at Hampden to win the Scottish Cup for the first time in 114 years.

Some time before I had been diagnosed as suffering from stomach cancer and underwent an operation at the Edinburgh Royal Infirmary. Thankfully the operation was a complete success, although I was still to undergo several sessions of chemotherapy. I was recovering well, but on the day of the final I didn't feel strong enough to make the trip to Hampden and watched the game from the house.

Probably like most Hibs supporters I had honestly not expected them to win, but they got off to a great start and I was particularly impressed with the play of Anthony Stokes who took his first goal superbly. On the chances missed in the early stages of the game, Hibs should have had it won in the first 20 minutes, although I suppose the same could be said for Rangers after they had equalised. When Stokes scored again late in the second half to level things, both my wife Agnes and I were on our feet celebrating and had hardly sat down when Gray scored the winner and I am not ashamed to say that we both had tears in our eyes.

At the final whistle we were dancing around the living room cuddling each other. My daughter Sonia, her husband Alastair and grandkids Owen and Lucy were all at the game and what made it even better was when the cameras panned around the ground at the end we could see them in the crowd.

We had all waited more than a hundred years for this moment. A lot of Hibs supporters have said that they would rather have had promotion, but not me; for me winning the cup was something very special.

The Scottish Cup was not such a big thing when I played, but with the length of time since the last win, plus the ridiculing we have had to put up with from Hearts supporters year after year, the monkey was now off our back. It was particularly pleasing, especially after our comeback from two goals behind at Tynecastle of all places in an earlier round.

I was really pleased for the players. Some great Hibs players have never won the cup and it would be impossible to describe in words the emotion of the moment.

The scenes in Edinburgh the following day, when the cup was paraded through the streets of the city and down to Leith Links were absolutely incredible. It was estimated that over 150,000 people had turned out to witness the occasion, perhaps the biggest crowd ever for any event in the city, and the surrounding streets were packed solid not only with Hibs supporters, but with the ordinary people in the street who all realised what a momentous occasion it was for the city. Everywhere you looked you could see kids and grownups alike with tears running down their cheeks, the amazing celebrations continuing well into the night.

The players that took part in the historic victory will be treated like gods down Easter Road way for the rest of their lives, particularly the scorer of the winning goal, captain David Gray, who will still be applauded in the street even when he is 70.

The players of the Turnbull's Tornadoes side of the early '70s who won the League Cup against Celtic in 1972 and defeated Hearts 7-0 at Tynecastle a few weeks later are still rightly considered legends, but to my mind nothing can compare with this Scottish Cup win.

Watching the players at Hampden receiving their winners' medals made me wish I was still playing, but you can't turn the clock back. As already mentioned, I was at least fortunate enough to have realised my life's ambition of wearing the famous green and white jersey.

Some other books published by **Luath Press**

Hibernian: From Joe Baker to Turnbull's Tornadoes
Tom Wright
ISBN 978 1908873 09 1 HBK £20

The Alex Cropley Story
Alex Cropley with Tom Wright
ISBN 978 1 910745 73 1 PBK £9.99

In *Hibernian: From Joe Baker to Turnbull's Tornadoes*, club historian Tom Wright marks a new dawn for the game and the end of an era for Hibs.

Hibernian begins in the turbulent 1960s, when relegation was avoided at Easter Road on the final day of the 1963 season.

The appointment of the legendary manager Jock Stein in 1964 saw an immediate improvement in the relegation haunted side. The Hibs side of the mid-'60s featured an all-Scottish international forward line, and the return of player Eddie Turnbull in 1971 saw the emergence of possibly Hibs' greatest-ever side – the magical Turnbull's Tornadoes.

Packed full of detail and interesting information, Hibernian is a must not only for Hibs supporters, but also for the general football fan who is interested in this defining period in the history of our game.

Signed to Hibernian aged just 16, Alex Cropley soon made his name as one of the legendary Turnbull's Tornadoes. In the 1970s he played for Hibernian, Arsenal, Aston Villa, Newcastle United, Toronto Blizzard and Portsmouth, before injuries forced him off the pitch. From football-mad kid playing on the streets of Edinburgh to member of the Scottish national team, his career epitomises both the aspirations and the bitter disappointments surrounding the game.

Crops is a testament to the passion of generations for the beautiful game. Updated to include Cropley's most up-to-date thoughts on Aston Villa having been relegated from the Premier League, and peppered with anecdotes about the footballing legends Cropley played alongside – this new edition of Crops is a must-have for any football fan.

With his educated left foot, Alex was a tremendous talent, but I have to say he could also be a real pain in the neck. A nippy sweetie, he was always moaning, but that is often the sign of a great player – a real determination to succeed and a refusal to settle for second best. – From the Afterword by PAT STANTON